Early Bird

by

Richard Mack

Red'n'Ritten Ltd.
Editor: Joan Stanley

Published by Red'n'Ritten Ltd,
17 Kings Barn Lane, Steyning,
West Sussex
BN44 3YR
© Red'n'Ritten Ltd. 2008

ISBN 9781904278665

A CIP Catalogue record for this book is available from the British Library.

Printed by Marston Book Services Ltd.

Cover Artwork by Mike Avery

Illustrations by Jill Mack

Editor Joan Stanley

To Georgina,

with love.

Early Bird

by

Richard Mack

Earlybird is a tongue-in-cheek tale based on the author's fifteen year time as a postman. By turns humourous and disrespectful, the author takes us on a journey into the world of the Royal Mail - introducing us to the eccentricities of its arcane working practices, its employees, its customers and their dogs.

Prior to his employment as a postman, the author was already an *Earlybird.* Throughout this book he brings us delightful yarns of his past life as a market gardener/farmer and other country cameos. And despite the author's scepticism, his enjoyment of his farming years and his time as a postman are evident.

The market town of Bramton could be anywhere in England, and the characters therein could be found in many a rural locality. The story starts one dark, August morning at four a.m. ...

One

The electronic beeping of the alarm clock penetrated my skull with all the subtlety of a high-speed dentist's drill. Groaning, I raised myself on one elbow and turned the racket off, blinking in disbelief at the time the luminous hands indicated: four a.m. It was an ungodly hour to rise and, glancing towards my wife who had not stirred, I made my way into the darkness of the bathroom.

Later, drinking a cup of coffee and still half asleep, I reflected on the awful night I had spent retiring at the unnaturally early hour of nine thirty, and pursued in a semi-sleep by long forgotten demons from my childhood alternating with vivid apocalyptic dreams from which I awoke covered in sweat. But I must have slept; I had been unaware of my wife coming to bed.

Finishing my coffee I went out into the night and extracted my ancient moped from the garage. I had not ridden it for years, but surprisingly it had burst into life the previous day, with a shattering roar that belied its tiny engine and its age. Donning my skidlid and goggles, I set off for the market town of Bramton, three miles away. The feeble headlight barely illuminated the tarmac ahead, and I had time to reflect on the bizarre circumstances that had set me on this road.

Sudden financial disaster had forced me to find employment quickly, any kind of employment, but preferably local. At forty five, I could not afford to be discerning. I thought of the Post Office. The local paper had reported staffing problems at Bramton and irregular deliveries, so I rang the Sorting Office. The manager, courteous and encouraging, had invited me to start work the following day.

"It involves a very early start," he warned me, "but if you want to try work as a postman we shall be pleased to see you."

1

I had been involved with farming for most of my life, so I thought I could cope with the early start - though rising at four a.m. did seem a little extreme.

"What about an interview?" I asked the manager.

He hesitated. "I will get an application form to you today, and we'll worry about the interview later. I might as well tell you, I am desperate for postmen at the moment. You make sure you are at the office at five a.m. tomorrow and we'll sort out the details then."

True to his word an application form mysteriously appeared on the little hall table during the afternoon. I was in the garden and the door had been left open, but I never saw a soul.

I filled it in that evening; it seemed wise to take it with me.

Weaving my way through half a dozen untidily parked Post Office vans I coasted my moped down the slope in the yard to the Sorting Office at the bottom. Three men were pulling bags from a stack inside a large high topped vehicle, letting them fall from the lip of the van to the ground, with scant respect for their contents before dragging them through open double doors and piling them in a heap on the floor.

I parked my moped in a lean-to. A large balding man in his fifties was incongruously sitting on a white plastic, garden chair drinking a cup of tea. I removed my skidlid and goggles, feeling very much like a new boy on his first day at school.

"That's illegal, that skidlid," the man observed. "You has to wear a proper helmet now, with a proper visor, not them goggles."

I already knew that, but felt disinclined to pursue a discussion on the legality of motorcycle headgear at that hour of the morning. He drained his tea, placing the cup on an adjacent garden chair and rose to his feet.

"I'm Sydney," he said, shaking my hand vigorously. "Not Sid, but Sydney. You're the new bloke, Richard. I knows all about you, because I'm your postman. I've been your postman for years."

I had never set eyes on him before, but it was hardly surprising as our post usually arrived before I was up.

"You'd better come in. We could certainly do with some more postmen 'ere."

He led me inside, introducing me to nobody. He indicated a distant door. "That's the locker room through there. Put your what's 'is names on a chair and come back in 'ere."

I deposited my gear and returned. The same three men I had seen earlier were cutting the bags open with curved scissors, and tipping the contents into large wheeled skips. These were then pushed to a central stand, where empty bags were hooked onto individual holders that had an area name attached. I had little time to take in what appeared, at first glance, to be a scene from hell: the work fuelled from the enormous pile of bags lying in the middle of the floor; bundles of letters and packages flying through the air to the accompaniment of foul language and a strong smell of sweat.

"'Ere, take these scissors," Sydney instructed, "and open some of them bags. 'Iggings'll be along directly and 'ee'll want a talk with you. But at least one of them others can go sorting."

I assumed 'Iggings was the name of the Manager. And ten minutes later a portly, avuncular looking man came through the doors. It was exactly five-fifteen. He went to each man - there were about fifteen - wishing him a good morning, and was answered with a grunt or complete ignorance.

Sydney materialized by my side and started cutting open bags, emptying them into the skips with unnecessary enthusiasm, "That's 'Iggings," he said equally unnecessarily. "'Ee'll be over to 'ave a word with you when 'ee's finished fartin' about sayin' good morning to us all." I was surprised by the blatant rudeness of everyone towards the manager.

Eventually he made his way over to us, "What's it like this morning, Sydney?"

"'Bout average," he mumbled by way of reply, concentrating furiously on cutting and emptying the bags.

Mr. Higgins turned to me and extended his hand. "I am John Higgings, the Sorting Office manager." We shook hands. "You had better come with me to my office and we'll sort out a few details."

I placed my scissors on a nearby table and followed him to his office, glancing back I noticed Sydney had abandoned his efforts at bag opening and disappeared. There was a low hum of conversation and some laughter.

John Higgings opened his office door, turned on the light and hung his coat on a circular wooden coatstand of the sort that was popular decades ago. The whole office, down to the wicker waste paper basket and the tubular steel chairs, looked like a film set from the 1950's, and the manager, sitting comfortably in his own plush chair behind the desk, completed the illusion.

"As I told you before on the telephone, I am desperate for postmen." He paused, shuffling some papers in front of him. "It's a social problem really," he continued, only half speaking to me. "Bramton is an area where people come to retire, housing is expensive and the younger generation tend to move away to the larger towns, where the cost of living is cheaper and there are more job opportunities. Working for Royal Mail is not everybody's first choice of employment, because of the unsocial hours and relatively low pay. But we have addressed that problem in two ways: by increasing allowances and, to attract workers from outside the area, by offering a special area definition allowance of twenty pounds."

I hadn't the faintest idea what that was. He went on, "This has prompted some discord amongst those who have come from further afield when they discover those already living in the area automatically receive the allowance as well, but the union insists that everyone gets it. The union is very strong within Royal Mail, and I expect Sydney Tuck

4

will try to get you to join. He is a good man, but he does know his rights."

He sighed, gazing at a point beyond my left shoulder. I remained silent. "We have a core of about eight people who have been with us for years, but the rest are either casuals or people I don't expect to stay long-term. Have you brought your application form?"

I pulled it from my pocket and handed it to him. He took a spectacle case from his top pocket, opened it, and carefully placed a pair of half-frame glasses on his nose. After briefly scanning the form, he placed it on his desk and rose to his feet. "At least you are local," he said smiling. "Perhaps you will stay for longer than most. I am going to put you with Dave Anderson on the Topleys round."

Slightly bemused by John Higgings's welcoming speech I allowed myself to be ushered from his office.

"Wait here," he indicated a row of curious looking contraptions, which reminded me of upright looms, "and I will fetch Dave."

I looked more closely at the strange pieces of office furniture. They were, I soon discovered, called sorting frames, the very cores of the existence of Royal Mail; the single most important feature of the office. Without them, there could be no sorting and, therefore, no delivery. Each house had its own slot, separated from the next by three-inch high, plastic dividers. The houses were neatly labelled, and the gaps varied according to the amount of mail received each day; the grander houses receiving more than the lesser, terraced houses. Some numbered houses shared a slot and each area was clearly marked, under the strip denoting the house names.

John Higgings reappeared with Dave and formally introduced us. He was a spotty, thin man of about twenty-five, with greasy black hair and a large gold earring twisting and dancing in his left earlobe. He had a distracted air about him, and as the manager made his way back to his office Dave inducted me into the mysteries of the sorting frame. It did not take long. There were four tiers of these named slots.

"The bottom here's Lower Topley, startin' left to right. Then you go back left again and it's Middle Topley, and so on."

It seemed easy enough.

"You can sit," he said swinging out a moulded plastic seat from under the frame, "and it's adjustable for height, like this."

He handed me a bundle of Sun bingo leaflets. "Households," he said enigmatically. "You stick 'em in the slots here, one each, and you might start to learn your way around the frame. I'll go back on primary and come back when we've finished."

There seemed a whole new lexicon to learn. Looking round, I saw that the huge pile of sacks on the floor was almost gone, and most of the men were standing, sorting into much larger frames.

Sydney came over to me. "You won't learn nothing from Dave. 'Ee's only interested in getting 'ome early to go to 'is other job. You ought to be with me an' I'd show you how to do the job proper, but ..." He backed away as John Higgings emerged from his office.

"We don't stand on formality here. We all use Christian names, and I am always available to see you, at any time."

I swung out the moulded plastic seat, carefully adjusted the height and gingerly sat on it. It was surprisingly comfortable and swung from side to side to give easy access to the wings on either edge of the frame. Picking up the bunch of the bingo leaflets, I cast a glance around. Everyone was concentrating on their sorting. I felt like a guest in a hotel allowed a privileged peep into the kitchen, the inner sanctum of the whole business. Only I was no intruder here, it was my job.

I recognised mail shots for what they were: unaddressed junk mail. I started fitting them into the slots, looking with interest at the house names. There were several Rose Cottages, three Keepers Cottages, a few houses suffixed with Farmhouse, denoting a non-working farm. I could picture them, the houses separated from their land and used as commuter retreats. Intriguingly, there was one Hell's Bottom.

I was awakened from my reverie by the taciturn Dave dumping an armful of letters on the flat plastic surface in front me. "That all you done? Shift over an' watch me throw this lot out."

Throw out? It seemed a good idea, for most of the letters looked like advertising rubbish. But the term apparently meant putting the letters into their individual slots. Dave was dextrous at it, and I admired his casual skill.

Sydney was not impressed. "'Ee won't learn nothing unless you let him do it 'imself. That's no way to train 'im, just letting 'im watch."

"Piss off, Sydney," Dave replied, without breaking his rhythm, "and let me train him my way."

So I was being trained. I thought that was something that happened to dogs.

An elderly man of sixty-five, well dressed and well spoken, appeared at my elbow and enquired whether I would like tea or coffee. He explained that I would have to pay ten pence a week for the cup of tea for which I opted. Half an hour later he reappeared carrying a large tray, laden with cups of tea and coffee. It was a civilised touch in what seemed to me a chaotic and anarchic scene. He was, I found out later, Jack the cleaner.

When there were only a few letters left to sort, Dave said, "You finish off."

I sat on the seat and started slowly sorting.

"No, no," he said impatiently. "That's the wrong Rose Cottage you done there, and the wrong Gardeners Cottage you done here." He muttered something to himself that I was grateful not to have heard, before raising his voice, "And you've only sorted half a dozen letters."

It was not an auspicious start.

I followed Dave to the stand containing the packet bags. He heaved the one marked 'Topleys' off its hooks and tipped it out unceremoniously into one of the, by now, empty skips. "You sort the

7

flats from the packets while I put the passenger seat back in the van."
Adding under his breath, "I hates this training lark."

"Lester!" he yelled. "Where the hell's the spare seat for the Marina?"

"No idea," came the reply, followed by unbroken cursing from
Dave.

I concentrated on sorting the flats - catalogues, magazines and large
A4 envelopes - from the packets. Sydney materialised from nowhere
and absentmindedly started helping me. I wondered if he had any work
of his own to do; he seemed to be taking a paternal interest in me so I
did not object.

"That Dave's a wrong 'un," he said. "'Ee don't like training 'cos it
puts 'is day out."

Changing the subject, I asked Sydney why the van apparently lacked
a passenger seat.

"Because we put the trays of letters on the floor. It makes it easier to
reach the bundles. When you're training they 'as to go in the back, an'
that can be a bit of a blighter."

Dave reappeared, presumably having installed the seat, glared at
Sydney and wheeled the trolley over to the sorting frame. He rapidly
inserted the flats behind the letters already in there, and placed the
packets in order. "Now watch me carefully, while I tie up."

Tying up was evidently an anachronism from the time when letters
were bundled up and secured with string. Dave, rapidly pulling the mail
from the frame secured the bundles with rubber bands, placing them in
fibreboard trays. The contents of the frame yielded two and a half trays
of letters, which Dave balanced precariously on top of the narrow
trolley. He stood back to check that nothing had been left behind, and,
satisfied, turned to me. "We'll go to the cage now and collect our
registereds from old Murdoch." He hesitated. "You might find
Murdoch a bit odd, being new and that, but don't take any notice.
You'll get used to him in time."

8

I followed Dave through the Sorting Office to the cage, wondering what mysterious creature lurked within. Most of the other postmen were still tying up, and we were the first to arrive at Murdoch's lair. It was well named, for it was just that, a cage situated at the end of the office; totally enclosed in wire mesh, with a door, similarly clad, standing wide open, negating any vestige of security that the area might have offered.

It was, Dave whispered to me just before we entered, officially called the Registered Letter Enclosure. And the door was supposed to be closed at all times, except when postmen were admitted one at a time to collect their registered letters and packets. "Murdoch don't bother with that. He only locks the door when he goes home."

Inside the cage was a huge and very old fashioned safe, several cabinets with their doors hanging open revealing rows of keys, and sitting at a desk in front of metal framework containing twenty or so large pigeon holes, with his back towards us, was old Murdoch.

"Morning, Lenny," Dave said amiably. "We've come for our registereds and keys."

There was no response. Murdoch was writing laboriously in what appeared to be a large ledger and he ignored Dave completely.

Dave cleared his throat and tried again. "I've got the new bloke, Richard, with me."

Murdoch carefully laid down his pen and turned in his swivel chair to face us. I goggled at him. He looked like a wizened monkey, a true inmate of the cage. He regarded me through weak, slightly watery, staring, blue eyes and I stared back at him. He was a slight man, with light brown wavy hair, and his resemblance to a monkey was remarkable. But it was those eyes that fascinated me: they were without soul.

He was of indeterminate age, anywhere between fifty and seventy-five -I found out later his true age was forty-eight. There was something about him that unnerved me, but I was at a loss to know what.

His examination of the newcomer complete, he grunted and turned back to his desk. Reaching forward he gave Dave two bunches of keys from one of the pigeonholes and three registered letters, for which Dave had to sign, carefully placing the counterfoils in his pocket. Dave looked at me, jerking his head towards the door and we left. The interview was over and Murdoch had spoken not a word. Somewhat shaken for a reason I could not readily identify I asked Dave if he was always like that.

"Mostly, but then he's a P.H.G." Sensing my bafflement he explained. "Postman Higher Grade. He's the same as us only he had to pass an exam and he's paid more, but don't you get thinking he's any authority over us 'cos he ain't. He might think he has, but he ain't," he reiterated forcefully.

We wheeled the trolley load of letters and packets through the doors into the yard, where Dave had reversed his van down from the top of the slope. It was a very old Morris Marina, liberally covered with small dents and gashes and in a filthy state.

"They were no ruddy good when they were new," Dave observed. "And when they get elderly they keep on breaking down. This one's covered ninety-eight thousand miles, and it's only fit for the scrap heap."

Looking at it, it was difficult to disagree. Dave loaded the contents of the trolley into the rear of the van, taking three bundles of letters from one of the trays and stacking them on the dashboard.

The van started with a cloud of noxious blue smoke pouring from the exhaust pipe and Sydney, alerted by the noise and, no doubt, the smell, came out of the Sorting Office. "Make sure you use your seat belts, mind."

"Sod off, Sydney. You know no one ever puts them on, leave us alone and go back to your work."

"Nosey blighter," He went on as we lurched out of the yard. "He

10

has these bouts of getting all official just because he's the union man, but no one takes any notice of him. He never wears a belt, nor do any of us drivers. It's too much trouble takin' 'em on and off every two minutes."

He chuckled to himself. "He'll be telling us to lock our vans every time we make a delivery next. We're supposed to, but our delivery would take all day and night if we did."

It was half past six and dawn had just broken, revealing heavy dew on the small areas of grass that had managed to survive man's intrusion of tarmac and concrete. The day seemed set fair.

Dave had noticed me glance at my watch. "We're early. It's been a light day, but there's never much on this round compared to some of the others."

Two

We roared down the main street of Bramton, suddenly swinging across the dropped kerb, over the pavement and down a drive that led between a row of terraced houses and shops. About two hundred yards along the drive was a small bungalow. Dave halted the van by the front door, grabbed a bundle of letters from the dashboard, peeled off the top four or five, and flung the bundle back, deftly stretching the rubber band over the top of the gear lever - which was festooned with bands, rather like the rings some African women used to stretch their necks. He leapt out of the van, pushed the mail through the letterbox and returned.

He seemed to be having trouble, muttering to himself and heaving at the spindly gear lever. Eventually, with an awful grinding noise, he found reverse, backed the van round and retraced the journey down the drive to the main street. I could only assume the occupants of the bungalow had become so inured to this racket at half past six in the morning that they accepted it as part of the daily routine; to me it was an unwarranted disturbance at such an early hour.

Dave's driving appalled me. Despite the fact there were already a few people about in the town, he recklessly drove across the pavement without appearing to glance left or right; drove the wrong way down the main road for about thirty yards and repeated the exercise, driving down another concealed driveway to a much larger house. He ripped off a few more letters and handed them to me. "It's your side; I'll turn round."

Climbing out of the van I walked to the front door and carefully pushed the letters through the letterbox. Dave was waiting for me. "You'll have to move faster than that; else we'll never get home."

Somewhat crestfallen by his reaction to my first delivery as a

13

postman I resumed my seat, and Dave let out the clutch, spinning the wheels on the loose gravel and leaving a cloud of dust in our wake.

We repeated this performance three times along the main street of Bramton, Dave showing scant regard for pedestrians or the Highway Code. The last house had a dreadful exit onto the road on a completely blind right-hand bend, but he confidently drove out, on the correct side of the road for a change, and we left the small town of Bramton for the depths of the country. I was rapidly becoming a nervous wreck.

Pride prevented me from wearing a seat belt; an arrogance as reckless as Dave's driving.

"We do these few houses on the way out so the town rounds - the bikes and trolleys - don't have to go all the way down to those places. If they put boxes at the ends of their drives it'd make life a whole lot easier. Come to that, they ought to do that on the rural rounds, too."

"Then you would never meet anyone," I said mildly.

"Blow that. 'Cept at Christmas for the tips, of course. All I want to do is to get back. People natter all the time and hold you up."

It was an interesting point of view, but not one to which I subscribed. I said nothing.

We shot out of Bramton and took a narrow lane to the left, about a mile out of town.

"This is where the round really starts," Dave swerved violently off the road to the left, down a narrow, rough drive. Nettles growing in profusion on either side brushed the sides of the van and slapped the wing mirrors, throwing dew and pollen onto the windscreen. "It's a sod in winter, because you have to back out in the dark and you can't hardly see a thing."

We stopped by a pretty house beside the river. "If he didn't park his car there we could turn round easy. Here," he continued, thrusting the bundle at me, "I'll call out the names and then you can have the letters ready when we get to the door. Adams," he said laconically.

I removed the top four, handing them to Dave. He handed them back. "Your side."

Mindful of the apparent need for speed I hurried to the door and thrust them through the letterbox. I had read somewhere, many years ago, that pushing letters through letterboxes was a form of sexual gratification, but it certainly gave me no thrill.

As the morning wore on, and I encountered stronger, potentially finger removing springs, I wondered what psycho-idiot had conceived such a notion. I said nothing about it to Dave.

He backed the van expertly through the encroaching nettles emerging at some risk blind onto the road. The untrimmed verges appeared to narrow the road, which was meagre enough in the first place, but Dave kept his foot on the throttle. "Don't meet much at this time of the morning," he said dangerously. "But sometimes there's the odd car or tractor. It pays to keep alert."

I hoped he was.

I had lived in the area for years and had thought I knew it well, but half the little lanes Dave took me along I never knew existed, let alone had houses on them, albeit lonely places. On reflection, in my misspent youth my time was spent driving from pub to pub, and though I knew all the shortcuts they were only to the next watering hole.

After a while I had no idea where we were and said as much to Dave.

He laughed, "It looks worse than it is. You'll get used to it, though we had one new bloke once, Charlie, and he really did get lost. Kept going when he should have turned round and ended up halfway to London. He didn't return to the office until it were very nearly dark, at half past six in the evening."

We drove down a long gravel drive, at the end of which was a large and opulent house. Even Dave drove more slowly than usual on the loose gravel.

"The local parliament bloke," he said conversationally. "Don't see much of him, but his wife's always pissed. Can't blame her really, living in a huge house with her kids and the nanny, and the old man away most of the time."

I was intrigued. It was only seven o'clock and no one was about.

"How do you come to see her when it's still so early?"

"I get lots of stuff for signature for them, registered and that. It ain't no good trying to get an answer at the door now, so I call in again on my way back when she's up. We'll be doing that today. There're two here for them. Stinks of booze she does and her handshakes so bad she can hardly write her name. Sad really, but you wait till you see the nanny."

We bumped down a dreadfully rough, deeply rutted track a few minutes later, the sump of the battered Royal Mail Marina frequently bottoming on the fortunately soft ground in the middle.

"Belle Lodge, worst call on the round."

The track must have been over a mile long and Belle Lodge was at the end of it: a disappointingly dilapidated abode set on the intersection of a number of other muddy tracks, impassable to motor traffic, in the middle of a thick wood.

"Hate this place. Gives me the creeps. Often can't get here in winter, and they never tip, though they should do for the efforts we make to deliver their mail."

A little old woman, wearing a faded dress, with a shawl over her head came to the window. "Got a mate today, I see," she cackled, peering closely at me.

"Yes, Miss Drake, he's a trainee."

"I hope he doesn't get lost in these woods." The house and the little old lady seemed lost in a time warp, miles from anywhere and I reflected there could hardly be any profit for Royal Mail delivering mail to such an outlandish place.

At last we left the warren of side roads and came to one I recognised leading to Lower Topley. We had a clear run couple of miles before we came to the first house on the outskirts. The Topleys - Lower, Middle and Upper - were depressing reminders of how village life had changed over the last twenty years or so, straggling drawn out communities lacking the soul of a proper village. There was no shop, and only one pub amongst the three of them. The shops had become houses.

And there were too many dwellings with names suffixed by 'farmhouse', indicating what had once been thriving family farms, now absorbed into a huge agricultural estate; with the houses sold off, for this was commuter and weekender land, with the railway station only ten miles away. 'Conveniently situated within easy reach of the station with frequent services to the capital,' was how estate agents described properties in these once lively villages, thus sounding the death knell of another piece of rural England.

There was an Old Schoolhouse and an Old Rectory in each of the Topleys, too, standing as mute monuments to the ridiculous phrase, 'The Way Forward', so beloved by politicians and big businesses.

"Dormitory area," said Dave, breaking into my thoughts. "Don't see no one much here 'cept at weekends. They like to be herded like cattle into trains and go to bloody London each day. Beats me why they want to do it."

We stopped outside the Old Post Office where, appropriately, there was a post box and I took the letters from the top of the bundle. "Watts?" Dave asked and I nodded. He handed me one of the large bunches of keys. "One eight eight," he said "and don't forget to change the tab from first collection to second. Do it before you take the letters out and that way you won't leave it on one. They all complain like mad round here if the tabs aren't changed!"

I pushed the letters through the letterbox of the Old Post Office and selecting the correct key, opened the box. Heeding Dave's advice I changed the tab over and collected the letters. There were about eight.

"Who does the second collection?" I asked, settling into my seat.

"That's done on scheduled attendance in the afternoon." Dave said. "I expect Higgings'll have you on it soon – we're always short of afternoon drivers, but the money's good. I never do it, can't, because of my other job." Scheduled attendance. It sounded like a form of school detention.

There was still a large number of little lanes leaving the main road - it was a "B" road, not an "A" road - looping up and around the villages, returning and, crossing the road, repeating the process the other side. I gloomily wondered how on earth I would remember the route - writing it down seemed the only answer.

"You only have three days to learn this," Dave said surprisingly. I looked at him, startled, wondering for a brief moment whether he was psychic. "That includes learning the sorting frame," he added, "and after a few days grace you have to go on I.P.S., too."

I.P.S.? Incoming Primary Sorting, apparently; when all the other postmen had been sorting the mail from the van into the large frames from which Dave had extracted the mail for Topley. It all seemed impossible to me, to learn so much in three days, but I reasoned if others could do it then so could I.

We turned off the main road, yet again, down a short stretch of tarmac that led to a very old, very quaint, thatched cottage. "Keepers, Upper Topley," Dave said, with a malicious smile. "We've got a packet so you'll have to knock on the door while I turn round. It's your side, see," he added, still smiling.

I climbed out of the van and knocked loudly on the door. After a long wait it opened and I was confronted by a very old man, with piercing blue eyes and a very red face. He was immaculately dressed, with razor sharp creases in his trousers and highly polished brown brogues. He had a small, neat moustache and looked everything a retired high-ranking army officer should be. His name was Colonel Mackinnon, I had learnt from studying the address on the box while I waited for him to answer the door. He looked from me to the van, where Dave, having turned round, was waiting, still grinning, and studying me and the old colonel with interest.

He took me by surprise. "What is your name?" he asked in a voice that was evidently used to giving orders. I told him. "Now, you listen carefully, there are three Keepers Cottages on your round. My name is Mackinnon, and the names of the inhabitants of the other two are Mitford and Reilley. I know that, because I constantly receive their mail and they mine. I spend a lot of time on the telephone to the postmaster complaining about this state of affairs, and I have suggested that if we have a regular postman, instead of an incessant selection of moronic youths like your grinning friend in the van, we might expect the accurate delivery that is our right. The postmaster assures me this will be the case, but I do not believe him for one minute."

He peered closely at me. "You seem more mature than the rest. I hope you will remember - Mackinnon, Upper Topley."

He turned smartly on his heel and closed the door. I made my way back to the Marina, the name Mackinnon, Upper Topley, emblazoning itself into my brain like some mantra. How could anyone forget, I wondered?

"Did the old blighter give you an earful?" Dave asked, still grinning.

"Well," I began wondering how the immaculate colonel, used to commanding hundreds of men, would react to the news that this moronic youth had referred to him as an old blighter, "not exactly. He..."

"Always complaining, he is, ringing up Higgings every day even when we do get it right. Miserable old sod, got nothing better to do."

While I was digesting the import of this statement Dave let out the clutch and we continued on our way. It was now half past nine and the sun was warming the air. There was a noticeable increase in the amount of traffic, but no corresponding decrease in the speed at which he hurtled along the narrow roads. The harvest was in full swing at this time of year, and every so often I noticed enormous combine harvesters surrounded by their attendant tractors and trailers, and groups of farm workers chatting, greasing the combines ready for the day's work.

"Ruddy tractors," Dave said, noticing my interest, "I hate those things. They slow you down when you catch them up and never let you past, and when they come the other way they're always in the middle of the road and usually on a blind bend. That's the trouble with a rural, 'specially at this time of year."

I refrained from comment. "We turn here," Dave announced, pulling past a house set about six feet back from the road and reversing perfectly into a narrow entrance. "It's a beast to come out of if they aren't here 'cos you come out blind and have to put your bonnet half way out before you can see. They're usually here and see you out, but not always."

Fortunately 'they' were at home and saw us safely out of their lethal access on this fast stretch of road. One feature of the round I had noticed was the preponderance of deathly accesses, some situated on the insides of almost blind bends, others, like this one, on fast stretches and just as diabolically dangerous.

"Are there many accidents on these rural rounds?" I asked Dave innocently.

"I'll say," he replied enthusiastically, "we've had some beauts, but never anyone hurt so far 'cos we seldom gets the chance to build up speed on these roads – they're too dodgy to belt along flat out."

I turned to stare at him in disbelief, but he continued, a note of pride creeping into his voice. "We've got the worst driving record in the area, which is why we have such crap vans. Three blameworthy accidents and we're taken off driving for six months and made to do a bike walk (that sounded interesting, but I didn't interrupt him). Sydney, he's on two blameworthies. He drives like an idiot, that man." He paused, laughing softly to himself. "I'd like to see him taken off driving. It would serve him right, the ignorant sod."

We had finished the Topleys, and continued deep into the country, down long farm tracks and visiting remote homesteads.

"We got our first registered here," Dave announced as we drew up outside a picturesque cottage on the outskirts of one of these hamlets. "You'd better come with me," and he opened the Marina door. It was not tremendously exciting. An elderly spinster answered Dave's knock and looked suspiciously at the registered letter while he explained a signature was required.

"I wonder what that can be," she said, signing the scrap of blue paper.

"They always say that," Dave informed me as we returned to the van.

"They send away for parcels, get registered letters that they know are coming, yet they always say, 'I wonder what that can be?' Mind you, them registered is sacrosanct. Lose one of them and you're in big trouble."

It was a quarter past ten and we were nearly at the end of the round.

"A couple of farms, one more box to empty, back to the parliament bloke's house and then to the office to collect our parcels. We do a small parcel round in the town when we return. We've done well this morning."

I held no illusion that I was being used to hasten Dave back to the office as quickly as possible so he could go home. Any 'training' on this round would have to come from my questions, not from Dave's interest in his trainee.

The box was my side and as I inserted the key I noticed the time of emptying was given as eleven o'clock.

"We're a little early on this box, aren't we?" I said, as I flicked a ubiquitous rubber band around the few letters I had collected.

'Sod it," Dave said as we roared away from the box. "I forgot to tell you. When we are too early for a box we take the tab out and put it back inside. That way people don't know when it's due for emptying. People's stupid anyway and they don't understand them tabs." he added contemptuously. That sounded rich coming from him.

He looked at me shiftily, "Don't tell Murdoch." I wondered why he was more afraid of Murdoch discovering the misdemeanor than John Higgins.

We returned to the parliamentary candidate's house. A glamorous young girl of about twenty was standing on the lawn smoking a cigarette. She was wearing a short mini skirt that showed her lovely legs off to full advantage, and a revealing top. She had shoulder length dark hair and a remarkably pretty oval face. She looked anything but a prospective M.P.'s wife and I said so to Dave.

He laughed shortly, "That's not her, that's the nanny. Polish or something I think, but a gorgeous bit of stuff; wouldn't mind getting in there. Full of working mothers this round is, hence the nannies. Don't do the kids no good, though," he added perceptively.

The young girl signed the slips and we sped back to the office. And that was, I reflected, one nanny who did not look after children for a working mother, and it was difficult to escape the thought that the husband might be tempted.

We stopped briefly at the office to collect the parcels - ten of them - and Dave drove round to a part of Bramton I had never visited, nor even knew existed: The Estates. Bramton was fortunate that it was not endowed with the awful housing estates of the larger conurbations, but tiny in comparison though they were The Estates were just as depressing. Much of the grass had been worn away on the wide verges by the footpaths, thoughtfully provided by the council, with a misguided view of giving the illusion of space. The bare earth was fouled with dog mess, and most of the trees had been snapped off at

22

their bases. And the houses looked poor and shabby.

It was a fine day and there were a lot of people about, talking over fences, tending their gardens and cleaning their cars. It was still the school holidays, and bored children were idling their time away on skateboards or bicycles. I was struck by the number of men of employable age lazing around, giving a lie to John Higging's pronouncement that it was difficult to find employees in the town.

"Unemployed and mostly unemployable," Dave told me in answer to my query. "Lazy sods playing the system," he added disapprovingly.

Everyone appeared depressingly stereotyped, as if they were moulding themselves on television soap series instead of the other way round. In fact the whole estate, on that fine summer day, reminded me of a film set; all that was missing was the crew.

And there were dogs everywhere, not small dogs, but German shepherd dogs, Dobermans, Labradors and collies, both of the last two horribly crossbred. I wondered how on earth the owners managed to feed them and their families. But they were playing the system, as Dave had observed, and that explained everything.

"They're well into mail order here," Dave said, "and come Christmas there are more parcels than letters to deliver."

We delivered our parcels, not without some banter, and returned to the office.

"That's it for today," Dave rubbed his hands together. "We're an hour before our time. It's only quarter to eleven. We work on a job-done basis at the Post Office. Murdoch doesn't like it. But if we've done all we're supposed to we can go, and there's nothing he can do about it. And if you're interested," he added unexpectedly, "we've travelled just over forty-two miles and made about two hundred calls. There're two fifty on the round, but we don't go everywhere every day."

It seemed more like four hundred miles to me, and a rough calculation showed we had achieved it at an average speed of just over ten miles per hour. I would never have guessed.

We returned to the cage and Dave handed the signed blue registered counterfoils to Murdoch. He grunted, placed them on his desk and spun his chair round.

He fixed his eyes on me, "I hope you don't think you'll get back this early every day, because you won't. And I don't want you claiming overtime when it's not justified, because I won't pay you. I know what Dave's game is, the two of you getting in early, because you've shared the round. But when you claim overtime, you remember the times you got back early."

He swivelled his chair round again, resuming his work.

"Miserable sod," Dave said. "Think he runs this office, but he doesn't. He's only a postman, same as us."

Murdoch's attitude puzzled me, but as it was only my first day I was disinclined to give it much further thought.

John Higgins came out of his office. "How did you like it?"

I muttered something conventional and he smiled.

"Dave's a good lad at heart. Just listen to him and you will find the job is not as bad as it first appears."

I collected my gear, kicked the ancient moped into life and rode home. Sydney, for once, never appeared.

My wife asked me how I had fared. It seemed an age ago that I had left home in the darkness, and my brain felt overloaded.

"There's a lot to remember," I said cautiously, and then realised that others could easily do what was essentially a simple job, added, "I think it'll work out. After all, it's only a stop gap."

"It's lovely to have you home so early," she said later, "even if it might be different at other times. What are you going to do about your sleep?"

This was something that had bothered me. Rising at four in the morning meant going to bed at eight o'clock in the evening if I was to get the eight hours I needed. And to me that was ridiculous. The question was a vexed one. I discovered after I had been there for a while that most postmen at Bramton were coy about it. Few of them admitted to having an afternoon nap and equally only one said he went to bed regularly at eight o'clock.

Doubtless there were those who could manage on only a few hours, but I was not amongst them. For the rest, it was a matter of reverse machismo to confess to sleeping in the afternoon. I compromised on that first day, dozing uneasily in a chair for a couple of hours. Later, I would go to bed and slumber soundly for two or three hours, finally retiring at about half past ten, but it took time for the body clock to adjust to such irregular sleep patterns.

I had a dreamless night and, in the morning as I coasted down the slope to park my moped, I reflected that at least I had an idea of what to expect; rather like the second day of school. For some reason the analogy was still strong in my mind.

Sydney was sitting drinking his tea. "You really didn't ought to be wearing that skidlid and them goggles," he began. But I ignored him and wished him a good morning; that confused him.

"How did you get on yesterday?" he enquired, and I told him. "You'll get used to it," he said, finishing his tea. "Time to go in now, there's more mail than yesterday." He indicated the mound of mailbags being hauled off the van. "Be late today."

I sat at the sorting frame concentrating furiously on learning it. Dave handed me a bundle of letters and I began sorting. After a while it started to make some sense and the pile began diminishing.

Dave returned with yet more letters. "You've got a mate today, called Stephen. Started this morning." He indicated a rather lost looking young man standing by a sorting frame, being inducted into its mysteries by a tired, much older postman. At least I was not the only new boy.

We left the office twenty-five minutes later than the previous day, partly because there was more mail and partly because I had been doing the majority of the sorting. I had found an old school exercise book that had belonged to my son, which had 'Poetry' written on the front cover in large letters. It had never been written in. My son was evidently no bard. And I had appropriated it for making notes on the round.

This was not as easy as it sounded, for note taking while Dave drove proved nearly impossible. One minute my pen was hovering impotently, almost weightless, a few inches above the page, the next the point was digging deeply into the paper, as heavy as lead. The resulting hieroglyphics would take some interpreting when I came to write them into a coherent sequence. Dave was amused by my attempts to commit the round to paper. "You'll never make head nor tail of that," he said, peering at my scrawl. "You'd be best off just trying to remember it."

"I wish you would keep your eyes on the road," I retorted huffily, but this only amused him further. "I can do this round with my eyes shut."

"The way you drive, it's the passenger who needs to keep his eyes closed."

The morning passed in a blur, but I was satisfied I had written most of it down correctly. I had no desire to end up like the postman who had driven half way to London, and said as much to Dave.

"Old Cedric," he said. "Funny thing was, he took his wife with him the next day and he still went wrong."

I introduced myself to Stephen on our return. He looked exhausted, and explained he was being trained on a bike round. "I'm completely out of condition and the sorting frame's a nightmare. You're lucky to be in a van."

John Higgings happened to catch his remark. "No one in this office is on a set round. We work in sections of three people in each section and the rounds rotate weekly. When you are both trained into your

26

rounds you will learn the other two and become fully integrated. Yours is the Junior Section," he added as an afterthought.

I felt that, in my mid forties, I was a little old to be a junior, but I was learning that the Royal Mail paid scant regard to the outside world. It really was like school again, especially when he informed me that everything in the office - from which section one was in, to choice of holidays - was based on seniority.

It was all a far cry from having been a self-employed farmer.

Three

Even our small farm was better organised than the Post Office - most of the time. I wondered what old Bert would have made of it all.

Bert was our octogenarian, occasional helper on the farm. He was a man of medium build, with an astonishingly ruddy, bucolic face. Seldom separated from his cap and his pipe, he pottered around happily doing the small, but useful jobs of which he was capable. He had been a carter all his life, a real carter, working with horses for a farmer whose enthusiasm for them had survived the ascendancy of the tractor. Bert loved our farm, readily proffering well intentioned, but often inaccurate advice.

Our first lambing had gone well, and watching the energetic lambs playing tag on the lines of bales laid out for shelter, in the early spring sunshine, made up for all the hard work and traumas that go with lambing time. The young ewes that refused to take to their offspring, regarding them with horror rather than maternal love. Lambing a ewe in the night pen by torchlight in the pouring rain; kneeling in the wet, clinging mud. Losing a precious ewe and trying to foster her orphan. And the dead lambs.

Alan, the shepherd on the farm where I had worked as a student years before, had told me, "First job youse does before lambing is dig a hole. Anyone who tells you 'ee don't have no dead lambs is a liar."

He was right, but it is human nature to remember the bad times and forget the better moments. It was a joy to watch the gambolling lambs and the contentedly grazing ewes, and to reflect it had all been worthwhile. But something was bothering me. We only had forty five ewes at the time, and we could hardly expect to live off the sheep until we had increased our flock to the hundred and fifty we envisaged.

We had made a start with calf rearing, and in the winter I had spent an interesting time with Bert repairing the asbestos roof of the old dairy. The previous owners had been outrageous botchers, and some of the rafters had been tied to nails on the wall with baler twine. How the whole roof had not blown away in the winter gales was a mystery to me. I have no great head for heights, and the dairy had a concrete floor.

"I'll tell you when you falls," Bert had said encouragingly.

I finished the roof, knocked out the concrete milking partitions with a sledgehammer, repaired the doors, re-glazed the windows, and we had a presentable calfrearing building.

Bert often came with me to market when I bought the calves. He loved it there, talking to all his old friends, reminiscing and drinking beer. He always went to sleep as soon as he had lowered himself into the seat of my mini pickup for the return journey, waking with a start when we drove into the farmyard.

"Good snooze, Bert?" I asked him once.

"I never go to sleep in a car," he retorted indignantly. "I never have been able to drop off in they things."

We reared twelve calves in our first winter, and they thrived. Feeding them on dark winter evenings was an almost biblical feeling; the wind driving the rain horizontally at the windows, the calves greedily slurping their milk from buckets, lifting them up in the air with their heads to drain the last drops, before contentedly bedding themselves down in the warm straw. My young daughter had almost total responsibility for them during lambing time; one of the benefits of a small family farm that made it such a good place for children.

None of this solved my problem. With the lambs from our forty five ewes, and the calves, we still desperately needed some enterprise, a cash crop to provide extra income for the summer. I wandered around the farm one morning, deep in thought. Corn was out of the question; we were not large enough for that. Root crops were too late in the year for the income that was needed.

Then I had a flash of inspiration. Beans. Of course! Market gardening, on a small scale. The idea was bound to catch on; there were hardly any pick-your-own farms in the area. I rushed to tell my wife, but she was sceptical.

"How are you going to sow three acres of French beans in nice neat rows in a comparatively short time?" she asked me.

I hadn't considered that one; so I consulted a friend of mine, David, who had done some work on market gardens, and who had a smallholding of his own.

I explained my dilemma to him, adding I did not want to spend a large sum of money on a specialist, tractor mounted precision drill.

"You need a hand operated version," he told me. "You load it with seed and push it up and down the field. Special belts, with holes in them to suit the size of your particular seed, from carrots to beans, space them at precise intervals in the row. You'll soon sow three acres with it. I've always hankered after one for my smallholding, but they are not cheap, and I doubt you'll find a second-hand one."

He was right. I carefully studied the leaflets I picked up from our local agricultural engineers, and decided to order a new one. David was correct in thinking they were not cheap, but I reckoned I would easily cover its cost, and still turn in a good profit.

While I was waiting for the machine to arrive, I cultivated the ground for my market garden enterprise. The ground was rather heavy and stony, but I was enthusiastic and expanded my plans to include leeks, to follow the beans and courgettes. That should be enough for our first year.

Everything was prepared for our vegetables, and the drill arrived on the exact day the manufactures had promised. It was a magnificent piece of machinery. Even the normally taciturn Bert was impressed. "If we'd 'ad they things when I were a nipper, it would have saved an 'ell of a lot of 'ard work."

It had two wheels, in a fore and aft configuration, and two handles for steering and pushing; a small double-sided plough behind the front wheel, adjustable for height; behind this was the seed box, with the special belts below taking the drive from the rear wheel. And there was a device for covering the seed at the rear. There were even marker poles on the sides, ploughing a small furrow to indicate where the next row was to go. The whole contraption was propelled and powered by me.

I eagerly loaded it onto the trailer, and we all went up to the field to try it out. I filled the little seed box with beans and set off. It worked perfectly, dropping them exactly spaced, at the correct depth and neatly covered over, just as the manufacturer had promised. There was, however, one major snag; it was incredibly hard work. I was aware our ground was not market garden quality, but I was unprepared for the enormous exertion required to push it along. It was evidently designed for light, stone-free, friable soil.

I managed ten yards at my first attempt before collapsing, exhausted, beside it.

"The trouble with you is you're not fit," Sarah informed me. But she declined my offer to try it out.

Bert remained silent, puffing on his pipe and surveying the clouds.

"It was your idea, so you'll have to persevere or we'll have to write the whole operation off, and we can't afford to do that. Don't worry," she added, "you'll soon get fit using that thing."

With that she walked back to the farmhouse, leaving Bert and I to somehow sow three acres of beans. And persevere I did, pushing the contraption up and down the field, nearly horizontal with the effort, pouring sweat, arms and legs shaking from the strain. I felt almost medieval using that thing. It was an anachronism, something a French peasant would have used in the middle ages.

It was duly christened The Peasant by my family, and drilling those beans was some of the hardest work I have ever done. If it struck a large stone, of which there were plenty, it would stop dead, almost pitching me over the handles. The obstacle would have to be removed,

The Peasant started again - and it was the hardest work of all gaining momentum - until the next bit of flint revealed itself, with a resounding clang on the nose of the plough. Gradually, I improved from ten yards without a break to twenty, and even to thirty. It was impossible not to count one's progress, but a thirty-yard stretch was my absolute limit without a rest. When I finished I must have been super fit.

I brought the courgettes on in little pots, but used The Peasant for drilling the leeks. There was no denying it did a good job, but I had my doubts about market gardening the following year. Sheep were much easier. The beans flourished, as did the courgettes, but the rabbits ate all the leeks. I used The Peasant to sow some late beans where the leeks had been, and they, too, did well; the rabbits apparently were not so keen on French beans as they were on leeks.

When the vegetables were ready for picking, I placed a prominent advertisement for pick-your-own beans and courgettes in the local paper, and sat by the phone in case there were any enquiries. And it did ring, once. It was a woman requesting directions; I gave them, but she never turned up. Nor did anyone else.

I inserted the advertisement in other papers. Still not one person came. The beans and courgettes, which had cropped heavily, too, would soon be old, stringy and useless unless we could persuade people to pick them.

Depressed, my wife, Bert and I retired to the local pub for a drink and a snack. My wife disappeared for a while. I assumed she had retired to powder her nose, but she had not. And when she reappeared she was bright eyed and smiling. "I've been in the kitchen," she said, "talking to the landlady. I found out how much she pays for beans and courgettes, and I've done a deal with her, undercutting her supplier. She says she will take as many as we can bring her. She'll freeze the surplus."

"You'll have us shot," I grumbled, "undercutting like that. Besides, we've enough to fill every room in the pub."

"And there're plenty of pubs and restaurants in the area. Let's go now and see how we get on."

We got on almost too well. We picked beans and courgettes all day long, and it was almost as hard work as pushing The Peasant. We delivered in the evenings - the only time we could manage - the mini pickup stacked out with boxes of our produce.

Bert often came with me on these runs, and he was in his element. Whilst I was in the kitchen unloading and taking payment, he slipped into the bar for a quick half. As the delivery progressed, it proved increasingly difficult to extract him from his various havens.

"'Aven't enjoyed myself so much for years," he told me after one call.

"I don't suppose you've drunk so much beer for years either."

"No," he agreed happily, "I bain't."

It had been a long, hard slog, but at last the crop was finished. We had made money from it - good money - but not quite in the way I had intended.

On our very last delivery, Bert leant towards me and said, anxiously and with feeling, "These beans 'ave been delicious all summer. I 'opes you keeps that Peasant 'o yourn and does the same next year. I told you it saves a lot of hard work, and I was right, and you'll find it even easier next year." There was really no answer to that.

But that was all in the past. Gone was the freedom of working when I pleased, however long and hard, replaced by the institution of Royal Mail, with its set hours, overtime and peculiar working practices and its curious ethos of 'The Way Forward'. If I were to remain a postman I would have to become used to it. Bert, I decided, would have made nothing at all of it.

Four

To my wife's amusement I carefully interpreted the notes I had taken and wrote them up on some free pages in the poetry exercise book.

Armed with this and a certain confidence, I rode down the slope where Sydney was sitting as usual, parked my moped and removed the exercise book from a saddlebag.

"What's that?" asked Sydney intrusively.

"It's a poetry book," I answered truthfully and walked into the office, leaving a nonplussed Sydney finishing his tea.

"It's your last day of training," Dave told me unnecessarily. "You'd better make the most of it and ask me anything you ain't clear on. You're on your own tomorrow." He pointed to my notebook. "That bloody thing won't help you none, how the hell can you expect to read that when you're going along?"

"It's only an aide mémoire," I said loftily, but the expression was not familiar to Dave. He shrugged and thrust a bundle of letters in front of me. "You'd better get sorting; it's the only way to learn."

Again, I concentrated on the route; it seemed easier now, and I made a few corrections in my notes. It was really a form of education by repetition, but the trouble was it had been years since I had done any learning. By the time we returned to the office at eleven o'clock I was reasonably confident.

Before I went home I talked to Stephen who had just returned from his first delivery: the bike rounds had a short break and then went out on a second delivery. The rural van rounds only made one delivery, and it appeared no one took the half hour break we were allowed, but worked straight through. It seemed a sensible arrangement.

With our very limited experience we were discussing the various merits and demerits of our respective rounds when Stephen noticed

35

one of his shoelaces had come undone. He went down on one knee and started retying it, and I was watching him idly when suddenly a voice said, "Get on your feet. I 'ate to see anyone kneeling in this office."

Stephen gazed up, frozen in the act of tying his lace, and his eyes met Murdock's stare.

"Go on, get up. No one kneels in this office."

Stephen slowly rose to his feet.

"That's better," Murdoch said, and repeating, "I 'ates to see people kneeling," wandered off, the yellowed stub of an unlit roll up cigarette protruding from his mouth.

"What was all that about?" Stephen asked in bewilderment.

"I don't know," I replied, but I was reminded whom Murdoch resembled in his manner. It was the depraved, bachelor headmaster of my preparatory school who had conceived a virulent loathing for me; at the impressionable age of eight, a hatred that was fully reciprocated. The analogy with school was complete.

"On your own today," said Sydney as I arrived in the morning. "Think you'll manage?"

"Yes," I replied rather shortly, irritated by his statement of the obvious.

I collected the letters from the main sorting frame, took them back to the Topley frame and started sorting. For a moment, I looked at it and my mind went totally blank; I couldn't remember a thing. I gazed at the first letter in my hand: Mr. and Mrs. Courtney, Lower Topley Farmhouse. Where the hell was that? Gradually memory reasserted itself and recollection returned.

Soon I became less hesitant and more fluid, carefully remembering the pitfalls of mixing up the three Keepers Cottages and the Rose Cottages, though my sorting was painfully slow compared with the more experienced hands.

Speed would come later, I told myself, concentrating on accuracy.

Sydney came over and leant against the frame, observing me. "I'd help you if I could, but I ain't done this round for years. That's the wrong Rose Cottage, by the way."

Outraged, I removed the letter and checked the name and address. It was correct.

"Like I said, it's years since I done this one," Sydney was unabashed, "but once you've done a round it comes back to you soon enough."

I wished he would go away, and eventually he did, moving on to see how Stephen was faring. He certainly took a proprietorial interest in newcomers.

I went to collect some more letters from the frame where the other postmen were still sorting. There was an inexhaustible supply this morning.

"Don't you go getting lost, like Cedric," one of them taunted me, and there was some laughter. "He went halfway to London, you know."

I did know, but Sydney said, "He won't get lost, 'ee's got his own map with him."

Dave came over a couple of times to see how his protégé was getting on, but mostly I was left to my own devices. I was languishing far behind the others, despite the fact I had done none of the primary sorting, and was beginning to despair of ever getting out, when a cheerful man of about forty joined me. He introduced himself as Peter.

"I know what it's like when you're on your own for the first time," he said. "No one else here gives two knobs of goat dung for a newcomer, they're only interested in seeing how far behind he gets. You'll find that out for yourself if you stay long enough."

He placed my van keys on the bench in front of the frame. "I've taken the seat out for you and stacked it away in the bike shed. Dave should have done it, but he couldn't be bothered. Now, if you shove over a bit I'll give you a hand."

Gratefully, I moved over and Peter helped me throw out letters for a quarter of an hour, until we had nearly finished them.

"That's all I've got time for. I'm on overtime again today so have to shift a bit myself to get back in on time. I've sorted your packets, they're over there," he indicated a trolley further up the office.

I thanked him profusely, but he just shrugged, and was gone.

When I had finished my sorting there was no one left in the office, apart from Jack who was collecting empty mugs, and John Higgings who, with a frown of concentration, was studying the signing in forms. These were placed on an ancient Dickensian-style, waist-high, sloping desk. They occupied a disproportionate amount of a manager's working day, I was to discover.

Jack passed by with his tray and picked up my mug. "Almost there. I see Peter helping you, but I'll tell you one thing. He's the only one who will. No other blighter'll bother. It's every man for himself in this place, always has been and always will be, but you'll be all right so long as you don't worry about getting behind. Everyone here is all rush and tear: who can get back fastest, who can get the most overtime, and how fast they can do it. I've worked in plenty of offices, but I've never come across one like this before."

I collected a couple of registered letters from the uncommunicative Murdoch and loaded up the Marina, carefully placing the box keys in the glove compartment where I wouldn't lose them.

John Higgings came over to me. "I expect I shall be gone when you return, but there should be someone in the office. Dave showed you how to fill out your overtime docket, I expect."

I nodded.

"You'll need to today, but after a few days you'll get the hang of things and cut your time down."

He walked away, and, starting the Morris Marina with some trepidation, I drove out of the yard. It was much later than I had left with Dave, about seven thirty, and the sun was evaporating the early mist as I drove, with considerably more care than Dave had exercised, across the pavement and down the drive to my first call, unimaginatively called The Bungalow. It was a curious feeling, being on my own, rather like an intrusion on somebody's privacy, and it persisted for several days until I was more used to the job and realised this was an accepted intrusion. But it was still a slightly uncomfortable sensation.

I parked the Marina, delivered The Bungalow's letters, returned to the van and tried to select reverse. Nothing, it appeared, would persuade that stubborn, clapped out gearbox to engage reverse. I tried every combination of tricks I could remember from the many vehicles I had driven over the years: pushing the gearlever down, pulling it up, searching in vain for a sprung collar to lift under the knob, and every permutation of positions I could think of, but nothing worked. The markings on the gear knob had long since eroded away.

I desperately tried to remember how Dave had done it, but apart from the first morning when he had roundly cursed the gearbox, he had experienced no trouble and I had taken no notice of how he put it in reverse. It should, after all, have been a pretty basic movement.

I cursed Dave, as fluently as he had uttered obscenities at the unfortunate van, for not letting me into its secret. How he must have laughed at the thought of his trainee struggling with the Marina's recalcitrant gearbox on his very first call. Eventually, with a crashing grinding of gear cogs, I found the elusive gear with a desperate lunge and flukey twist of the irritating, spindly lever. I hastily turned round and fled back down the drive, wondering what on earth the inhabitants of The Bungalow had made of my performance.

It had not been an auspicious start.

I had no further trouble with reverse once I had got the knack and, rather to my surprise, I never had to resort to my poetry exercise book. Evidently Royal Mail was correct in its assumption that three days training was sufficient. Encouraged, I started to relax and enjoy the round. Belle Lodge came and went, with no appearance of its eccentric occupant, and I was waved hastily onto the road from the house on the lethal straight. I was a long way behind the time Dave had set, but I was not worried. If there was one good thing about this job it was that there was no pressure - unless a driver became worked up and anxious about getting back on time, which seemed to be Dave's main objective.

Once again I was struck by the lack of people; it really was a dormitory area and it was not until I arrived at the Keepers Cottage where Colonel Mackinnon resided that I had a proper conversation. The old colonel, evidently well aware that after the third day a new recruit was on his own, came to the door immediately he heard the van. He was immaculately dressed again and solemnly took the letters I gave him.

"I trust they are not for Messrs. Mitford or Reilley."

I assured him they were not; I had double checked them before I left the van.

He carefully went through them and, satisfied, said, "I hope I am seeing the beginning of a decent service now. At least you have made a good start."

On that patronising note he closed the door, leaving me standing on the threshold, perfectly certain I would never become his permanent postman. Much later on, when I came to deliver Mr. Mitford's letters to his Keepers Cottage I found I had missorted two of Colonel Mackinnon's into his. There was little that could be done. It was too late to return to the colonel, and the colossal loss of face involved would have been too much to bear, so I put them to one side. I would sneak them into the sorting frame on my return and the old boy would receive them in the morning, none the wiser. But it bothered me how easy it appeared to make such a basic mistake. I put it down to inexperience, but it was the sort of blunder I thought I could never make.

The remainder of the round was uneventful. A few dogs barked behind closed doors, the harvest had restarted and the traffic had correspondingly increased. At least I was in charge of my own destiny, provided the rickety van did not shed a wheel, which, given the alarming vibration that transmitted itself to the steering wheel, was always a possibility.

I returned to the parliamentary candidate's house with a registered letter. Despite the comparative lateness of my earlier arrival there had been no one in view. I was fully expecting to meet the glamorous, cigarette-smoking nanny, but, to my surprise, the door was opened by the man himself. He was urbane and polite, as one would expect from someone who probably regarded everyone as a potential voter. He signed the little blue scrap of paper and carefully handed it back to me, remarking politely on the fine weather. I would sooner have met the nanny.

I emptied the final box, conscientiously turning the tab over to 2 and returned to the office. Murdoch was preparing to leave and I gave him my registered slips, which he took without comment. Then I loaded the parcels for delivery to the estates into the van. John Higgins had evidently departed, and apart from Murdoch the office was deserted.

I arrived back at one o'clock, tired after the effort of concentration, but pleased there had been no major problems. I put Colonel Mackinnon's letters in his slot and turned to find Sydney entering the office.

"You done well. That book of yours must 'ave helped. Course it makes it easier, driving yourself them last two days of training. Better than any book, doing it yourself."

I was puzzled, "I never drove at all until today." I wished I had, but the idea had never occurred to me.

"You should 'ave driven," Sydney replied. "The regulations say one day's observation followed by two days driving. That bloody Dave's no good, only interested in getting home. Too late now," he added, with unconscious irony, "but I'll 'ave a word with Uncle John about it, though 'ee won't do nothing. Never does, too frightened 'ee might lose someone."

I liked the Uncle John and asked Sydney if everyone called him that.

"Always been known as Uncle John, ever since 'e came 'ere as manager."

I couldn't have thought of a better sobriquet for him.

"'Ere, I got something for you." Sydney fumbled around in his top jacket pocket and produced a piece of paper. "It's a union application what's is name. All you 'ave to do is fill it in and return it to me, and I'll see to the rest. We're going on strike, so you may as well join."

I took the form and glanced at it. I was not a union man. The only one I had ever joined had been the Auckland Gas Workers Union, for three weeks, and it had brought me no benefit - even when one of my labouring colleagues had threatened to knock me into the trench we had just dug, for refusing to collect his tools for him.

"I'll report you to the union," I had told him mischievously.

"They won't do nothing," had been his dismissive reply. "They's bloody useless, only interested in strikes. Now get them tools."

I had refused again, and fortunately his threat had been as empty as the trench, but it had reinforced the notion I had harboured for years, that unions were a waste of time.

I turned the form around in my hands. "I'm not sure I want to join," I told Sydney, but he held up his hand to stop me.

"Everyone in this office belongs," and to emphasise the point as if I had not taken it in, "we are a fully unionised office."

I placing the form in my pocket, "I'll think about it."

I thought about it that evening and decided, rather against my better judgement, that I would join. I had only just 'started' and did not wish to become a pariah in the office, despite my conscience dictating otherwise.

I handed Sydney the completed form the following morning, as he was finishing his tea outside the office. He glanced at it and stuffed it into his pocket. Standing up, he surprisingly shook my hand.

"Consider yourself a member," he said formally, "and welcome to the Communication Workers' Union. You'll not regret it, an' I reckons you're a stayer now."

I was uncertain about the staying bit, but if it satisfied Sydney that was good enough.

"When and why are we going on strike?" I asked him.

"About a fortnight, and for the usual what's 'is name, pay. It's always pay, but it won't last long, less than a week, and then management usually sees sense. What you lose in wages you makes up in overtime clearing the backlog."

It sounded a tenuous argument to me, but I did not disagree.

"What about strike pay?" I enquired.

"Won't get none of that. We're not a rich union, can't afford no strike pay. Your subs will be deducted automatically from your pay."

Slightly puzzled and now, apparently, a fully-fledged member, I went inside and started sorting.

"How did you get on yesterday?" Dave asked. "You have any trouble with reverse?"

I glanced at him, standing over me, grinning inanely. "I finished about one, and I had no problem with reverse. Should I have?"

"You're on your own tomorrow," I later told Stephen.

"I'm on my own today," he replied. "Murdoch said because we're so short staffed I could only have two days training. I still don't know the sorting frame properly, so God knows what time I'll get back. Murdoch says he won't pay me if I claim overtime, whatever that means."

I was beginning to wonder who ran the office and whether Murdoch owned Royal Mail. "He can't do that. You have to be paid for the work you do. Has Sydney seen you about joining the union yet?"

"He did mention it, but at this rate I shan't be here long enough to bother."

The office was patently understaffed and it was difficult to justify Murdoch's attitude, but I guessed there was more to it than merely trying to curb the overtime, which was not his concern in the first place.

After I had been doing the round for a week, and was beginning to return to the office in reasonable time, Uncle John, I could think of him as none other now, approached me. "You'll have to learn the main sorting frame, I know it will delay your going out in the morning, but everyone has to sort on the main frame and I think it's time you started." He hesitated. "You might find it hard to begin with, more difficult than your Topley frame, but it has to be done. I'll start you on it tomorrow."

He was right. The frame was a nightmare. There were about thirty odd pigeon holes, large enough for sizeable letters, all labelled, and one person was supposed to stand and sort into this contraption. There were six of these, all identical, but there were more sorters than frames, which meant that often two people had to share. In addition, though the pigeon holes were clearly labeled by the round names, there were many anomalies. Some routes overlapped each other, and until someone had actually done a round it was difficult to know where one finished and another started. The altruistic Peter positioned himself next to me and explained all this. "You'll have to look out for the factories, too, they've their own separate boxes."

'The factories' were a bit of a puzzle. I was unaware of any factories in Bramton, and on further investigation it turned out the word was a misnomer, referring instead to firms that received large amounts of mail, such as estate agents and insurance companies. It was, apparently, an anachronism in the same vein as tying up; it seemed that Royal Mail was deeply embedded in the past.

I had also noted there were no computers in the office even though it was 1988. It was probably just as well for I was perfectly certain that

Uncle John would not have had a clue how to operate one, any more than I.

Peter was a fast and fluent sorter. He had been at Bramton for seven years. "Anything you are unsure of, leave on a pile in front of me, and I'll sort them. You'll make plenty of mistakes to start with, but after a while you'll get the hang of it." The pile in front of Peter grew to an alarming height, but at last we finished sorting the letters, and he speedily re-sorted the ones I had not known.

"Anything larger than a letter goes into the packet bag," he told me as we returned to our respective sorting frames, "but I hear they're thinking of changing that and making special frames to take A4 sized mail. It would make life much easier if they did."

I was slowly coming to know some of the people on the round, though I had yet to meet the parliamentary candidate's wife. I was also meeting some of their dogs. It is a well known fact that dogs and postmen do not get on, and there has never been a convincing reason for it, but it is, nonetheless, perfectly true.

There were two dogs on the Topleys that particularly bothered me. One was a black Labrador in Lower Topley, which was allowed the run of its owner's garden while he was away at work. The path to the front door, with the garden to the right, was crudely fenced with pig wire stapled to rickety posts. And the dog, which knew the sound of the van, was waiting for me when I stopped.

It raced dementedly up and down, barking furiously, hackles fully up, and white froth flying from its mouth. I sometimes wondered if it had rabies. It would hurl itself against the insubstantial netting, which rocked alarmingly, following my progress to the front door, a matter of ten yards. When I delivered the mail it stood on its hind legs, the front feet firmly planted on the top strand of the pig wire, barking hysterically, before turning and repeating the performance for the return journey.

Dave had said, "Just ignore it and push the letters through the box," but I gained the impression that underneath his bravado he was just as nervous as I was.

It is said that dogs can smell fear and being terrified of this black, demented monster certainly did not help, though it would probably have behaved in the same way regardless. As far as I was concerned the animal was beyond redemption and would probably have torn me apart, had it broken the inadequate fencing.

What I particularly disliked, and it was something I could never completely erase from my memory, were the flecks of white foam flying from its mouth, which landed on my trousers, and the drawn back top lip displaying all its canine dentistry. I carefully wiped the revolting mess off with grass when I made my next call and was safely out of the animal's range.

It was beyond my comprehension why people kept dogs like this, but, as I found out in my time at the Post Office, it was a truism that dogs are like their owners. It was fortunate I never met this particular owner, for if he had only been half as bad as his canine friend I would have run a mile.

The other dog was an Alsation that belonged to an elderly couple further up the road. The wife doted on the animal, but I hated it. Again, it had the run of the garden, but the only view of the postman it had was through a wooden gate adjacent to the post box, which was screwed to the wall. Like the Labrador, it went beserk when it heard the van arrive and alternately hurled itself at the gate, which rattled and shook, and whirled around in circles chasing its tail. Again its hackles were fully raised, its top lip drawn back and white foam flew from its mouth. It was a gruesome sight. Sometimes the woman tried to placate it, but her dog was beyond control, ignoring her completely.

"He's a lovely dog really, we've had him for five years and I adore him. He won't hurt you; he just gets a little excited when he sees the postman."

Her husband was more peremptory, grabbing it by the collar and hurling the horrible thing to the ground and, sometimes, swinging a well aimed boot at the beast. But this, unsurprisingly, only served to inflame it to even greater excesses.

He was more realistic than his wife. "Don't you come near it or it'll have you in small pieces quicker than a piranha."

I didn't doubt him for a minute. I cut a stout stick from the hedgerow and suitably armed, walked up the respective paths with slightly more confidence, though I doubted it would really have made much difference had I been confronted by these animals if they escaped; they were far too quick and agile. It was the stuff of nightmares, but fortunately the fences and the gate latch always held.

Five

Stephen stormed into the sorting area, "That's it. I've made up my mind, I'm leaving. It's a terrible job. The hours are dreadful, the people unfriendly and that ruddy Murdoch gets at me all the time. I've had enough."

Murdoch I could handle, but he was right about the hours. The job was a social killer. And it was one of life's mysteries how postmen were able to procreate for total exhaustion; with only a Sunday off to recover, the working week was scarcely conducive to encouraging a rise in the postal birth rate.

I reserved my judgement on unfriendly colleagues, for I only really knew Sydney and Peter. But my first impression, reinforced by Jack's comments, was that everyone in the office was completely selfcentered - with the notable exception of Peter. I decided to give the job a fairer trial; after all I needed the money and there was a bonus - I felt fitter than I had for a long time.

I mentioned this to Sydney. He laughed. "You'll be fitter than ever after next week. You're on a bike then. Fit to drop you'll be."

Sydney appeared to know everything, and his words were confirmed by Uncle John the following morning. "I'm putting you on a town walk next week," adding confusingly, "you'd better see Sydney about a bicycle. And that's another thing, if you give him your measurements he will organise a uniform for you."

He sighed. "It's going to be difficult next week. I'm losing my three students, and Stephen is leaving, so you'll have to work some overtime or we'll never get the mail out. The trouble is we keep advertising for postmen, but no one applies." He gave a tired smile. "We'll manage somehow. We usually do."

I gave my measurements to Sydney and he stuffed the piece of paper in his pocket. "That'll be through in a couple of weeks, an' I'll fix a bike for you on Monday."

"You seem to have a lot of responsibility in the office."

"I'm union representative, uniform officer, bike officer and 'ealth an' safety officer," he said proudly. "Apart from the union rep bit, I gets paid for the other duties, an' I tells Higgings what to do most of the time. 'Ee ain't got a clue about the rounds, but I've been 'ere for twenty years an' I know em all. 'Ee'd be lost without me."

There was no false modesty to Sydney.

My last day on the Topleys - a Saturday - was a dreadful day. It poured throughout, torrential, unremitting rain. I was drenched by the time I arrived at the office on my moped, and I remained wet all day. Sydney gave me some Royal Mail waterproofs, which let in water almost immediately and after an hour I was soaked down to, and including, my underpants.

The Marina didn't like the conditions any more than I did, threatening to expire at any minute. It was hardly surprising considering the huge puddles and miniature lakes it had to negotiate, often on three cylinders and sometimes, it felt, only one. Frantic revving for a while restored all four to some sort of health, only to be doused again when I was forced by another car into the running river of water flowing down the side of the road. The van was thoroughly miserable, and so was I. There were very few people around, which was not surprising, and even the irascable colonel never ventured from his Keepers Cottage to check his mail before accepting it as correct.

I did meet the parliamentary candidate's wife. She was standing in the porch smoking a cigarette, and when I arrived she emerged from the shelter of the porch, without a coat, and walked over to me before I had a chance to get out. It was raining harder than ever and I was so wet that the very act of levering myself out of the seat was one of acute discomfort; my saturated clothing had chafed my skin, and I was grateful that, for one call at least, I could remain in my sodden seat.

She bent to take the registered letter and slip, and I heard an audible hiss as the rain extinguished her cigarette. I looked at her as she attempted to sign the receipt, which was rapidly turning to pulp. She was about forty five and once she must have been beautiful, but she was a wreck now. It did not help that the rain was coursing down her hair, and dripping off the end of her nose. Her face was ravaged from the effects of drinking. She had heavy bags under her bloodshot eyes and deep lines on her cheeks, which were an intricate network of tiny red veins.

Her hand shook violently as she attempted her signature; she had clearly indulged in her first drink of the day. She gave me a ghastly smile as she returned the disintigrating receipt and, sodden herself, she turned and, groping in her pocket for a packet of cigarettes, shambled back to the house. I felt an immense wave of pity for her, my own miserable condition forgotten as I watched her.

Who knows what could have reduced a previously attractive woman to this dreadful parody of a human being. Whether it was something in her genes, or just the fact that she was the wife of someone who had a high profile, and the strain caused her to seek refuge in the bottle, I would never know. But, as I drove back to the office, I suddenly felt dreadfully depressed.

Sitting hunched on my moped, the rain bouncing off my goggles, water penetrating every body orifice, shivering violently from the cold and wet, all I could think of was a hot bath.

My daughter was home from university for the weekend and had spent the morning languishing in a constantly topped up bath, filled to the overflow. There was no hot water left, so I settled for a brisk rub down with a towel and a very large Scotch.

There was chaos in the office on Monday morning. In addition to the departure of the students and Stephen, two others had phoned in sick.

Uncle John showed me my new frame. "I can't spare anyone to train you. You'll have to work it out for yourself. It shouldn't be too difficult. At least you have some idea from the Topley frame."

I glanced at it briefly. It was straightforward enough: closes, streets and, from what I remembered, upmarket estates. Most of the houses were numbered, two sharing a sorting slot, with only a few businesses at the end of the round. The trouble was, though I had heard of some of the areas, I had not the remotest idea where they were. I knew the general layout of Bramton - it was pretty basic, the whereabouts of the shops and the pubs - but not the sprawl, which lay around it.

I told Uncle John, and he thought for a minute. "I'll get Lenny Murdoch to take you round in his car. It won't take long and then at least you will know the route."

He was right about the sorting frame. With my experience of the Topley frame, this was easy, though by the time I had finished I was almost the last man left in the office.

Jack passed by, engaged on his endless task of collecting empty mugs. "We're both beginners today," he said with a smile. "They've got me on delivering. That's quite something, the cleaner delivering letters. Things must be desperate, even old Murdoch's doing a round."

I bundled up my letters, carefully packing them into the bags, which were designed to fit on the flat platforms at the front of the bicycles. Sydney had found me a bike: a standard Royal Mail Pashley. I viewed it with some suspicion. It was years since I had ridden such a contraption, and this one had no gears. It looked like hard work - all the machines I had used before had at least been graced with three speed gears.

Sydney undid the straps on my first bag - I had three - dumped it on the carrier and tied the ends firmly together just under the handlebars.

"Plonk your other two over there," he indicated a pile by the door, "make sure they're clearly labelled and 'Iggings'll drop them off later, one at the shop and the other at number two Badger Close."

I went into the cage. Murdoch was sitting with his back to me, again writing in some sort of ledger. I noticed his hands. They were huge, and the pen he was holding looked awkward, and insignificant, in his sausage-like fingers. It was odd to see such enormous hands on so slight a person.

I cleared my throat and he slowly swivelled his chair round to face me, I gazed into those terrible eyes, "John Higgings said he would have a word with you, and that you would take me round Town Four in your car."

He swivelled to face his desk, put down his pen and pushed the chair back, slowly rising to his feet. He picked up his car keys from a side table and walked out of the cage. I followed him. He really was a very odd man.

We walked to his car, a brand new Ford Orion and, opening the door, he lowered himself into the driver's seat. Hesitantly, I followed suit. I felt like an uninvited guest at a party. The car and the interior were blue, and the seats were plush. There were a pair of white fluffy dice hanging from the interior mirror, a couple of plastic nodding dogs on either side of the back shelf, and a small vase of plastic roses attached to the top of the dashboard. The whole interior smelt overpoweringly of air freshener.

He started this monument to bad taste, drove out of the yard, and took me to the opposite side of Bramton to where I had delivered parcels to the estates. This end of town was quite different, executive homes, executive closes and executive mansions.

"You starts 'ere," Murdoch said suddenly, the first words he had uttered, "Foxgrove."

We drove round Foxgrove, Shepherds Close, Willow Tree Drive and many more, each time Murdoch jabbing one of his porky index fingers soundlessly at the sign proclaiming the reminder that, not so very long ago, these developments had been green fields, copses and woods. It was more disheartening than the Farmhouses, Old Vicarages and Old

Post Offices of the Topleys but, as current jargon dictated, it was the way forward.

Apprehensively, I judged the gradients. That standard Pashley would take a lot of pedalling, especially with a full bag on its carrier, and it was a fair distance, even in Murdoch's car. We finished in a long road containing some assorted pre-war bungalows, and a few small industrial units and workshops.

"That's your last call," Murdoch said, "and then you comes back and does a second delivery."

He must have been joking. It would take me hours to get round, and if I had to do a second delivery I would not be home until about four o' clock, but I said nothing.

We drove back to the yard and Murdoch indicated the bicycle leaning against the wall, the bag on its carrier, ready to go. "You'd better get mounted and sod off, else you won't be back till nightfall. And don't forget your second delivery."

He locked his car and shambled back to his cage.

I swung my leg over the crossbar of the Pashley and very nearly kept going; the weight of the bag on the front acted as a pendulum, unbalancing the machine and, nearly, me with it. Pedalling hard, standing on the pedals, I wobbled my way up the slope leading away from the Sorting Office, and pushed on more confidently to my first call. There was no doubting that, for one as unused to cycling as I, the Pashley was incredibly hard work. Puffing and blowing, feeling hot and flushed, with legs that felt like lead, I arrived. I had ridden half a mile, and firmly decided that Murdoch could forget about his second delivery. I was starting to doubt I would ever see the Sorting Office again.

Gradually my muscles eased - though how they would be in the morning was quite another matter - and, alternating between leaning the bicycle against a wall whilst walking around a close and pedalling to the next one, I was able to take an interest in the round. In a curious way it represented, in miniature, the progression of the middle classes: from first house, first mortgage and first wife to promotion, a larger house, then executive house and finally the retirement, mock-Georgian mansion. The round faithfully followed this middle class pattern. There were none of the upper classes here, they and the landed gentry lived on the rural rounds.

Heaven knows where I fitted in - an ex public schoolboy and farmer, pedalling an overloaded, outdated, sit-up-and-beg Pashley around these roads. The housing layout was no doubt the same in most towns and cities in the country. Living in such stereotypical conditions was certainly something I could never countenance.

Bramton was a small town where nearly everyone knew everyone else and, on the estates at least, a lot of them were related, often dangerously so. And small towns bred small town attitudes, not all of which were healthy. Bramton was probably not unique in having developments situated at either end, with the grey areas where they joined occupied by a miscellany of older houses and run down businesses.

Nearly all of these up-market streets were open planned, making it easy to walk round them and cut across the beautifully tended lawns, either lovingly maintained by bored executive housewives or expensive gardeners.

Sydney had warned me of the dangers of stepping on these strips of perfection. "You can ravish their wives, seduce their daughters or have an affair with the nanny," he had told me, "and they'll forgive you. But never take short cuts across their lawns."

He was right, at least about that.

One elderly man was waiting for me at his door, watching me walking on his grass. "You're new, so I will tell you this once. When you deliver my mail you walk down my drive, not over my lawn. Is that clear?"

"Perfectly," I replied, wondering what was so sacrosanct about it. He snatched the letters from my hand, turned on his heel and slammed the door.

I decided the sensible way was to continue crossing unfenced gardens until I was advised not to, and to avoid any confrontation. I found out later that this was the attitude most of my colleagues adopted.

A couple of hours into the round I encountered a problem far more acute than that of trespassing on grass. I was desperate to relieve myself and I could see nowhere suitable to go. These open planned developments and estates were all very well, but not particularly private. Mostly they had borders around the edges and the odd shrubs planted here and there, not nearly dense enough to afford the cover I needed. Eventually, I found a large clump of pampas grass and carefully manoeuvering myself close to it, where I reckoned I could not be seen from the house, not twenty yards away, I noisily and gratefully relieved myself. It was a far from ideal place, but I was past caring by then. Later I found out that both the infant school, a short detour away, and the shop were quite happy to let the postman use their facilities. Other rounds were more difficult; ingenuity and a strong bladder were needed for this job, especially in cold weather.

I made my last delivery, and was faced with a long uphill pull back to the office. My legs felt as though they could not complete another turn of the crank. Somehow, quite exhausted, I thankfully coasted down the slope to the Sorting Office and parked the outrageous, gearless Pashley in the bicycle shed.

There was no one in the office, which was unlocked. It was one forty five, so I quickly gathered my gear and rode home on my old moped before there could be any argument about a second delivery. Never had I appreciated the power of the little Puch's 49cc engine more.

I suffered dreadful cramp in my legs that night, and in the morning it was not only my legs that were stiff; most of the other muscles in my body had rebelled against the unaccustomed and violent exercise. Gradually they eased and, as the elasticity returned, I became a little less of a wooden man. To my surprise, no one said a word about my failure to take out the second delivery. They probably had not even noticed.

It wasn't until much later that I discovered a second delivery hadn't been taken out for weeks. When we were so short staffed, and where so many rounds had been split up and taken out on overtime, there simply had not been time for it.

The longer I did this round, the faster and fitter I became, and the more pieces of other rounds were put on me. The trouble was that the sorting of these was done in a hurry by others, and often left much to be desired. I was sometimes faced with the choice of cycling down a hill to deliver a missorted letter to a house I had just visited, and sweating my way back up the hill again, or putting the letter to one side for delivery the following day. At first I was conciencious, but later, more cynically, put them aside.

It was not difficult to be cynical. We were dreadfully overworked, often returning home after two o'clock in the afternoon, six days a week. And having a disrupted sleep pattern was no help. And none of us was getting any younger.

Uncle John kept me on this round for several weeks. He had somehow managed to engage two temporary postmen. This eased the burden of work for a while, and I found that at least I could finish at a more reasonable time. It also meant I could leave the office earlier and, as it was October now, this was often in the dark and cold, with early frosts turning cars into igloos of frozen glass and metal.

In the mornings, the young, keen, would-be executives living at the beginning of the round overcame this problem by starting their vehicles and turning the heater up to full power, and then disappearing back into their houses to turn on the television and eat their breakfasts. Delivering letters in the freezing cold was unpleasant enough, but walking through a fog of petrol fumes and vapour rising from numerous cars, left unevenly ticking over and slowly defrosting, made it even more so. The curtains were always pulled back, revealing children slowly masticating whilst gazing vacantly at mindless cartoon features on the TV, ingesting nourishment for the body and rubbish for the mind before they were whisked off to school. It was scarcely an intellectual start to the day.

I wondered, too, at the intelligence of the architects of these brick and building block houses, flung up in no time at all and probably with a design life of about thirty years. They appeared to be of a basic, standard design, with a few variations depending on the size of the house. Each incorporated a small porch at the front door, with the downstairs loo to one side. Pushing letters through the letterbox was not an edifying experience, with the occupant of the loo only a foot or two away. It was also not improved by Bramton's recently acquired Indian takeaway.

The more expensive properties were not immune to this design quirk - or it could have been the architect's perverted sense of humour. Worse, the houses were deteriorating, too, though they were not more than four or five years old. In one particular close of twenty five houses some had cracks in the brickwork and, on virtually every house, all the window frames were rotten; so much so I could easily push my finger into them. And these 'desirable' houses changed hands for phenomenal amounts of money.

Six

My uniform had arrived. I do not like wearing uniform, it reminds me too much of school, mostly something I would rather forget, but there was little option other than to wear it. Self conciously, I entered the office and had to endure the expected, but good humoured, comments.

Sydney, for some reason, was immensely proud of me in my new attire. I was not so sure.

"You're a proper postman now."

Uncle John approved, too. "Very smart. By the way, I've been sent a date for your interview and aptitude test. Next Wednesday at two o'clock in the main Sorting Office at Buddleshaw."

I was aghast. Interview? Aptitude test? I had no idea what he was talking about, so I asked him to elucidate.

"The interview for your job here," he explained patiently. "You must have an interview, and the aptitude test is to ensure you're suitable for the job. It's a matter of form. You must have both before Royal Mail can employ you."

"But I've been here for two months," I protested, "employed and paid by Royal Mail and now supplied with a uniform. Surely there's no need for either."

He was adamant. "You must have them both, before you can be employed."

There seemed little point in persisting against this logic. It was part of the system, and working for an institution like Royal Mail I had to go along with their rules and set procedures, which were, apparently, inflexible. I hated interviews, but the aptitude test intrigued me. I asked Sydney about it all.

"Well, the interview's what d'yer call it," he said enigmatically.

"What do you mean?" I was puzzled. I had noticed that Sydney hid behind 'what d'yer call it' or 'what's 'is name' when he was unsure of a word - which was quite often.

"Well, it's a what's 'is name thing. You 'as to do it."

He was more revealing about the aptitude test.

"That's dead easy," he said. "No one 'as ever failed it. Never. A couple of students failed it once," he added perplexingly, "but no one fails that, you won't 'ave no trouble there."

But he was less forthcoming when pressed as to what constituted an aptitude test.

"You matches things up and that," he answered vaguely. "It's years since I took mine, but I don't expect it 'as changed much. 'Ere, ask Dave, 'ee took it more recently than me."

I had become quite friendly with Dave since he inducted me into the workings of the Post Office. He had worked for Royal Mail since he had left school and, apart from Uncle John, was the only person in the office who had not experienced life in the real world. He was crafty and cunning, always trying to turn events to his advantage but, in an odd way, he was naive. He had worked at the main office at Buddleshaw for a few years before coming to Bramton, and he knew all the gossip - from both offices - almost before it happened. But he was unable to keep a secret for more than a few minutes, often turning supposition into fact, and, amazingly, he was nearly always right.

It was a useful trait. Much later, I invented an anonymous friend at Buddleshaw, whose name I could never divulge, and, when it suited me, I swore Dave to secrecy and fed him the most outrageous misinformation, certain that within a day everyone in the office would know. It was a form of counter-craft.

Dave confirmed all that Sydney had told me.

"You has to be a complete idiot to fail that. You should pass it all right." It sounded a doubtful compliment.

"Them temporaries," he went on, at a tangent, "they's going next week and we've got two permanent postmen joining. About time, too, with Christmas coming."

I asked him how he knew.

"Higgings told me," he said , smiling. "He tells me everything."

I was unsure of that, but there was definitely a bond between Dave and John Higgings; they were, in a way, isolated as the only career postmen in the office.

Buddleshaw was ten miles away, a prosperous town of some seventy thousand people. The Sorting Office was huge; the floor area of the Bramton office would have comfortably fitted into one small corner. Row upon row of sorting frames stretched into the distance. I was impressed.

For all its faults, and there were many, Royal Mail was a huge and generally well organised machine. When I surveyed this vast Sorting Office serving only a medium sized town, and then thought of the other sixty-odd million people that Royal Mail served, multiplying the number of Sorting Offices by …

It was almost too much to take in. To send a first class letter to any one of the twenty seven million addresses and, mostly, have it arrive the next day was, to me, a minor miracle; far more than the advances made in the intangible and invisible field of instant communication, such as the mobile phone or e-mails, instantly received and instantly forgotten.

The only pity was that Royal Mail delivered so few genuine letters, now a relic of the past, and devoted this huge machine to the delivery of vast quantities of junk, universally and derisively called crap mail by all postmen. We were constantly told that this intrusive, unsolicited rubbish paid the wages and subsidised the whole affair, which was undeniably true, but it still seemed an awful shame that this incredible system was largely devoted to the delivery of wasteful rubbish.

I was ushered upstairs where I was interviewed by a dour Scot after which I was taken to a small room with several school-type desks and chairs arranged in rows. He handed me some question sheets and indicated a desk. "You have half an hour to complete the test," he said and left the room. All that was missing was a Royal Mail invigilator.

I was evidently the only person taking the Aptitude Test, and I looked at the papers. There were two, one pictorial and one written. The latter appeared to be aimed at delinquent five year olds rather than responsible adults. I completed it in about five minutes and turned my attention to the pictures. They were of the type, 'What is wrong with this?' What really took my attention was the dated appearance of the drawings. There was a car, which I identified as a Triumph Mayflower, answer- no steering wheel; a Spitfire - no propeller; a bicycle even older and heavier than the standard Ashley - no chain; a double decker bus of great age: no hand pole on the rear platform - some of the younger generation might just have missed that one - and so on.

I judged the paper had been printed sometime in the late nineteen forties, and Royal Mail must still have had a large stock to use up. After ten minutes I had completed the task and, lying back in my chair, lit a cigarette. I couldn't see an ashtray, but, unbelievably, the desk contained an inkwell, a porcelain inkwell, which fitted into a hole at the top. It still had a crust of dried ink, and it made an excellent ashtray.

After half an hour James MacBride returned to collect my papers. He sniffed the air, "Have you been smoking?" he enquired, with some hostility.

I admitted I had.

"Royal Mail has a strict no smoking policy on its premises. There are designated smoking areas in some buildings, but otherwise smoking is forbidden."

He gathered my answers and huffily marched out of the room, at the same time indicating I was free to leave. It was the only time in my life I was certain I had scored one hundred percent in an examination.

At no time in my interview had he asked me if I could ride a bicycle.

Dave's information had been correct. Two new postmen duly arrived and started work. Ted was a young man of about twenty five, with a bemused air about him. It was scarcely surprising, for previously he had been a gardener. And Duncan was a man of my age who had worked in the construction industry. Both had joined Royal Mail by a more conventional route than I, and arrived kitted out in their uniforms, having passed both their interviews and aptitude tests.

Three weeks later Uncle John handed me a letter, saying I had been accepted into the Royal Mail and would start work the following Monday. Uncle John formally shook my hand, "Welcome to Royal Mail." I was speechless.

It was just as well Ted and Duncan had joined us; it was now November and Christmas, that famous feast, which was a harvest for Royal Mail and all the junk mail firms, was not far away. I had heard terrible stories about it, but reserved my judgement: it sounded no worse than the three concentrated weeks of lambing and probably a good deal easier.

The advent of Ted and Duncan restored some sort of normality in the office. I had been on a bicycle for weeks and my legs were becoming muscled like some rider on the Tour de France. I was finally allowed to return to the Topleys, but after the town rounds, where I was meeting people all the time, I found it an uninspiring and soulless round. At least the old colonel was pleased to see me return.

"I had hoped to see you on this round permanently," he informed me, "but there seems little chance of that. That grinning lout who has been delivering here still cannot differentiate the three Keepers Cottages, but I suppose in these days of lowered standards I shall have to accept it."

The Junior Section, comprising Ted, Duncan and myself, settled into a rotation of three rounds, made up of Topleys and two 'walks'. One I had not done before, a semi rural round, which involved a mile and a half ride out of Bramton to a village called Norton, followed by an afternoon van collection. It was not a particularly happy arrangement, finishing at about half past ten and returning to the office at four o'clock to make the afternoon collections. But I was allowed the luxury of someone to train me.

My trainer was a man of similar age to myself, called Gavin. He was, very thin and almost as taciturn as Murdoch. He wore a small almost, but not quite, Hitler moustache. His abrupt manner and intolerance of my mistakes made me ask him causticially if he had once been a schoolmaster and, rather to my surprise, he admitted he had taught little boys. He was less than amused when I advised him that I was not one of his pupils and if he and I were to get through the day, without coming to blows, he had better stop treating me as one.

After this unsatisfactory start he gradually unbent, becoming less didactic, and I ventured to ask him about the relationship between Sydney, Murdoch and John Higgings - something that had been intriguing me.

He considered for a minute before asking me, unexpectedly, "Do you, by any chance, have a fag on you?"

I offered him my tin and he slowly made himself a roll-up. I watched him as he struck a pose, one hand on hip, the other slowly lifting the cigarette to his lips. He fumbled for a lighter and, having lit up, maintained his position, staring at the sky, inhaling deeply. He was really rather a scruffy individual, pretentious in a slovenly way. His sweater sported large holes and the shirt underneath appeared unironed. His fingers were stained yellow with nicotine, and his shoes had not seen any polish for months, if ever.

Slowly he lowered his cigarette, ceased staring at the sky and met my gaze.

'Sydney, Murdoch and Higgings?" he asked rhetorically. "It's just that they all think they run the office."

He looked at his watch. "Time we were moving. We've along way to go."

Evidently I would glean little information from Gavin; I did not press the point. We mounted our bicycles and continued on our way.

Two and a half hours later, after five more of my cigarettes, Gavin pushed the last letters into the last door of the last house and we cycled back to the office.

Duncan, Ted and I fitted comfortably into our three round routine. Dave had moved into another section, unwillingly and threatening to return to the Junior Section as soon as he could. He evidently had his motives, though it was difficult to guess what they were, except that they were of benefit to Dave and Dave alone.

The Topleys had had its soul removed by its proximity to the railway station, and its country heart torn out by the advent of prairie type farming; one of these vast estates was, ironically, owned by the Post Office Pension Fund. Norton was a pleasant round, marred by the broken shift, and the town bicycle round was relatively easy, now that my protesting muscles had eased into some sort of harmony with the rest of my body. Despite the official 'walk' title they were referred to as rounds in the office. What I especially liked about it was the second delivery.

There was an excellent bakery in the town, and I had fallen into the habit of buying a hot pie on my way back and taking it up to the tea room to eat at leisure while reading Jack's newspaper. Sometimes I was joined by other postmen; it was a useful way of getting to know them.

Having finished the pie and returned the newspaper, it was time to sort and go out on the second delivery. This was seldom a great amount and did not replicate the first for some reason, but involved a walk - a proper walk for once - through the centre of town, with a bag on my shoulder delivering to the shops and offices, and the scattering of houses tucked away behind the main thoroughfare.

Whilst on one of these second deliveries I noticed the franked slogan on one of the letters bore the name of my old public school. It was addressed to a Mrs. Reynolds. Certainly, I could remember a master of that name. He had often endeavoured to explain the mysteries of trigonometry and algebra to me, with limited success - but he had been a bachelor, even then in his late fifties. Besides, I remembered reading in one of the bulletins the school persisted in sending their old boys that he had died some years ago.

Recollection came in a rush. Of course, to everyone's surprise he had married late in life, long after I had left the school: this Mrs. Reynolds must be his widow.

When I arrived at her house she was outside, tending her window boxes in the early winter sunshine: a sprightly old lady, probably in her early eighties, her face alert and full of character, her eyes bright and intelligent. I handed her the single letter and cleared my throat.

"I couldn't help noticing the name of the school on the envelope," I began as she took the letter in her still elegant hand. "I went there in the early sixties, and your husband used to teach me mathematics."

She looked at me for a long while, her eyes level and unwavering. I guessed that she must have worked at the school, perhaps a matron or even a librarian, and the late marriage must have been for companionship in old age.

"You say you were there in the early sixties and my husband taught you mathematics?" she repeated at last in a tone of voice, which clearly expressed disbelief. There was another pause, while she regarded me suspiciously. "What is your name?" she asked crisply, "and which house were you in? Who was the headmaster while you were there?"

I answered her questions, rather regretting I had broached the subject at all, and mentally upgraded her to a teacher. Only a teacher could ask questions in that manner.

"And you are a postman," she said, slowly shaking her head. She turned and, still holding her letter tightly in her hand, returned to her house through the still opened front door, which she closed firmly behind her.

Thoroughly chastened by the implied rebuke, I gloomily continued on my round.

I saw Mrs. Reynolds a few days later. She came hurrying out as I approached. I formed the impression she had been waiting for me.

"You were quite right," she said without preamble, "you did go to my husband's school, and he did teach you."

She leant forward, her face close to mine, before announcing triumphantly, "I looked you up."

It would have been nice to have related that we became firm friends, that we had cups of tea in front of her fire while discussing the old school and her departed husband, but I never saw Mrs. Reynolds again. Shortly after our meeting she was rushed to hospital, where she died some days later. Whether it was the shock of learning that one of her late husband's pupils had ended up as a postman or not, I would never discover.

But Mrs. Reynolds had unconciously taught me a lesson. I resolved that, unless directly questioned, I would keep my past to myself.

Seven

Murdoch had taken a dislike to Ted. An insidious, gratuitous aversion. He had evidently decided that Ted - good natured and willing, but a slow starter - had arrived solely to exercise the mordant wit that was Murdoch's speciality, honed to perfection over the years. It was not a pleasant spectacle, and Ted appeared incapable of standing up to him.

"It's easy for you," Ted said to me one day. "You're older than me and Murdoch leaves you alone, but I need this job. My wife's expecting a baby soon, and being a postman pays better than gardening, and it's more secure. I wish he'd leave me alone. He's not in charge of the office anyway, is he?" he finished lamely.

Murdoch had, on the other hand, taken an unhealthy interest in Duncan. Murdoch had few, if any, friends at work, and with his unattractive personality it was doubtful he had many outside either. But, he went out of his way to cultivate Duncan, with cringingly embarrassing attempts at humour, which were designed as overtures for friendship.

Smoking had been recently banned at Bramton, in common with all Royal Mail offices; a regulation, which was flagrantly disobeyed in the afternoons when there was no one to enforce the ban. Both Duncan and Murdoch were smokers and they were often seen together outside enjoying cigarettes. Duncan appeared uneasy at this excessive attention, and the new relationship attracted much humorous comment, especially when the hapless Duncan decided to leave his sorting frame for a quick smoke, only to be followed a few minutes later by Murdoch who must have been watching through the wire mesh of his cage.

It was no coincidence that Duncan lived in Bramton and Ted in a village a few miles distant.

Ted's rhetorical question had been intriguing me for some time, but, in this closed shop of a workplace, where the attitude was to let newcomers find out for themselves, no one appeared eager to answer it.

There were only two people in the office who were independent of the common rabble of postmen, who delighted in watching people fall flat on their faces, and they were Uncle John and Jack. It was hardly a question I could ask the manager, but when I found myself alone in the tea room with Jack, I put it to him.

He carefully folded the tea towel he had been carrying, and placed it on a table and sat down opposite me.

"I told you before that I have never worked in a place like this, and that no one except Peter cares about anyone else." He pushed his glasses back onto his nose and stared hard at me. "Everyone here is a failure; teachers, greengrocers, lorry drivers, cooks and," he added with a smile, "failed farmers. We have cheerful failures and gloomy failures. And they chose the Royal Mail, because it is an institution that looks after them. Rather like the welfare state. And they all delude themselves they are skilled, indispensable workers. Well, they're not. They're semi skilled at best, and some of them, encouraged by the union, spend their time conniving and plotting against their colleagues, and the management, because they have little better to do. Sometimes I think this place is like an infant school."

He leant back in his chair and stared at the wall. "John Higgings runs this office. He has gone as far as he can in his career and is due to retire in a few years. Murdoch thinks he runs it. Sydney knows he runs it. And Gavin is planning to run it. But, in reality, the office runs itself. Everyone knows what to do, and if someone goes sick his round is automatically covered. It's been like that for years."

He smiled again. "Does that answer your question?"

I laughed. "I never realised it was so complex, I said. "I was only a simple farmer and I've no idea of office politics. It's all a far cry from green fields, livestock, crops and the interference of real politicians, if they are more intelligent than these office politicians, which I doubt."

"You'll find out," Jack replied. "I used to be in the merchant navy, so I've seen some of the world. Most of these individuals have never been out of the country; they've seen nothing, they're small minded people living in a small minded town. I doubt Sydney, Gavin or Murdoch have left the area this year; they'd be too frightened someone would be plotting behind their backs. But I'll tell you one thing," he said, leaning forward, "they all let themselves down in the end. They have to show their hands. For some reason they can't help it, but you'll find out."

Unfortunately Murdoch walked into the tea room, finishing our conversation.

I liked Jack. He had led an interesting life. After many years in the merchant navy he had been persuaded by his wife to 'come ashore' and had taken a variety of employment, much of it office jobs. Jack was far more highly qualified than his humble position of cleaner cum teaboy suggested.

"I just wanted a retirement job to keep me out of trouble, and out of the house," he replied when I asked him why he was working for the Post Office. "I've never been proud, and this suppliments the pension and keeps the brain active."

He had most of the office accurately summed up, for he had acute powers of observation. "Most of them aren't worth a light. That Dave, he hunts with the hounds and runs with the hare. Gavin's always scheming for his own advantage. And Murdoch, he's unbelievable."

I pressed him about Murdoch and he thought for a moment. "He sums this place up. Not the Post Office, but Bramton. He was born here, went to school here, has worked only here, has lived all his life here and he'll die here. He's a miserable sod and underneath that prosperous, middle class, market town image, Bramton's as miserable a place as Murdoch's a miserable person. He knows just about everyone in the town, and most of them know him, and if you watch him he'll put on another face to his customers to the one you see when he's at work. Just like Bramton."

A trite thought crossed my mind. I almost dismissed it as ridiculous, but nevertheless asked Jack. "Is that why he dislikes Ted, me and one or two of the others, just because we don't come from Bramton?"

"Yes, you've got it," Jack replied with a smile. "It's as simple as that. It's why he is trying to cultivate Duncan. He lives in Bramton. You are at a double disadvantage, living outside the town and having a public school accent. That really grates on him. He finds it difficult to handle anyone beyond his experience. That's why he's after you. You and I are like exiles in this office," he continued, "but at least I can stand back and observe whilst you are in the thick of it."

It was not a comforting thought.

Eight

The normally ebullient Sydney was uncharacteristically subdued one dark November morning. I coasted down the slope, parked my purple Puch, removed my skidlid and goggles and wished Sydney a good morning. He was sitting, as usual, on a white plastic, garden chair drinking his cup of tea, which he lowered from his lips and placed on a wicker bamboo table in front of him: a recent acquisition, found by Peter dumped in a ditch. Always keen to keep the countryside clean and put something to good use, he had retrieved it and brought it back in his van.

Sydney ignored my greeting staring straight ahead into space. I shrugged and went into the office. It was nothing unusual; they could be a moody lot, these postmen. It was probably something to do with the unnaturally early start. And, besides, Sydney had a large number of extra curricular jobs he undertook around the town after he had finished working for Royal Mail. He was probably tired.

Inside the office there was a certain discernable levity. For some reason there were often different atmospheres, instantly dectectable on entering. Unsurprisingly, an excessive amount of mail produced a gloomy ambience, but when the local football team had won a match there was an air of inordinate happiness. Having no interest in football at all I was immune to that one, but this particular morning something seemed to have put everyone in a good humour. I had not yet encountered Murdoch, but it was doubtful anything short of total catastrophe would have changed his humour.

It was best, I had discovered, not to ask questions about these matters, but rather to let events unfold in their own good time. They were not long in so doing when Sydney walked through the doors. The

73

low hum of conversation ceased as he took up his sorting position and overloud comments were made, such as, "I wonder where Sydney's having his breakfast this morning?" and, "That's a bloody good round, breakfast thrown in. Wish mine were that good."

Sydney ignored these unsubtle remarks, furiously concentrating on his sorting. When Uncle John came in at exactly five fifteen he abandoned his usual practice of futilely wishing everyone a good morning, and walked straight over to Sydney, tapped him on the shoulder and together they disappeared into his office.

We watched this performance in fascinated silence, but as soon as Uncle John's office door closed a roar of conversation, speculation and laughter erupted. There were no secrets in this place and I rapidly found out the cause of Sydney's unease.

There was a large manor house on his round, which was owned by an immensely wealthy couple. He was reputed to be 'something to do with banking', and they owned several further homes around the world. He was based in America where he lived, presumably in great luxury, with his wife, but the other properties were all kept fully staffed in case his work took him to the relevant country. The manor house was one of these, and was maintained in a constant state of readiness should the couple decide to visit England. In fact their visits were so infrequent and brief that Sydney had never met them, and the changeover of staff was considerable - probably as a result of boredom.

Sydney was a great friend of the gardener who, in turn, was a great friend of the housekeeper, whom Sydney also had never met. It was rumoured that the gardener was 'carrying on' with the housekeeper, which probably explained why Sydney had never met her. Or it could, more simply, have been that he arrived at the manor house to deliver the mail at such an early hour she was still in bed. But his arrival was not too early for the gardener, and the two of them had, for a long time, enjoyed the indulgence of a full English breakfast, cooked by him on the oil fired Aga in the kitchen; the ingredients supplied from the well stocked fridge, the daily delivery of bread, and the chickens he kept, at his employers' expense, on a piece of waste ground behind the compost heap. If the housekeeper noticed the large quantity of bacon, eggs, sausages, baked beans and bread her staff consumed each week, she never intimated as such to anyone.

There was usually warning of the owners' return for a visit. And on these occasions the gardener informed Sydney who forewent his full English breakfast, delivered the mail and departed to his next call, with an empty stomach.

On this occasion there had been a breakdown in communication. Sydney arrived at the manor house, but his partner-in-crime was nowhere to be found. Never a person to pass up an opportunity, nor one to ponder the gardener's aberration, Sydney walked into the kitchen, found the large frying pan, lifted one of the heavy lids covering a hotplate on the Aga, placed the frying pan on top and started cooking breakfast for himself and his absentee friend.

He was just cracking the third egg when the lady of the house, wearing a full length dressing gown, entered the kitchen. Sydney, assuming her to be the housekeeper, greeted her in his inimitable way. "Hello, gorgeous, you looks lovely in that gown. You fancy a bite of breakfast? Fred usually cooks it, but 'ee ain't 'ere yet. I can do you another egg, easy, and when Fred turns up we can all enjoy breakfast together." It was not difficult to imagine. I had heard Sydney attempting to impress the fairer sex before.

The lady of the house was unamused and once the misunderstanding was cleared up - it took a little time - Sydney departed from the manor house in a cloud of dust and flying gravel.

I pieced all this together over a period of several weeks from conversations with Sydney by pretending to symparhise with him. He genuinely felt he was the innocent victim of a monumental injustice, for

"I can do you another egg, easy …"

the lady of the house, hardly surprisingly, complained bitterly to Uncle John, telling him she didn't want Sydney - that bloody postman - to set foot on the grounds of the manor house ever again.

Uncle John, probably relieved that she had not taken the matter higher, was faced with a dilemma. He could scarcely sack Sydney, the office was barely fully staffed and Christmas was not far off, and Sydney had been working for Royal Mail for over twenty years with, at least officially, an exemplary record. In any case, to fire someone there were laid down procedures, which involved Head Office, and it was best they never got to hear of the incident. So he took the easy way out and demoted him to a bike round, at least for the time being. It meant Sydney would lose out on his Christmas tips. He had been on the round for years.

"Pity he's on a bike over that," Dave was heard to remark, "I was looking forward to his next crash when he would have been put back on a bike anyway. That would have been justice."

The housekeeper and the gardener received the sack. He never spoke to Sydney again.

Nine

Ted had had problems of his own. Cycling down a steep path on our town round one rainy day, he discovered, too late, that the rim operated brakes of the Pashley were totally ineffective when wet. Knuckles white from the effort of pulling both brake levers flush with the handgrips, he hurtled through the glass front door of the house at the end of the path, demolishing a telephone table and buckling his front wheel on the wall beyond, fortunately without injury to himself. The terrified and naturally angry occupants were used to having their letters brought to them in a more circumspect manner, and heedless of the white and shaking Ted, retrieved the telephone from the floor and complained vociferously to Uncle John.

If there was one thing more miserable than a van round on a wet day - where at least there was a heater to temper the worst effects - it was delivering mail on a bicycle in torrential rain. It was four hours of unmitigated misery, with clothing becoming heavy and saturated as the morning wore on. Mounting the bicycle became a nightmare, with the heavy waterproof trousers Royal Mail thoughtfully provided. They were stiff and unyielding, the condensation they generated made the garments worn underneath soaking wet, too, and it was debatable whether they were worth wearing at all. I hated the things.

Fingers became numb with cold and it was almost impossible to separate the sodden letters from the bundles and themselves. Then, chilled to the bone and often in the teeth of a biting gale there was the long, leg chafing pedal back to the office. That was not the end of it. After a brief break to warm up and eat a pie in the tea room there was the second delivery trudging out, still drenched, to repeat the process. It was uncanny how often the rain ceased at the precise moment work finished. A postman earned his wages in such conditions.

79

The Royal Mail meant everything to Uncle John. He had known no other life: starting as a telegram boy when he left school, progressing to postman, a job he held for years before moving into junior management via a succession of positions as diverse as security and planning. He was as much of an epitome of Royal Mail as the bulldog was of England. He was tenacious, faithful and entirely stubborn. He had nearly always worked locally, mostly at Buddleshaw where he started his management career.

He advanced steadily, promoted after long intervals to higher levels, until he was offered the managership of Bramton. Many of his younger and more go-ahead colleagues would have regarded such an appointment as the end of their careers, a dead end job with no further prospects. But to Uncle John being Sorting Office Manager at Bramton was the very pinnacle of his career.

He was fifty seven years old and realised that this was as far as he could go, and he was supremely happy about it. There were changes coming, not least the introduction of computers and all the technology that went with them. For the first time, with three years to serve before retirement, he was content; reasoning the old fashioned way would last him out to his retirement before the new technology arrived. On his own admission, he would never have been able to cope.

He was not so happy when Sydney, his troublesome union representative, informed him there was a strong possibility of a strike before Christmas, possibly in the last week of November, just as the office would start to become really busy.

Uncle John was a great worrier, and Sydney, still smarting from the breakfast fiasco, sensed this and, with an animal cunning, played on it. It was a shame. Uncle John was essentialy a decent man who had dealt fairly with him, probably more so than he had deserved. But this was not the way Sydney viewed it, and in the days preceding the strike he managed to work Uncle John into a dreadful state of worry and despondency.

The strike itself was, of course, about pay, and in those days of union brinkmanship, particularly with the Communication Workers Union, was almost an annual event. Some years there was a strike and this played heavily on Uncle John.

The strike did take place as forecast, in the last week in November. We learnt this from Sydney on the Monday morning, with some difficulty, as he was not only a terrible public speaker, but handicapped by his unique use of the twin words 'what's 'is name' and 'what d'yer call it'. In times of stress, they surfaced with increased frequency. After a while we understood the strike was taking place, as from that morning.

Uncle John, standing apart, listened to Sydney's excruciatingly halting speech in a dignified silence, and returned to his office at its conclusion - presumably to telephone for instructions. The rest of us discussed it while Sydney went outside, picked up one of the garden chairs standing behind Peter's salvaged, wicker table together with a homemade placard he had brought with him, he marched up the slope and sat down by the entrance gates, the placard prominently displayed. I looked at it later. It read: OFFICAL UNIUON PIKET. OFFICAL STRIKE. BLACKGARDS KEEP OUT. Contemplating Sydney's calligraphy for a while, I decided any comment was unnecessary.

Bramton was not a hotbed of militantcy, but the general consensus of opinion was to support the strike, at least for the time being. The only dissenter was Peter who announced he had no intention of striking or of losing out on his pay – there was no such thing as strike pay. It might have been enlightening to have discovered exactly where our union subs went, but apparently it was not politic to ask. Rather ashamed of myself for going against my principals I joined the rest and went home, leaving a grim faced Sydney sitting by his crude placard, and Uncle John, Peter and a couple of part timers who were not union members. There was some decorating, which needed doing. I consoled myself that money I saved by doing it myself would more than

81

compensate for the loss of wages. Besides, no one thought the strike would last long.

The strike ended after five days with the usual compromise that could easily have been worked out before, had it not been for the bloody minded union officials. The whole thing had been a monumental waste of time, and it left a trail of bitterness and wreckage in its wake as surely as the strongest storm.

Uncle John handled the strike very badly. It was scarcely surprising. He had been involved with desputes before, but never as manager of an office on his own. He panicked, and sent Peter on a futile mission to Buddleshaw to collect the Bramton mail. Who he thought would sort this mail had it arrived was a mystery.

Peter never collected a single letter. Buddleshaw was a militant office and, as it turned out, a vindictive one. He was met with a torrent of abuse and threats by the pickets there, all of whom knew who he was, and wisely decided not to cross the picket line. It was union intimidation at its worst. When he returned, empty handed, Uncle John promptly and unfairly suspended him, his only non-striking, full time postman.

A furious argument ensued and eventually Peter was reinstated, but it was all too much for Uncle John. His whole life seemed to him to be falling apart in front of his eyes, all the standards he had treasured over the years had disintigrated as well; all his staff, with the exception of Peter and the part timers, had deserted him and he took it all to heart - quite literally. On the third day of the strike he collapsed, with a heart attack.

Ironically, it was Peter who discovered him slumped across his desk and called the ambulance. He would be out of action for at least two months, probably more.

Reaction to the heart attack was mixed. Sydney was childishly and crudely delighted.

'Serves the blighter right," he said to anyone who would listen. "Never could stand him. 'Ee deserves all 'ee got."

He was like a schoolboy celebrating some terrible misfortune befalling an unpopular headmaster, completely overlooking the fact that Uncle John was an honourable man, caught completely out of his depth. Peter held his own counsel, but he did elect to come out of the union and he refused to collect or deliver mail to Buddleshaw.

Feelings still ran deep there over the strike, and the grapevine, usually surprisingly accurate, said there were people 'out to get him'. So much for a civilised society.

The general reaction was a shrug of the shoulders and the often heard comment from most postmen, "He was only a manager. We'll get another one."

In that they were wrong. We got Murdoch.

Ten

One day in December when I had returned from my round Sydney said to me unexpectedly, "I remembers your farm. You was neighbours with what's 'is name Langton, and I used to be your postman. Never saw you, though. You 'ardly ever 'ad any mail. Didn't make the connection till a few days ago."

It was hardly surprising there was little mail for Sydney to deliver, for we did not live on our farm. We had bought it for the land, not the decrepit old bungalow, which went with it. We 'camped' in the bungalow at lambing time.

"What became of it all?" asked Sydney.

"It became part of a larger farm," I replied, "and the old bungalow was bulldozed. The site is awaiting planning permission."

'Shame really. That bungalow could 'ave been made real lovely.'

I smiled to myself. Nothing could have made that bungalow 'real lovely.' I remembered the eccentric plumbing, the lethal wiring and, particularly, the outside - and only - loo. The concrete floor was some four inches below ground level; and when it rained it flooded, the water level reaching the step. We developed the necessary habit of wearing Wellingtons when visiting it - crunching through the ice in winter and sharing it with the frogs from the nearby pond in the summer; they seemed to appreciate the cool dampness of the concrete.

There was a six inch gap at the top of the door and, while sitting there, it was possible to contemplate the jumbo jets lumbering their way to Heathrow, hoping their passengers did not enjoy a reciprocal grandstand view. In addition, from time to time the pipe, which joined the overhead cistern, had a habit of becoming detached, drenching the unfortunate user when it was flushed. It was something I was never able to fully cure. We used to lean round the door and pull the chain from the outside. And once, forgetting to warn her, I was rewarded by the sight of my mother-in-law emerging soaked and furious, at a speed that belied her many aches and pains.

"Matthew, that were his name. Matthew Langton," Sydney said suddenly. "Nice man, a proper gentleman. Always tipped well at Christmas. Does you see him now? Kept cows, didn't 'ee?"

"Yes, I see him often. He's a good friend of mine. Always asking when I am going to become his postman."

"Well, you just might at that. Stranger things 'ave happened. Gunners Castle, a good round that. Did it for years before Gavin, Lester and Dave 'ad it, but they was after your time. You shouldn't get in there really, seniority and that counts for a lot 'ere, but you never knows."

I stared at him, wondering whether he knew something I didn't. "Know Mary and Ben?" he asked.

I shook my head.

"Lovely people. Lovely people."

"Remember Johnsons in Bramton?" he continued. "Packed up about three years ago. I worked there afternoons an' I 'as a feeling I seed you in there sometimes getting building materials for your farm an' 'all. At least, I think it were you."

He was probably right, though I couldn't remember seeing Sydney there.

"They 'ad a driver called Robert," he went on. "Bone 'ead we called 'im. 'Ad to take a lorry load of bricks to an 'ouse for an hextention and delivered them to the wrong place. 'Ad to re-load the lot the next day. Disorganised outfit they was at Johnsons."

It was difficult to disagree. I had my own particular memory of Johnsons. It was Christmas Eve and Sarah's mother was coming to stay for Christmas. Unfortunately, our plastic lavatory seat had cracked in half and, probably mindful of the fiasco with our farm loo, my wife

86

despatched me to Buddleshaw for a replacement. Surprisingly, the only lavatory seat for sale in the whole of Buddleshaw was a flimsy affair, totally unsuited for mother-in-law's ample proportions. Driving home, I suddenly remembered Johnsons. They stocked a line in hardware and they might just have what I required.

I parked the mini pick-up and opened the shop door which, instead of ringing the usual bell, activated a scratchy electronic version of Rudolph The Red Nosed Reindeer. Startled, I closed the door. A bizarre sight greeted me. An aged crone dressed as a bulging fairy, complete with wand and covered with sparkle dust whom I had never seen before pranced alarmingly towards me and thrust a glass of sherry into my hand, at the same time taking another from the table and swigging it back in a single swallow. It was clearly not her first of the day.

A motionless Father Christmas sat on a garden chair by a gaudily decorated, plastic Christmas tree festooned with flashing lights, his chin resting on his chest. His right hand clutched a glass of sherry, which had tipped forward, spilling half the contents over his red cloak. He was either asleep or dead. It was difficult to know and I hastily drank up in case it was the latter condition.

The ancient fairy immediately presented me with a full glass and took another for herself, taking a generous sip. Staggering slightly, she steadied herself by pressing her wand firmly on the table that held the drinks. I looked at it with interest. In addition to about fifteen glasses of sherry, already poured, there were a bottle of scotch and a bottle of brandy.

It was four o'clock. There were no other customers and judging from the weather - it had started to rain heavily - not likely to be any more. The fairy and Father Christmas looked set for a hung over Christmas day. She remembered herself and asked me what I wanted.

I hesitantly explained my requirement. She listened carefully, thought for a moment, put her head back and bellowed, "DAD," in a sopranic

Father Christmas and an ancient fairy

88

tone that took me completely by surprise. "GENT 'ERE WANTS A LAV SEAT. 'AVE WE GOT ANY LEFT?"

I could not believe a woman of her years could have a father still alive, but Father Christmas jerked his head off his chest. It was impossible to judge his age under his white beard and red hood. He slowly and wordlessly rose to his feet and led me to the rear of the store. There he found a stout, lilac coloured, plastic lavatory seat, more than a match for my mother-in-law's considerable weight. As I paid him, the fairy passed me another glass of sherry. I drank it in a single swallow.

"You don't get stores like Johnsons any more," said Sydney. "More's the pity." He looked at his watch. "I must get along. If you gets on Gunners Castle I shall 'ave to object," he added enigmatically. "It's my job as union rep, see."

Eleven

It was generally reckoned that Christmas tips would be down that year as a result of the strike, but most of Royal Mail's customers seemed to have accepted the strike with a stoical cynicism that came from living in a country where winters of discontent were no novelty.

"It made no difference to me," one told me. "All I get is junk mail, which goes straight in the bin. You can strike as often as you like. No rubbish and no bills suit me."

Uncle John appeared to have been written off, with a metaphorical shrug of the shoulders as uncaring as the literal one people gave on hearing of his misfortune. No card was sent, no inquiries made, and no one went to see him in hospital.

The Bramton office did not usually rate as a priority with the higher management of Royal Mail. The fact that it only served a small town and a scattered rural community, with a total population of five thousand, probably meant it operated at a slight loss, in contrast to the larger offices in the big towns that made huge profits from the lucrative business mail. Little of that money found its way to Bramton, which was often referred to, only half jokingly, as the forgotten office, but it explained all the clapped out vans and lack of decoration in the office.

The same applied to Uncle John's indisposition; it was one of, 'We've got the aftermath of the strike to cope with, and Christmas is only three weeks away. They'll just have to get on with it.'

So we did, with Murdoch in charge, though, to his chagrin, he was never given the title of Temporary Manager. He moved into Uncle John's office and life went on as before, with the added spice of knowing the unpleasant Murdoch had some real authority over us, though with luck, only on a short term basis.

In truth, no one of merit who aspired to top management level would contemplate a career with Royal Mail, hidebound in its old fashioned working practises and saddled with an intransigent and vicious union. The only exceptions were the likes of Uncle John who had progressed through the ranks and were promoted to management level more by right on length of service than on ability.

The backlog from the strike was soon cleared, and in the first week of December Murdoch announced the Christmas arrangements. These, apparently, were the same as they had been in the past. We kept to the same rounds, which ran for approximately two and a half weeks and were quaintly referred to as 'Christmas pressure'. Two extra vans were provided: one a brand new hire vehicle, the other a resurrected 'time expired' Post Office van. The hired van was used for the delivery of parcels around the town and for any other extra work that cropped up; it was my misfortune to be lumbered with the other.

It was a dreadful machine. The term 'time expired' was clearly a euphemism for completely worn out. It was the inevitable Morris Marina, with erratic brakes, wobbly steering and, worst of all, only a quarter of an inch of movement in the clutch pedal before it engaged. When I first attempted to drive it I promptly stalled it three times in quick succession to the vast amusement of the watching group of my so called colleagues.

Furious, and ignoring their ribald comments, I stormed into what was now Murdoch's office and complained bitterly. There seemed something horribly wrong seeing him seated in Uncle John's chair, at Uncle John's desk and with his coat hanging on Uncle John's coat stand, but I ignored his staring eyes and firmly stated that the van was a deathtrap, and that was before I had discovered its other eccentricities.

He slowly rose to his feet and came outside.

"Get in, Lennie," someone shouted, "and give him a driving lesson."

He lowered himself into the seat, started the engine and, to my enormous satisfaction, stalled the infernal machine. He tried again, with the same result and, unwilling to lose more face, climbed out and said,

"They drove it up here, so it must be all right. You'll soon get used to it. We can't change it now, there just aren't any more vans available, not even for 'ire, as it's Christmas."

I was covering Norton over the Christmas pressure period and I said, "I would rather stick with the bike than have the luxury of this van."

He gave a short laugh. "When you sees the amount of mail you'll 'ave to take out there you'll realise why we got you a van." He turned and went back to Uncle John's office.

The three of us in the Junior Section, in common with the other sections, had agreed to pool our tips, if any. Duncan was doing the Topleys and Ted the town round.

There had been one other change following Uncle John's heart attack and that had been the introduction of a new incumbent in the cage. He was Neville, a withdrawn man of few words whom I always thought of as young, because he gave the impression of lacking any worldly wisdom. He was a well built man in his early thirties living as one of life's bachelors in a house he was buying on a mortgage, a few doors down from his widowed mother, with whom he ate all his meals. He was a curiously intense character who, when drawn on his favourite subjects - archeology and obscure forms of music, would discourse so intently that it was possible to walk away, leaving him talking to thin air for quite a while before he realised his audience had departed.

This same intensity had affected him in another, potentially lethal, way. He had worked for Royal Mail for fifteen years and had decided he was destined for better things, so he had enrolled on an Open University course, with the objective of becoming a schoolmaster. So much did the course affect him that it occupied all his thoughts, all the time - thoughts of revision, his next paper, his future prospects - he thought of nothing else.

This was unfortunate, for this intense concentration came to the exclusion of everything else and affected his driving, with disasterous results. Within a week of his enrolment he had written off two Post Office vans and badly damaged another. It was a record as bad as any, and he was banned for life from driving a Post Office vehicle of any sort. This was later commuted when Bramton ran short of drivers. He was banished to a bicycle round, but fared no better. Pedalling furiously, his mind on his studies, he carreered full tilt into the rear of a parked car - sailing over the roof and landing on the bonnet, writing off the Pashley and causing considerable damage to the car in the process.

Royal Mail, which had rules and regulations to cover most eventualities, had never come across someone of Neville's self destructive instincts, and there was nothing in the rule book that said a postman could be banned from riding a bicycle. So, with a fresh Pashley he promptly repeated the performance two weeks later, this time breaking his nose, amazingly the only injury he or anyone else suffered during his studies.

If he had been delivering around the town on foot he would probably have knocked people over. It was with some relief to the office, those people who knew him in Bramton, and his victims that he was incarcerated in the cage. At least for the time being.

We were all set for Christmas. Just before the Christmas rush started, I was peacefully sitting on my own at a table in the tea room eating a steak and kidney pie and reading Jack's newspaper when the door opened and Murdoch walked in.

I looked up briefly and endeavoured to concentrate on the paper, but it was not easy. Murdoch had a way of making me feel edgy; besides, my moment of tranquility had been destroyed. Over the top of Jack's newspaper, I watched him make a cup of tea, fully expecting him to take it downstairs to his new office. Instead, to my horror, he ignored the other places in the tea room and pointedly seated himself opposite me.

There was little option. I folded the newspaper, laid it on the table and concentrated on finishing the remainder of my pie, reasoning it would be better to sort the second delivery than to be stuck in the tea room alone with the odious Murdoch.

I looked up and his pale blue eyes met mine. They were devoid of expression. Suddenly, he started speaking, the thick fingers of his right hand wrapped tightly around his tea mug, threatening to crush it. I was never quite sure whether he was talking to me, despite the fact I was the only other person in the tea room and his terrible eyes were fixed unwaveringly on my own - like a snake hypnotising its prey before it strikes. With an awful fascination I listened to him, without interruption, as he started his discourse.

"I should 'ave been made manager of this office two and a half year ago when Bradley left. 'Ee were a good manager, and I knows 'ee recommended me to take over when 'ee left. We got on well. I been 'ere for twenty four years, I knows every round and I knows exactly 'ow this office works, and I knows nearly everyone in the area, and they knows me."

He was a bit optimistic on that score; I knew plenty of people who had never heard of Murdoch.

"I'm experienced and it was common sense to make me manager. This office should 'ave been mine two and a 'alf year ago. So what does they do? They makes 'Iggings manager. 'Iggings. I knowed 'ee when 'ee were a postman at Buddleshaw and 'ee weren't no good then and I tell you something," he went on, leaning alarmingly over the table, his eyes still fixed on mine, causing me to instinctively lean back. "I'll tell you, 'ee ain't no bloody good as manager neither. 'Ee knows nothing, nothing about the rounds, nothing about the customers, nothing about the office. They must 'ave been mad when they made 'im manager 'ere when they 'ad a ready made one already in the office. They all laughs at him behind 'is back 'ere. They wouldn't laugh behind my back, I tell you."

95

He leant back in his chair and I relaxed slightly, almost as if I had been reprieved, but there was more to come. He banged his mug down on the table, and the now cold tea slopped over his hand, but he never noticed. "We's one of the top offices in the county, and it's nothing to do with that sod 'Iggings. It's all because of me. I've made it the best office. I've been doing it for years, first with Bradley and now with 'Iggings. It's all because of my 'ard work in the cage that we're so good. So do they reward me with the office when Bradley goes? Do they 'ell. They gives that useless blighter 'Iggings my job, because they doesn't know what to do with 'ee. 'Ee ain't no clue how to run an office. If it weren't for me, we'd be sunk, completely sunk, I'm telling yer. When 'ee 'ad his 'eart attack I 'oped the sod'd die, and they'd give me the office. My office by right anyway. But they never did. They makes me temporary manager and then doesn't confirm it. I can't even take that bloody sign I 'ates so much off his door. That one what says 'John Higgings, Office Manager'. It should be 'Lennie Murdoch, Office Manager', but they won't let me do that, not even temporary. And now, and now..."

He paused, searching for words, his pale blue eyes watering profusely, whether from emotion or not was hard to tell. "And now they 'phones me and tells me the blighter weren't as ill as they thought at first and 'ee'll be back mid January. And I'll be back in the bloody cage again, carrying him and carrying the office."

He banged his mug on the table again, "They's no bloody sense. They should 'ave retired him and made me manager while they 'ad the chance. No bloody sense at all." He scraped his chair back and left the tea room. His half empty tea mug remained on the table.

Thoroughly shaken, I made my way downstairs in his wake, at least comforted by the knowledge that Royal Mail did, sometimes, show some intelligence. I was beginning to understand what Jack meant when he had enigmatically told me, "They all let themselves down and reveal themselves in the end."

Christmas was revealing itself, too. It had been for months in the form of catalogues and the usual junk mail, but now there were outward signs: wreath on doors, Christmas trees with flashing lights, coloured lights strung on trees in gardens and, as far as Royal Mail was concerned, the odd early Christmas card. All far too early in my opinion: decorations should be put in place on Christmas Eve and taken down promptly on the sixth of January.

There was a Post Office 'Do' at the end of the first week in December, in a pub in Bramton. I was undecided whether to go or not. If office politics were anything to go by the event was likely to end in a bloodbath. But it was surprisingly well supported, the staff of 'the front office' - the main Post Office, which was connected to the Sorting Office by a single door - joining in. It would have been churlish not to have participated, so I reluctantly added my name to the list. I had experienced office Christmas parties before and they were seldom edifying experiences.

I noticed Sydney's name was missing, and also Gavin's; they were the only ones, apart from the incapacitated Uncle John, who were not attending, and I asked Sydney why.

"Gavin," he said scornfully, "'ee won't never go to a do like that unless it's free. 'Ee ain't never got no money, and 'ee won't be no loss neither, all 'ee talks about is office politics, nothing else."

I thought that was rich coming from Sydney. He lapsed into silence. I prompted him. "Why aren't you going, Sydney?"

He hesitated. "I ain't never going to no Post Office do, not never again," he replied with some feeling. "The last one I went to, three years ago, they insulted my missus and I ain't never forgiven them, never."

Curious, I persisted. Dave was standing close by, grinning inanely.

"What did they say, Sydney?" I asked.

Sydney looked emotional. "You can bugger off," he said to Dave, "and wipe that smile off your face."

Lowering his voice, he said, "They asked 'er why on earth she married someone like me. And I wasn't 'aving that. I said, 'That's it, we're off.' And we left. And I ain't going to another of them do's again and neither ain't she."

"Why did she marry you, Sydney?" Dave, who had not moved, asked innocently.

It was too much for Sydney. He breathed deeply and walked away.

The 'do' was unmemorable. Everyone brought their wives or girlfriends.

I sat next to Lester, a softly spoken Yorkshireman with whom I had had little contact. He worked with the absent Gavin. And it was to join them that Dave had reluctantly departed from the Junior Section. Lester had served in the Royal Navy and had only been at the Post Office for a few months more than I. My wife was seated next to Jack and his wife.

Lester was more a man of the world than many at Royal Mail. He turned to me and, with infinite politeness, said, "I hope you don't mind my asking, but with your accent, did you by any chance go to public school?"

I affirmed I had.

"I thought so, I have been meaning to ask you for some time."

I warmed to Lester; the question had been asked without, malice, envy or further enquiry. Apparently I had passed some sort of test.

Later he said, "You know, Dave doesn't like working with Gavin and I. All he is interested in is finishing as fast as he can and getting off to his other job. It makes it look bad for us. We are older and slower, and when we book overtime Murdoch comes back with the comment that if Dave can do the round in such and such a time, why can't we? We all know Dave runs rather than walks when he delivers, and drives like a maniac. So, we were wondering if you would like to join our section after Christmas. We are all about the same age, and I know

Dave wants to return to the Junior Section."

Slightly flattered, I said I thought it sounded an interesting prospect.

"We'll talk about it after Christmas," Lester said. "We were thinking of asking either Duncan or you, but Duncan is a little too friendly with Murdoch for our liking."

A thought occured to me. "What about the seniority issue?"

"No problem," Lester assured me. "We can overcome that easily enough."

Perhaps Jack was wrong and I was not such an exile as I had first thought.

Presided over by Murdoch, the evening degenerated into risqué behaviour and ribald jokes, fuelled by an unhappy mixture of alcohol and fatigue - an occupational hazard at Bramton, where we worked harder than most offices. We adjourned to the bar for further rounds of drinks, feeling slightly ridiculous in our festive hats. The talk was exclusively shop, so to spare us further boredom Sarah and I slipped quietly out of a side door and made our escape.

The food had been indifferent, the company boorish, the festivities forced and artificial. It was no better and no worse than most office Christmas dinners I had had the misfortune to attend over the years.

"I liked Jack," my wife told me on the way home. "He was quite a gentleman, but he does seem to have a low opinion of postmen."

The 'Christmas pressure', so eagerly awaited by some for the extra overtime and dreaded by others for the extra work, started on the Monday following the dinner. It proved a false dawn, the mail being about the same as it had been at any other time of the year.

For a few days I wondered what all the fuss had been about. I had mastered the clutch in the awful van, which provided it was kept to a maximum speed of forty miles per hour was relatively safe, and I had temporarily been relieved of my afternoon collection. These rounds were being worked by four masochistic postmen for whom overtime meant everything and family life nothing. Gavin, Sydney and Lester were three of them.

For the first three days of that week I enjoyed the luxury of finishing at eleven o'clock, but on the Thursday the Christmas rush hit the office like a tidal wave. I had never seen so much mail and I was shocked by the sheer volume of it, pouring into the office at all times of the day as though a large dam had burst and was directing its wall of destructive water at Bramton. For it was destruction; it terminated free time, it destroyed the normal office banter and, in some cases, it totally obliterated the normal good humour of some of my colleagues. It disturbed sleeping patterns and, more importantly, it ruined social life. It was virtually impossible to enjoy Christmas parties: we were all far too tired.

It scarcely seemed possible there could be so much post, but we threw ourselves into the work with a will to try and keep pace with it. It was all the harder due to Murdoch's intransigence, refusing to employ any casual staff to ease the situation. It was the first time anyone could remember it happening, so I had nothing to judge it on, but Murdoch had insisted we could cope, and cope we did.

I was seldom home before four o'clock, often far later, and in common with most of the others I worked straight through without a break. The fourteen Post Office days of Christmas became a horrible grind: returning home late, quickly eating a snack, having a couple of hours sleep, waking for supper, blankly watching the television for a while - it was far too tiring to contemplate anything else, even reading - and retiring to bed early to sleep dreamlessly until the diabolical alarm clock rang at four o'clock in the morning, stridently announcing the start of another day. At least, I would think to myself grimy as I dressed in the cold bathroom, it was one day less of this purgatory called Christmas.

There were compensations, but they were few. Every day someone brought in some food, from traditional mince pies and Christmas cake to sausage rolls and, memorably, a revolting bread pudding, which Neville's mother had made. I gave my portion to Duncan who ate it with relish and appeared to suffer no side effects.

One morning Sydney brought in a large bottle of whisky. We added generous measures to our cups of tea, despite Murdoch exhorting Sydney not to let 'his drivers' have any. We ignored him.

And there were, of course, the tips. It was reckoned milkmen made up to eight or nine hundred pounds at Christmas. I have little idea if this is true, but it was an undeniable fact that for some reason they received more tips from more customers than postmen. Quite why that should be I do not know, but one of the low points of my Christmas was bending down to pick up an envelope on a doorstep only to find it read, 'To our milkman. Happy Christmas.' There never was an envelope for the postman from that house.

At the end of Christmas, exhausted, Duncan, Ted and I totalled our tips. We made £27.25 each, with three bottles of cheap red wine, several boxes of biscuits and seven brace of pheasants, probably the least popular tip at such a busy time as no one had the time to pluck them. Later, I asked Ted what he had done with his birds.

"I took them up to that wood, the one just out of town, and hid them behind some trees - someway apart so no one would be suspicious."

I said I hoped he had removed the string from their necks and he looked distraught. "No, I forgot. Do you think it matters?"

I replied that I doubted the grateful foxes would object as they gnawed their way through their very own Christmas tips, and he looked relieved.

If there was a cascade of inward mail, there was a floodtide of outgoing mail, trolley loads of the stuff were wheeled from the main Post Office into the Sorting Office and dumped on the ground, awaiting transport to Buddleshaw for onward transit. Bramton, as far as Royal Mail was concerned, was a terminus station on a small branch line, whereas Buddleshaw was a large mainline station from where all mail from the other outlying offices, as well as their own, was sorted and despatched on the first stage of its journey. It was a huge undertaking in normal times; at Christmas it was monumental.

On occasions there was so much inward and outward mail in the office that it was difficult to see the dividing line. Mounds of parcels and packets, bundles and bundles of Christmas cards, calenders in cardboard tubes and sides of smoked salmon lay on the floor awaiting their turn to be sorted.

Neville was not having a happy Christmas. It was not as if the work in Murdoch's cage was difficult, nor that Neville was an unintelligent man, but he was totally disorganised and the cage was in a perpetual state of chaos with him almost knee deep in registered mail, parcels and packets scattered over the floor in no sort of order at all. It was as if he had difficulty in disengaging his brain from his Open University course and concentrating on more mundane matters. To compound his misery, he was highly strung and sensitive, and everyone knew this. Some of his colleagues taunted him cruelly while they were waiting for him to sort out their registered mail and Neville - who should have known better, but was unable to help himself - unfailingly rose to the bait. He took to locking himself in the cage and we would watch him muttering to himself, endeavouring to make order out of chaos. There was no doubt he operated on another plane from normal human beings, and Dave succintly summed him up one particularly trying morning, with the comment "Neville's something else."

When we returned from our rounds, we sorted until we were too exhausted to continue, staring blankly at letters held in our hands like novices, wondering where they should be placed. Until, with relief, the mind cleared and normal sorting was resumed, only for the blankness to return once again. I seriously thought if this level of work was maintained for too long I might start hallucinating.

There were two Sundays in that first Christmas pressure period I spent with Royal Mail. The great day itself fell on a Wednesday. The first was spent sorting, on a voluntary basis. Had we not, there would have been two days mail to have sorted and delivered on the Monday. Not an appealing prospect, as the two people who decided a Sunday away from the circus was preferable to working discovered to their cost, finishing work the next day at six o'clock and half past six respectively. If anything, the volume of mail increased during the second week of Chrismas. "Never known it so bad," I overheard Sydney say one morning. "It'll be a record Christmas."

Quite apart from Sydney's paradoxical remark, I often pondered the negativity of the job. There was a certain pride gained from accurate and rapid sorting, maybe, and Lester always took a fastidious pride in his appearance, but that was about it. Being a postman was, like many jobs in the service industry, an essentially dead end job. And the fact that Sydney had said it would be a record Christmas - and it was, if Royal Mail's figures were to be believed - should have been greeted with some enthusiasm. But it wasn't. Perhaps we were all half dead from overwork to care.

"It's the overtime," said Lester, who was rapidly acquiring a reputation of becoming the office's overtime king. "That's where the satisfaction is, when you can see it on your payslip at the end of the week. That's the real satisfaction in this job."

But it wasn't. It was true the net amount was much greater at Christmas, but when I looked at my wage slip and saw the punitive amount of tax the government had extracted from it I wondered if it was really worthwhile. It would have been churlish to have refused to work overtime at Christmas, as we were entitled to, as too many people depended on the fragile links of the overstretched chain holding. If one was to snap at such a busy time a small office like Bramton would descend into real chaos. There was no extra man power to cushion the loss of only one postman, unlike the larger offices, which were better staffed and more easily able to absorb a sudden crisis. And ultimately it was the customer who would suffer most and, at Christmas at least, there was the fulfilment of knowing we were delivering useful mail, not junk, that customers actually wanted and looked forward to receiving. That, more than all the overtaxed overtime, which Lester valued so highly, was something worthwhile.

On the last Sunday before Christmas we made a delivery. It was, as far as I am aware, the last time Royal Mail performed this service, and it was an eerie experience. Most people had started their Christmas and New Year holidays and were relaxing, walking in the weak, late December sunshine, strolling down country lanes where the shaded verges were still crisp with hoar frost, before returning home to cook a leisurely Sunday lunch. They appeared unsurprised to see the postman out on his rounds; it was what they expected, rather in the manner they showed surprise when I told them we would not be delivering on bank holidays.

Some folk even asked if there would be a delivery on Christmas Day. They must have had long memories. Times were changing and I remembered the note delivered with our milk one day, which read, 'To improve our service to you, we are discontinuing our daily delivery and you will now have a delivery on Mondays, Wednesdays and Fridays.' Perhaps Royal Mail would, one day, follow Unigate's example.

I continued on my round, slightly depressed, feeling no part of the atmosphere or spirit of Christmas, something I always used to enjoy. Driving along roads almost bereft of traffic, delivering goodwill in the form of cards and parcels, with a feeling of gloom, which matched the lengthening shadow and fading light as the short winter's day drew to a close.

Sydney had been impossibly cheerful over Christmas and I only belatedly discovered the reason. Murdoch had reinstated him to his old round. Unnoticed by most of us wrapped up in the concentration Christmas mail demanded, he had decided to stamp his authority on the office and show who was the real manager. Sydney was schoolboyishly defiant. "That'll show that sod 'Iggings. I didn't ought to 'ave been taken off that round in the first place, I ain't done nothing wrong."

I rather doubted the lady of the manor house would have viewed his protestation in the the same light, and as she had specifically said she did not want 'that bloody postman near her home again', I asked Sydney how he managed to deliver her mail.

"Easy," he replied. "The stupid cow was so determined that no postman would set foot in 'er bloody kitchen again she went and put a box on the gate and padlocked it so no one could drive up to 'er bloody manor. It's one in the eye for that bloody 'Iggings, an' I'll get all my Christmas tips now, sod him."

Sydney had been outlandishly joyful throughout the Christmas pressure, with his heavy handed banter. He was one of those people who thrived in adversity, with a wearisome jocularity, which was as forced and irritating as it was insensitive. Yet underneath his bluff exterior, Sydney was really a sensitive and kindly man, always ready to help and offer well intentioned advice, even if it were so out of date and inaccurate as to be worthless. He took such grave offence when he was told, in no uncertain terms by the normally placid Lester, to be quiet so he could concentrate on what he was doing that he never said a word to anyone for the rest of the day and refused to speak to Lester for several weeks.

The clutch finally expired on my van the Monday before Christmas, not so there was no drive, but rather that it was welded permanently in drive.

"I can't possibly get 'old of another van, like I told you." Murdoch informed me. "Can you manage with it like that?"

I thought for a moment. It meant turning the engine off every time I stopped, and at road junctions, and starting off again, with the van in first on the starter motor, and using the gearbox like an old fashioned crash gearbox. I would also have to re-plan my round to avoid starting on hills. It could be done.

"I think so," I replied, "but it won't do the gearbox much good."

"Never mind that," Murdoch said. "That van's 'ad it anyway. It's either drive it like that or taking a bike and keep on coming back for your bags. I ain't got no one to take them out to you."

It was an unappealing prospect. I preferred to take my chance with the van. Sydney was not amused when he heard about it. "You won't be insured, driving it like that, and the union won't back you if you 'as a what's 'is name, knowing what your van were like."

I shrugged. "I'm not taking a bike, Sydney. I'll take my chance with the van and the union."

"It's your own funeral. And I'll tell you another thing. 'Ealth an' safety wouldn't like it neither."

I failed to make the connection with health and safety, but very soon I became quite expert at driving my time expired, clutchless van. Certainly, to start with, there were some awful noises from the gearbox, but I soon learned how to judge the revs correctly and change gear almost smoothly. Eventually, impressed with my improving skill, I developed a grudging respect for the clapped out Marina - so long as it survived the next two days.

The van did survive, and so did we all, including Neville who was only a few days away from a nervous breakdown when we finished on Christmas Eve.

I completed my delivery and retired to the tea room where it was rumoured there would be drinks available by courtesy of the tea fund, which was administered by Murdoch. There must have been a large surplus, for there was a plentiful supply of beer, and a bottle of whisky.

106

The well stocked tea room was deserted, the debris on the floor evincing the earlier occupancy of the town rounds - who, with no second delivery, had departed for their Christmas a long time before - in contrast to the Sorting Office which, for the first time in two and a half weeks, was completely clear of parcels, packets and bundles of Christmas cards and letters. It was as if a shutter had been sharply pulled down, signifying the end of Christmas at the Post Office: there was nothing left to deliver.

I had thought Christmas would be like harvest time on the farm, whether it was corn, potatoes or lambs. And in one sense it was. Although with farming there were always breaks for the weather or lulls in the lambing. But on the Post Office there was no let up, especially for the weather, and at the end there was nothing to show for all the hours of unremitting work.

I lit a cigarette and sat back, enjoying a well earned glass of beer, glad of the peace and quiet for a moment or two. Presently, Ted and Duncan came into the tea room and for a while we sat in companionable silence, smoking our cigarettes and drinking our beers, lost in a fog of fatigue and tobacco smoke.

Suddenly Duncan said, "You know what a woman on my round told me this morning?"

Ted and I shook our heads.

"She said, 'You postmen don't really have such a bad time at Christmas, just delivering the mail. The people I feel sorry for are the poor souls who do all that sorting. That's where the real work is.' Can you believe it? She thought all we did was deliver presorted mail. They've no idea, these people; they're stupid."

Sydney burst through the door, exuding forced cheerfulness and bonhomie. I suspected he was slightly drunk, but he poured himself an enormous whisky and before sitting down produced two more bottles from a carrier bag he had been holding.

"Tips," he said expansively, placing them on the table. "Did bloody well for tips this year. These, bottles and bottles of wine, brandy and stuff and nearly six 'undred quid. That'll teach 'Iggings."

I didn't believe him for a moment.

Returning home, I cut some holly from the tree in the garden, decorated the house with sprigs placed behind the pictures, ate a brief meal and retired to bed, requesting my wife to wake me in a couple of hours. I had a real fear if she did not I would probably sleep right through to Christmas Day. I was certainly tired enough.

Christmas Day and Boxing Day passed in a peaceful, family atmosphere. There was one big bonus for me. For the first time in years there were no farm animals to be fed, no chickens to be locked up to protect them from the predatory foxes, no bellowing calves impatient for their milk, and no house cow to be milked. Whatever regrets I might have harboured at leaving farming, I missed none of it that Christmas.

Twelve

Returning to work on the Friday, there was a nasty shock in store. Expecting a relatively quiet time between Christmas and the New Year, I was staggered by the amount of mail we hauled off the van from Buddleshaw that morning. It was junk mail, all of it. During the two days of Christmas holiday permitted by Royal Mail, I dimly recalled subliminally absorbing advertisments for various competitions on the television notably by the Readers' Digest, Which? magazine and some others for their prize draws, but I had no idea these ads would be followed by such quantities of rubbish. In addition, there were piles of unsolicited holiday brochures. Duncan, Ted and I were horrified, but the older hands laughed. "It's always the same after Christmas, all the rubbish comes out."

Which?, which should have known better, was a particular target for our ire, sending out mail for their prize draw in flimsy little envelopes that were difficult to hold and almost impossible to sort, so small were they. Also, many were addressed to people who had died years ago, moved house or simply did not exist. Plenty of the addresses did not exist either.

Royal Mail had a way of dealing with this dead mail in the form of small stickers, with appropriate boxes to tick - gone away, deceased, incorrectly addressed and so on. I took a malicious pleasure in setting aside these letters, with junk mail even a spelling mistake qualified as incorrectly addressed as far as I was concerned, and later applying the stickers, appropriately ticked. It was a small way of getting my own back on the perpetrators of this rubbish. And it had the added bonus of making more work for Murdoch when he was in the cage, and Neville when he was not, for the postman, higher grade, was also in charge of the dead letters.

These dead letters were returned to the sender who did not take the slightest notice of the information on the stickers, sending out the same garbage next time round to the same non existent people at the same non existent addresses.

I had a particular loathing for junk mail in all its forms. I hated the supposedly eye catching slogans printed on the front of the envelopes. *'Open Immediately.' 'Prize Numbers Enclosed.' 'Time Sensitive Material Enclosed* - whatever that might have meant. *'Dated Material Enclosed'* - so what, most mail bore a date. *'You Could Be A Winner.' 'Open Now.'* It was all designed to appeal to the baser human instincts of greed and wealth, something for nothing, and it was all an insult to intelligence.

It was no use saying the likelihood of winning the huge amounts of money promised was probably less than winning a national lottery, if indeed there were any prizes in the first place. I hated junk mail. There was far too much of it. Royal Mail would still have made a healthy profit on a quarter of the amount, but revenue was 'the way forward' and all reason was felled like trees in the rain forest in the pursuit of greater profits.

What was surprising was the number of gullible people who responded to these outrageous promises of instant riches. It was possible to judge this by the quantity of reply paid envelopes collected from the post boxes and from the mail on rural rounds, which was left out for us to collect - sometimes more than was collected from the boxes. This was revealing, for it showed the richest, and sometimes more intelligent members of society were just as gullible as the poorer and supposedly less knowledgeable classes to whom these cynical marketing tricks were primarily aimed. When it came to greed all class barriers were transcended and no one knew it better than the marketing chiefs of the firms involved. And the cynical postman. It was quite possible to work up a hate neurosis against the firms involved. The Readers' Digest, Dell, The Franklin Mint, Which? and many, many more. My outlet was to return as much as was legally possible to the sender, but others took more drastic action, either destroying or delaying it, both sackable offences by Royal Mail.

The Readers' Digest was head and shoulders above any other firms in the constant sending of unwanted advertisements and books. For sheer persistence they deserved a cardboard medal soaked in the collective sweat of thousands of overworked postmen.

Royal Mail deserved a medal, too, for the sheer incompetentce of their sales staff. A friend of mine worked for a firm taking its first steps into direct mailing, as it is jargonistically called. They were tentative steps, but important ones. They wanted to send out one million mailshots, not many by the standards of the large direct mailing firms, but significant. He approached the relevant department and, as he was a new customer, was accorded a meeting with the manager. A price was worked out and agreed. My friend had been told by his boss to ask for a discount: he was told to ask for five per cent, but settle for two and a half. He was staggered to be offered an immediate discount of thirty five percent.

"I couldn't believe it," he told me later, "no firm I have ever worked with has offered a discount like that, and, had I not been so shocked, I think I could have pushed him even further."

Royal Mail was riddled with incompetent middle managers who were not up to the standard required by the more cut throat organisations in the real world. Instead, they settled comfortably and complacently into the unreal, secure womb of this vast unreformed organisation, dispensing largesse with a casual abandon that would have shocked a private company. If the middle management were inept they were indolently so, and that was not an accusation that could be levelled at the hard working failures who were the postmen, without whom there would be none of these surplus middle managers in the first place.

In 1988, the whole of Royal Mail conjured an image of a fat waddling dinasour, riddled with parasites, lurching randomly forward to quite where it did not know, never believing anything could ever change.

Of all the junk mail the most hated by the postmen and - if their reaction was anything to go by - their customers were 'households', grandiosely called the Household Delivery Service by Royal Mail. These were the unaddressed leaflets advertising cut price insurance, water softeners, double glazing and Sun bingo competitions. Later, uninspirationally, they changed the name of this service to Royal Mail door to door service, but to us they always remained households. The larger charities often took advantage of this service, sending out their appeals for money in bulky envelopes containing free pens. These were a nightmare to deliver as they never fitted with the other post on account of their awkward bulk.

It is difficult to crititsize charities, but I always had an abiding suspicion there were people in full time employment working for them who had to justify their jobs. And one way of doing so was to use the Royal Mail household delivery service, at great expense, to send out an appeal blanketing the whole country, which was really achieving nothing more than preaching to the converted who would have contributed anyway. The worst offenders, by far, were the various cancer charities who, having ensnared someone by guilt followed it up with endless mailshots requesting even more money. I wish they could have witnessed, as I did on many occasions, the distress this caused many elderly widows and widowers - who had recently lost their spouses from cancer - some of them living on meagre state pensions, who felt obliged to contribute money they could ill afford. It was a form of moral blackmail I deplored.

These cancer charities would do well to realise, too, that every household in the country has a surfeit of pens, to the point where they are thrown away. We had a huge box in the office full of free charity pens, removed from surplus envelopes before the contents were incinerated, simply because no one had bothered to find out exactly how many people the Bramton area encompassed. The pens were no good anyway: they leaked and ruined countless Post Office shirts.

The whole charity conundrum was summed up neatly and succinctly by an extremely wealthy lady. When I handed her her mail one morning I separately gave her a household to which she said loftily, "I do not subscribe to the Macmillan cancer appeal, I subscribe to the charity of my choice." Whereupon she dropped the envelope directly into her rubbish bin.

There were several reasons why we hated these households. They did not constitute proper mail and as we were officially employed as purveyors of Her Majesty's mail this was hardly part of the job. True, we were paid extra for delivering them, but it was not in proportion to the extra work they created.We were, in effect, reduced to the role of leaflet distributers. Some firms appeared to become addicted to sending out the same leaflets to the same areas almost every third week throughout the year, and it was depressing to hear the inevitable comments from our customers as they hurled them into their bins. It was all a terrible waste and whether these firms ever recouped their costs from this exercise was open to debate.

We all had our own methods of dealing with this junk. Ted, supremely and often irritatingly consciencious, carefully placed his households in his sorting frame where the folded ones could easily have a letter accidentally slipped between the leaves and then get thrown away with the leaflet, assiduously annotating the ones where the slot was shared by two houses, with the number for each house. If, occasionally, he found he was short of two or three he would scour the office until he found them. Others, me included, took a more insouciant attitude, not bothering to place them in the frame, but taking them out in their bundles, whether on a bicycle or a van round, and peeling one off to add to the mail, at each house we visited. As far as I was concerned, I delivered one lot each day and if I missed a house I never bothered returning the following day to deliver one of these outrageous leaflets, the true fag end of the advertising industry.

Peter composted his. "I've never delivered one in my life. I take them home, remove the rubber bands and throw them on my compost heap."

I was surprised the altruistic Peter would go to such lengths, but he was very much a highly principled friend of the earth. A postman had been sacked quite recently for disposing of his households in a rubbish bin, but Peter was unrepentant, "Then let them sack me, if they find out. I hate those useless things. Best place for them. They make lovely compost, too, even the glossy ones. In two months there's nothing left of them."

It was, I thought, a fitting epitaph for the advertising industry.

Thirteen

Uncle John was making a good recovery from his heart attack and it was rumoured he would return to the office in the third week in January, doubtless to Murdoch's chagrin and Neville's relief.

Gavin and Lester approached me shortly after Christmas and we discussed the prospect of me joining their section. "That Dave's no good," Gavin said. "We want to get rid of him and he wants to join the Junior Section. That shouldn't be a problem, but it would be best to wait until Higgings returns. Murdoch doesn't like Lester and me, and I don't think he much likes you either. He's bound to make a fuss while he's in charge of the office, but we won't have any trouble from Higgings."

I was unclear why there should be trouble. It appeared perfectly straightforward. But this was the Post Office where nothing was as it seemed. Apparently, if someone senior to me wanted to join the section and objected it might throw the office into chaos, with all the rounds having to be re-allocated. It was all rather confusing and the analogy of school returned to mind, the sections representing houses with the Headmaster alone having the authority to sanction the transfer of a boy from one to another, seeking advice from his chief prefects in the guise of Sydney and Murdoch. It was odd, in the modern world, such an archaic system survived.

For the time being, until the return of Uncle John, I continued in the Junior Section. After Christmas we returned to our normal rotation on the rounds. Travelling around the Topleys, the gloomy aftermath of Christmas was in evidence everywhere; at first, overflowing dustbins, stuffed with the detritus of the festival, and later, after the twelfth night, dried up Christmas trees thrown out into gardens, and sometimes onto the road verges and even into fields, by uncaring people who appeared to think it was the duty of the unfortunate farmer or the council to dispose of them on their behalf. There, they often remained for months, gradually turning brown and shedding all their needles, resembling grotesque fish skeletons, picked clean of all their flesh.

Peter, who acted as a social concience for all of us, collected these discarded trees on his round, loaded them into his van and disposed of them in the skip thoughtfully provided by the council at the waste disposal facility in Bramton.

The first snow of winter came during the second week in January. I knew as soon as I was awakened by the alarm clock at four o'clock in the morning that snow had fallen during the night by the unnatural luminescence reflected from the ceiling and walls. But when I opened the door to get my Puch out of the garage the snow had ceased and the moon was illuminating the scene as brightly as daylight. There had only been a fall of some two inches, and cautiously riding into Bramton was a memorable experience. No other vehicle had violated the virgin surface and I felt like an explorer on an alien planet where no human had ventured before, the single wheelmark of my moped clearly visible behind when I glanced in the mirror.

"Must be bloody mad, riding that thing in this weather," was Sydney's greeting as I dismounted and heaved the machine onto its stand. He was, as usual, sitting on his plastic, garden chair, his tea on the wicker table in front of him. It was where we came out of the office to have a cigarette break, and as Sydney didn't smoke I always thought it odd he braved the winter cold to drink his rapidly cooling cup of tea outside.

"No madder than delivering letters on a Post Office bicycle," I retorted.

"The roads'll be gritted by the time them's out," he replied. "Besides, you can always push a bike."

I sighed. There was no arguing with Sydney. "'Ere, I got something for you," he reached under the wicker table and produced a crash helmet, with all the aplomb of a conjurer producing a rabbit from a top hat. He proffered it to me and, astonished, I made a step towards him and took it. It was a moderately up to date crash helmet, complete with visor. I mumbled my thanks and Sydney, suddenly appealingly bashful, said, "Well, I've seen it sitting in this old boy's shed for ages, and I knowed 'ee give up biking so I thought of you and that bloody cork lined skid lid you wears and I asked 'im if I could 'ave it. 'Ee were pleased to get rid of it. You make sure you wears it," he went on, "especially in this weather."

Surprisingly touched by Sydney's thoughtfulness, I went inside. No longer would the schoolchildren be able to rudely shriek, "Here comes Biggles," as I returned through Bramton on my way home - a daily ritual, which I found wearisome, but afforded them endless amusement.

Driving around the Topleys was a nightmare compared to my euphoric and slightly unreal ride into work. The council appeared to have abandoned any attempt to grit the side roads, and the Topleys were set mostly on and around such roads. By the time I had managed to start the reluctant Morris Marina other traffic had driven on them, compressing the virgin snow into a lethal, rutted, vengeful icy surface. There was no relief from the weather; it remained below freezing all day.

A Morris Marina, with its rear wheel drive and little weight in the back, was hardly the ideal vehicle to drive at such times. I struggled two of the heavy concrete blocks, with grooves moulded in them for parking the Pashleys, into the back of the van to add ballast and set off on the road. The weather had placed an entirely different perspective on the Topleys, and it required a complete re-think on how I was to tackle it. I had never realised how many steep hills ended with a T junction at the bottom, mostly with banks or brick walls facing up the hill, nor how many drives joined the road on the downhill; the main problem was trying to bring the van to a halt without skidding into the obstacle in front. With some of the steeper drives it was easier to park outside and walk in, but there was no escaping the junctions.

I was no newcomer to driving in ice and snow, and there was little relief from the intense concentration needed to survive these awful conditions. It was ironic to hear the warnings issuing from the radio - a rare luxury in the otherwise basic Marina - advising drivers to stay at home unless their journey was really necessary when the postman had little option other than to venture out.

But the post van was not the only vehicle on the road from necessity rather than choice and I had enormous respect for the drivers of the few, huge, articulated, grain-lorries I saw cautiously negotiating the rutted ice; I could imagine nothing more dangerous to drive in such weather, a potential jackknifing waiting at every corner. I pulled over as far as possible when I met one. The grim faced driver hunched over the wheel, with a concentration that showed he was fully aware his forty ton, flexible combination allowed not the slightest margin of error. Somehow, watching these monstrous vehicles, which were never designed to be driven along country lanes in the snow, gave a sense of proportion to driving a van, which was infinitely more manoeuvrable and a fraction of the weight of those grain-lorries.

The irascible Colonel Mackinnon of Keepers Cottage was one of the few people I met regularly on this otherwise dormitory round and he, grudgingly, appeared pleased to see me.

"It is good to know that not everything in this country ceases to function in a couple of inches of snow. I would offer you a cup of tea seeing the conditions are not as normal as they should be, but the power is off at the moment. The electricity company apparently cannot function when the temperature drops below freezing, nor has the ullage lorry arrived today. I don't suppose you have seen it?"

I shook my head uncomprehendingly, wondering what the old boy was talking about, when suddenly I realised he was referring to the dustcart. "Pity," he said. "They should have been here hours ago. You take care on these roads," he went on, "our mail delivery means much to us in these isolated rural communities."

As I continued on my round, the reasons for the electricity failure and the non arrival of the 'ullage' lorry became clear. The former was nothing to do with the weather, but rather the freak result of a macabre accident which, had I not seen it for myself, I would never have believed. A large tawny owl had alighted on a power line further down the road and, as it had regained its balance and straightened its head had come in contact with the line above it, instantly sending thousands of volts through its body and blacking out half of the Topley area.

The tawny owl was frozen, quite literally, in the rictus of death, the talons firmly gripping the lower line as almost its last concious movement, the head firmly in contact with the upper wire, ears still upright, eyes wide open and staring unblinkingly forever at an image of the snow carpeted vista, and the beak hinged grotesquely open.

My initial thought had been, what was a tawny owl doing in broad daylight sitting on a power line, and it was not until I had looked with greater perception that I understood the bizzare circumstance of its demise. There had been no evidence of the electricity company all morning: the old colonel would have a long wait for his tea.

He would have an even longer wait for his dustbins to be emptied. Half an hour later I discovered the 'ullage' lorry lying on its side in a ditch, with three disconsolate dustmen standing by it, silently smoking cigarettes, shivering from the cold, their eyes fixed on the icy road. It was difficult to reconcile this motley crew with the cheerful lot who, before Christmas, had been loudly toting for tips: one dressed as a burly and unlikely fairy, complete with wand, wings, tiara, bare hairy legs, hob nailed boots and a risque sequin covered outsized mini dress.

It was easy to see cause of their plight. Too idle to carry the bins the twenty yards from a house to their lorry, they had driven up a steep driveway and emptied the bins. On the way out, the driver had lost control on the icy surface, depositing his lorry and its load into the ditch. The old colonel would be lucky to have his bins emptied that day. Maybe, I thought, the mishap might persuade the council to grit the side roads where it was so sorely needed, but it was a folorn hope.

To my astonishment, the following morning, riding my Puch gingerly along the road to Bramton at a quarter to five in the morning with both feet lightly trailing on the road, I saw headlights in the distance accompanied by an intermittent orange flashing. It was a rare gritting lorry, twenty four hours late, and as it passed the lumps of salt and grit were flung against my new helmet and visor, and stinging my unprotected legs like thousands of dried peas shot from well aimed pea shooters. The cold weather was as transient as a heatwave in summer, and after three days the westerly air flow re-established itself, bringing warmer weather, a light drizzle and leaving a porridge of dirty slush and mud in its wake. The only casualty in the office had been Peter who, swerving to avoid a skidding car, had demolished a wall.

Fourteen

I had, quite literally, an unnerving experience on my town round, in a secluded close of some six houses, on one of the more exclusive developments. There was a packet, which was too large for one of the letterboxes, so I rang the doorbell. There was no answer apart from the barking of a dog somewhere within the house. I was not anxious to make the acquaintance of the dog, which judging from its deep bark was a large one. So after another half hearted ring and with some relief I investigated the possibility of leaving the packet in the garage. Scarcely anyone used their garages for their intended purpose and, carelessly, they were nearly always left unlocked, which considering the amount of expensive equipment often left inside, was surprising. This garage was a double one, with an up and over door and, as I had expected, was not locked, but it proved remarkably resistant to my efforts to open it. The handle freed easily enough, but the door stubbornly refused to open more than an inch or two at the bottom, not enough to slide the packet through. Determined not to be beaten, I placed the packet on the ground, firmly gripped the handle with one hand and, sliding the fingers of the other hand under the door, gave a terrific heave.

The result was startling. There was a thunderous cacophony, like a load of corrugated iron falling from a lorry onto a concrete surface, followed by strange sliding and grinding noises, which continued irregularly for what to me constituted an age. Just as I thought there could be no more clamour to come there were further minor crashes and bangs from within the garage, like aftershocks of an earthquake. Horrified, I let go of the door, which had only shifted by a foot, and nervously looked around the close, expecting windows to be flung open and suspicious householders to come storming down their paths demanding an explanation. Astonishingly, there was nothing, no reaction at all. The noise must have reverberated around half of Bramton, all the dogs in the close were barking dementedly and I could hear barking far into the distance. It was through the barking dogs that I knew at least two houses were occupied in that close. I heard their owners, either uncaring of the fate of their neighbour's garage or too terrified to venture out, clearly shouting at them to be quiet.

Stunned by the havoc I must have wrought to the unseen and unknown contents of that garage, I cautiously slipped the packet under the door and tried to close it, but it had jammed and attempts to close it only elicited more ominous grinding noises from the interior, so I left the owners to soft it out, pushing a note through the letterbox, which cryptically read 'Packet left in garage', and crept out of the close.

Strangely, there was never a word of complaint, only a silence as complete and calm as the delivery had been thunderous and discordant.

It was quite different with the fudge.

There was an elderly lady who lived in one of a row of terraced houses in the no-man's land, which lay between the estates and the developments in Bramton. She was a nice old girl of about eighty called Mrs. Compton, a widow.

Mrs. Compton had a friend who sent her a large box of home made fudge once a month and Mrs. Compton was very fond of her friend's fudge. It was something, which, in the loneliness of her widowhood, she looked forward to receiving and consuming. I knew all this, because some lonely people take the opportunity of the postman's visit for a chat and a contact with the world beyond their loneliness, and Mrs. Compton was no exception. We often used to chat on her doorstep, and I always made time for her. It was a part of the job I enjoyed. She told me all about her monthly delivery, her friend who made it, and her family and pets; and about her late husband and her family, and her life when her husband was overseas. He had been in the army and she was used to loneliness and she could cope with it. I always patiently listened to her, never in a hurry to move on, unlike some of the younger postmen like Dave who had no time for anyone other than themselves.

But Mrs. Compton was sometimes forgetful, and she did not always tell me everything. She either forgot or omitted to tell me she was going away for a few days. This was unfortunate, for her monthly box of fudge arrived while she was away. Post Office procedure dictated an impersonal note to be dropped through her letterbox proclaiming, 'We are sorry to have missed you, and are unable to deliver your packet/letter/parcel because …' followed by a number of reasons listed by little squares, which required the appropriate tick. It went on to state that the item of mail could be collected from the Sorting Office, or delivered again at a convenient day for the customer.

This was all very well, but took little account of the fact that elderly ladies with few friends, living out their remaining years in a not particularly salubrious part of Bramton, probably in circumstances that were considerably less opulent than they had been used to in the more halcyon days of their lives, found it extremely difficult to make the long track to the Sorting Office. Most had no transport, and Mrs. Compton certainly did not. And everyone, of course, wanted their parcels as soon as possible.

In these circumstances it was far better, and easier, to ask a neighbour whether they minded looking after the package, and receiving no reply from Mrs. Compton's door, I rang the bell of the next house in the terrace. A harrased young woman with unkempt hair, wearing a dirty apron, answered the door. Two snivelling young children, mucus liberally pouring from their noses, peered wide eyed around either side of her. I explained what I wanted.

"Mrs. Compton? Who's she?" she asked.

"Your neighbour," I said patiently.

"Which side?" I explained. "Oh, her. All right, I suppose so." She took the box of fudge and closed the door with a deep sigh. I continued on the round.

It rained that evening, heavy rain that bounded off the window panes and lashed the moss from the tiles into the gutters, which noisily overflowed onto the ground below, splattering the outside walls with a dirty, wet organic gruel. The skies cleared in the early hours and I escaped the soaking I had been expecting.

Mrs. Compton's fudge had not fared so well. When I arrived at her house it was on her doorstep and it was a sorry sight, the cardboard box in advanced stages of decomposition, sitting in a brown puddle of dissolved fudge. Evidently Mrs. Compton's sulky neighbour had waited until I was out of sight and deposited the fudge on her doorstep. Her reluctant duty discharged she had retired into her own house with her snivelling children, closing her door and mind to the fudge. There was nothing I could do. The fudge was beyond redemption, so I left the revolting mess where it was.

Unsurprisingly, on her return, Mrs. Compton complained bitterly to Murdoch. If anything, he had become even more taciturn. I was summonsed to his office and asked to explain, which I did, stating my opinion of the neighbour in no uncertain terms. Murdoch was not impressed, nor did he appear to care. I asked him what he proposed to do about it, and he looked askance at me for having the temerity to put such a question to him.

"Give 'er a claim form," he said, "but she won't get nothing. Fudge? That ain't got no value. She might get a book of second class stamps if she's lucky." He swivelled the chair to face the desk and continued with his arcane workings in his ledger.

But the fudge did have a value. It had a value to Mrs. Compton, in more ways than the mere eating of it. She must have contacted her friend, told her of the sad fate of the box of fudge she had sent and her sympathetic friend, mindful of Mrs. Cotton's circumstances, sent her a replacement box.

By a ghastly coincidence she was away again when it arrived, and again it poured with rain that night. I had to pass by Mrs. Compton's

124

house the following morning and I involuntarily glanced at it as I passed. There, on the doorstep, leaking a by now familiar brown liquid from the sodden cardboard box, was her replacement fudge.

Duncan was on the round that week and I asked him what he had done.

"Left it with her neighbour," he replied, "that sulky one with them snotty nosed kids."

It was a sorry state of affairs. Mrs. Compton never made a complaint about the second box of fudge; she probably didn't think it was worth it for a book of second class stamps. But she blamed the postman for its ruination. As a consequence, she no longer came to the door when her letters were delivered and we were both the losers for it. If Murdoch had told her what had really happened she might have been more forgiving, but Duncan and I were never given the opportunity to explain.

Fifteen

Uncle John returned in the third week in January. He was slightly thinner, though still portly, but otherwise unchanged in every way. Murdoch returned to his cage and Neville escaped to his Pashley on which he could revise his Open University course to his heart's content and indulge his daydream of bettering himself.

Worried he might be returned to his bicycle round Sydney was uncharacteristically quiet for a few days, inadvertently drawing more attention and loud comments from some of his colleagues who knew perfectly well what was bothering him than if he had remained his normal jovial self. Uncle John must have thought he had served his sentence.

I asked him how he was and he looked surprised.

"I am fine now, thank you," he replied, "or so the doctors tell me. I still get very tired, but I am assured this is quite normal." He sighed. "There's a lot to worry about, though. There are big changes coming here and they're appointing a new Area Manager, a tough man I hear, but I'll survive, I suppose."

I started walking away from him when he said, "Thank you for asking. You are the only person in the office who has bothered."

I genuinely liked Uncle John, who was working at the limit of his intellectual capacity as Manager at Bramton. The Area Manager was another matter. There had been two in the short time I had been at the office, ineffectual middle aged men who made fleeting visits to Bramton, pestering Uncle John with unnecessary persistence mostly about the amount of extra hours being worked. Royal Mail was obsessed by overtime, seeking any means possible to reduce it, failing to understand that in a permanently understaffed office it was a choice between having the mail delivered or leaving it in the sorting frame. It was not an enviable job being an Area Manager, constantly harassed by superior managers, passing this frustration on to the junior managers who, in turn, passed it down to the end of the line - the postman.

The postmen held all the trump cards. Royal Mail was totally reliant on them to deliver the mail: without them there would be no business, no managers and the postman had one unassailable right; he was not obliged to work overtime. Royal Mail was structured in such an extraordinary way that, for a guaranteed daily delivery throught the country it relied on, and expected, its postmen to work longer than a basic week. If they declined the whole system would descend into chaos. Management, postmen, and particularly the union, knew this. It seemed an odd way to run a business when the employer was obsessed by reducing the number of hours as much as possible, probably something that was deeply rooted in the past when life was more leisurely and there was no junk mail.

The postman suffered no stress, which was solely the privilege of management, at whatever level: pressurised from the top, pressurised from the next level down and, ultimately, pressurised by the postmen. It was scarcely a recipe for smooth operation and, again just like school, the higher a Royal Mail manager rose in the structure the more sadistic delight he took in bullying his underlings.

There was no trace of humanity in these men, most of whom were not very bright, the dross of the rejects of more go-ahead private companies. The sorry truth was that these men were, like the mail that sustained them, junk. Nothing on this earth would have persuaded me to become a Royal Mail manager. I valued my life and principals far more highly than that.

An honourable exception to the management rat race was the guileless Uncle John, who sometimes appeared bewildered by inhabiting the viper's nest into which he had been promoted, and it was undoubtedly this as much as the strike that had contributed to his heart attack.

The two Area Managers had succumbed in a different way. They both suffered nervous breakdowns. One had been a coach driver, the other a J.C.B. driver. They never returned to Royal Mail. I wondered how the new 'tough' appointee would fare.

Gavin approached Uncle John with his proposal for Dave and me to swop sections, and he raised no objection. Sydney muttered a few protestations that it was against accepted procedure, but we ignored him; he was hardly in a position to protest anyway. The rest of the office was completely disinterested.

My new section Gunners Castle was so called on account of a ruined medieval castle of obscure and largely uninvestigated antiquity. Every section had an awkward round, which did not fit well into the three week rotation, and ours was no exception. It comprised a rural round, also known as Gunners Castle, a town round and a late shift. This late shift was the unpopular one, and I viewed it with some misgivings.

The awkward round in the Junior Section had been Norton, with its split shift and the long bicycle ride out to it. The late shift at least had the redeeming feature that one could work straight through it. In addition, it was a five day week duty. So in theory one had every third Saturday off, but this seldom worked in practise. The hours were eleven in the morning until seven in the evening, again theoretically allowing its postman lie in, but this seldom worked in practise either.

The reasons were, of course, overtime. It gave Uncle John the option of using the late man to work a round in the mornings and a full round on Saturdays: these were the grounds for my misgivings. I viewed the extra hours as very much a two edged sword, because of the amount of tax deducted. If it had not been for the fact that the late shift was such an easy round I would never have entertained the idea of joining Gavin and Lester.

The other two were delightful. The town round was different in that it was a trolley round. The mail was loaded into a four wheeled Royal

Mail trolley and trundled around the old town of Bramton as it had been before the spread of the estates and developments arrived. It was a pretty walk through old streets lined with old houses, which led down to the river flowing along the bottom end of Bramton. There were no closes, gardens or crescents, though there was, perversely, a mobile home park. This consisted of forty outsized caravans, disguised by means of low walls and porches to resemble bungalows. Once delivered and parked these dwellings were no more mobile than the bungalows they crudely purported to be. This round had a second, parcel delivery to the shops and offices in the two main streets of Bramton.

It was the rural round I was really looking forward to, I was already familiar with the three villages it encompassed - Gunners Castle, Ruston and Ashley. Unlike the dormitory Topleys, on the opposite side of Bramton, all the villages were proper rural communities just far enough from the railway station to enable their characters to survive. There were commuters and the odd weekenders, but nothing on the scale of the Topleys and other villages unfortunately situated near a railway line.

Lester formally welcomed me to my new section, shaking my hand and wishing me well. It was difficult not to laugh, but he was perfectly serious. He was a dapper, short man, always immaculately turned out as befitted an ex-petty officer of the Royal Navy, and he favoured the formal peaked hat, which Royal Mail only issued on special request. I would not have been seen dead in it, but somehow it suited Lester.

The training was left to Gavin, as senior member of the section. I already knew most of the town round from the bits and pieces of overtime I had picked up on it. It was decided that I only needed to learn the late shift and Gunners Castle.

We started with Gunners Castle. Having become used to the way the sorting frames worked and it was really only a matter of learning the route and the idiosyncrasies of the round. The main problem was with Gavin, the failed schoolmaster, the same Gavin who had trained me on

Norton. He liked to think of himself as a complex character, but his views on life were really extraordinarily simplistic. He was an unreconstructed, latterday bohemian, whose attitude appeared to be that the world and anyone who inhabited it owed him a living, and this included me. He was always in the office, whether he was working or not, and unlike the majority of his colleagues who, when they had finished, went straight home, Gavin always lingered talking shop and office politics.

I mentioned this to Jack, who sniffed expressively. "If you saw his wife you would understand why he's reluctant to go home: always nagging him, forever telling him what to do. And those undernourished children of his, whining and crying."

He shook his head slowly, flicking his tea towel at a dopey fly on one of the tea room tables. "You would think they were poor, but Gavin works nearly all day long and she works from home, cleaning and restoring pictures. They say she's quite well regarded in the art world, so there must be money there."

Gavin, on his own admission, had been a late developer. He had learnt to drive late, married late and realised too late he was unsuited to teaching. His two young daughters aged two and three, were twenty years younger than the children of most people of his age. He was perpetually short of money and cigarettes.

"His wife won't let him smoke in his own house," Jack had said. "He has to smoke in the garden, and then he's only allowed one cigarette in an evening."

He compensated for his evening nicotine deprivement by having endless cigarettes during the day, nearly all other people's, as I discovered to my cost.

On the first morning of training on Gunners Castle, as we settled into the van, he turned to me and said, "Could I cadge a cigarette from you by any chance?" It was to become a familiar refrain, but one that I was only prepared to suffer in the short term. Tobacco was expensive enough, and it soon became clear Gavin was disinclined to return any generosity, or to reciprocate any favours he asked, and they were many. It was not only I who suffered from the demands of his unfulfilled bohemianism. Lester, Duncan and many other smokers were constantly targeted.

Gavin was addicted to incredibly strong coffee as much as he was to cigarettes. He took a flask with him in the van - I, more modestly, took a bottle of tap water - and announced there were two coffee stops on the round.

There were approximately the same number of calls on Gunners Castle as there were on the Topleys, but the route comprised three distinct villages rather than the string of Upper, Middle and Lower Topley, which more or less merged with each other.

The first of these villages was Ashley, which, had it not possessed a church, would have qualified as a hamlet. There were some one hundred and fifty inhabitants, but they were influential inhabitants. Ashley was an exclusive, much sought after village, hidden away far from any main road, with the river meandering gently through it. It represented, I thought ironically, everything that Gavin stood against.

Gunners Castle was a much larger village, which boasted a pub and a filling station that also doubled as a small shop and sub post office. It was set in rolling countryside at a much higher elevation than the low lying Ashley. And it was here we had our first coffee stop, though how Gavin could stomach any more after the foul smelling, diabolically strong concoction he had been drinking from his flask was beyond me.

"We always stop here," Gavin told me, "no matter how late we are. Mary would be upset if we didn't. She always gives us a slice of cake," he added with a smile, "and if she's out she leaves the cake and coffee cups on the table. We help ourselves. The house is always unlocked."

Mary was the wife of a retired farm manager, Ben, whom I seldom saw. After years of early starts he had discovered the delights of a lie in, something I envied him; even on a Sunday the habit of waking at four o'clock was difficult to shake off and sleep was fitful and elusive thereafter.

Mary was in her early seventies, a cheerful matter of fact woman, much involved with village matters. She greeted me with equanimity. "I hope I'll see more of you than I did of your predecessor. He never stopped. Ran in, wished me good morning and disappeared in a cloud of dust and flying gravel. He won't make old bones living at that pace."

She made three coffees and joined us at the table, pushing a freshly baked cake towards me. "Help yourself, I baked it this morning."

Carefully cutting a slice, I passed the cake to Gavin who cut a piece twice the size of mine.

"That wife of yours cannot feed you properly," Mary observed. "Look at him, there's nothing of him."

It was true. Gavin was painfully thin and I remembered Jack's comments about the children and his home life, but his next remark took me by surprise.

"Is Ben up yet?"

"Not yet, the lazy devil." She turned to me, "He enjoys his lie in, and he deserves it, too."

"Do you think he would mind if I had one of his cigarettes?" Gavin persisted.

Mary sighed. "Help yourself," she said, indicating a packet on the dresser. "It's one less for him, but one more for you. I don't know what you men like about cigarettes."

Gavin reached over, took the packet and extracted two cigarettes, which he placed in his pocket. I was astonished by his barefaced cheek, but Mary was unmoved. She finished her coffee and rose to her feet. "I must get on, I've a lot of baking to do."

We took the hint, finished our coffees and departed.

"She's a wonderful woman, Mary," Gavin said in a rare moment of praise. "She's a superb cook, too. I can't understand why Dave never stopped for his cake and coffee. She was really upset by that." He reached into his pocket and removed one of the cigarettes. "Ben's nice, too. You'll like him."

Gunners Castle wound on up a narrow twisting lane, thinning out all the time to isolated farms interspersed with a few cottages before culminating at a solitary pub on top of a ridge. High above the village it afforded magnificent views stretching into vistas of unspoilt countryside without a town to be seen, the many small villages almost lost in the immensity of the scene.

It was here that we had had our farm, and it was here that Matthew farmed. As we drove into his farmyard Gavin said, "You had better hand him his letters, Lester tells me you two are friends."

It was the nearest he had come to admitting that he knew I had had a farm in the area. He was probably appalled to think a farmer could become a postman; in his mind farmers were inherently rich, privileged and lazy.

As I clambered out of the van, Matthew came out of his front door to greet me - I had forewarned him that I was his new postman - and we shook hands. He had been farming there all his life, taking the farm on from his father. His land had shared a long boundary with ours. He had a dairy herd of some seventy cows.

Matthew was a good man, almost too good for his own sake. He was slightly built, in his mid fifties, always wearing a boiler suit during his working day. He was deeply religious and he carried his principals to an almost old fashioned extreme. Apart from looking after his stock, he refused to work on Sundays, and I once saw him sacrifice a field of prize hay, which was ready to bale one sunny Sunday; he left it and it rained continuously for the next four days. He was often in a state of crisis. It seemed that anything that could go wrong on his farm did so. But he and his wife, Florence, took it all with a philosophical shrug of the shoulders.

In the many years we had been neighbours and friends we had helped each other out throughout the seasons.

He smiled broadly. "Welcome back, even if it is as a postman."

"At least I shan't be helping you with your haymaking and silaging," I said in return.

He smiled. "I shouldn't be too sure of that. Haymaking is coming up and there's plenty to do around the farm. I hear you finish at midday."

This part of Gunners Gastle was fairly scattered and, apart from Matthew and our other immediate neighbours we had known few people there. Even Matthew, who had lived on his farm all his life, only knew Mary and Ben by name. They had never met, probably because they lived in the centre of the village and most of Matthew's friends lived beyond the postal boundary of Gunners Castle. "Do you ever see The Judge?" he asked me with a mischievious smile.

"We have the odd telephone call," I replied guardedly, "and a card at Christmas and I still shear his sheep each year, as you know. Apart from that I haven't seen him for a long time."

"I'm sure he'll be glad to see you back in the area," Matthew said, still smiling.

I, too, was perfectly certain that The Judge would be happy I was back.

"Well, you're quite safe at the moment, he's on holiday until next week."

I returned to the van and, with a disapproving glance, Gavin drove out of the farmyard.

The pub, the Gunners Castle, commanded one of the best views in the country and, isolated as it was, I had enjoyed many glasses of beer there as a young man. It had never been known to close its doors, except if one had arrived before twelve o'clock in the morning when it was inevitably shut. Now it was a pub-restaurant with strict opening and closing times and was much favoured by the upwardly mobile set who were prepared to drive for miles to sample its rugged isolation and staggering views. I had not enjoyed a drink there for years.

From there, the road descended to the village of Ruston, the other side of the hill to Gunners Castle, where we had our second coffee stop. It was at a hideously modern farm house, built in the early 1960's, where economy counted for everything in its construction. It was a monstrous building in every sense of the word, sprawling, ugly and completely devoid of character. The walls were pebble dashed and the windows metal framed, but the greatest paradox was that this outrageous habitation was built in the most beautiful position, situated in a clearing in the middle of a large oak wood, with its own private lake and magnificent gardens, which extended to the very edge of the trees. The drive was a mile long strip of tarmac, winding through the oak trees and leading to this flawed paradise.

We parked outside the kitchen door and went inside. There was no one about, but there on the table was a cup, teaspoon and a jar of coffee. Gavin found another cup and moved the large aluminium kettle onto the hob of the Aga. For a moment I recalled Sydney cooking his breakfast on just such a cumbersome contraption, but Gavin assured me all was in order.

We sat in silence, drinking our coffee. The kitchen appeared to be in its original state of decoration, looking as though it had not been touched since it had been built nearly thirty years before. It was also dirty and smelt strongly of dogs; there were some filthy dog baskets loosely arranged on either side of the Aga.

Presently, Gavin went across to a small serving hatch and called through it, "Anything to go, sir?" I was astonished by the servile 'sir' coming from Gavin.

A faint voice answered, "It will be ready in five minutes."

Gavin returned to the table and picked up his cup. "The Brodies are a little reclusive and don't like going out to the post office if they can avoid it," he said in a low voice, "so we always collect their mail."

At that moment three large black Labradors, claws skidding on the worn linoleum, burst through the doorway followed by two toy poodles and an elderly woman wearing a dirty, torn mackintosh. This was Mrs. Brodie and I studied her with interest.

She was about the same age as Mary, but she looked a wreck. Her hair was in urgent need of a hairdresser's attention; it was long and white, sticking upwards at strange angles and patches of it appeared to be missing, rather like the half blown seed head of a dandelion. Her country brogues were down at heel and in need of repair, covered in wet mud, and she wore thick woollen stockings, which had once been white and were now a grimy grey. There was a half smoked cigarette hanging from her lips. Her whole appearance gave an impression of decay, similar to the house she inhabited.

The dogs sniffed around us, and Gavin rose to his feet. I followed suit, half wondering if he was about to ask her for a cigarette. But he knew when he had met his match, instead introducing me to Mrs. Brodie.

"Just make yourself at home here," she said in an educated voice, vaguely indicating the kitchen with a sweep of her hand, her cigarette bobbing on her lips, the smoke drifting unheeded into her eyes. It was the end of the conversation.

"Go to your baskets, dogs," she said and left the room.

The dogs ignored her and Gavin returned to the hatch. I followed him. Seated at the end of a long and probably expensive dining room table was a distinguished looking old man, in contrast to his wife, immaculately dressed, surrounded by papers. He rose to his feet - he was a tall man - and approached the hatch, holding a bundle of letters in his hand.

"Would you be good enough to take these?" he asked Gavin, and then looked inquiringly at me.

As Gavin appeared to have dried up, I introduced myself and the old boy shook my hand firmly through, the hatch.

"My wife and I don't get out much nowadays," he said, "and we appreciate our postman taking our mail. Make sure you have your coffee each morning, and there are always biscuits in the tin. Just help yourself."

"They're a lovely couple," Gavin said when we were once again in the van, "I wouldn't try the biscuits if I were you. They are disgusting."

For Gavin to have condemned the biscuits, they really must have been horrible.

We returned to the filling station and little shop cum sub post office, collected the mail and returned to Bramton.

"Did you like the round?" Gavin asked me back in the office, drinking the dregs of his foul coffee.

I replied, truthfully, that I had.

He nodded his head. "I thought you would," he said with satisfaction.

I left him to wander his lonely way around the office until Heaven knew when and returned home.

For a reason I never fully understood, but was a foretaste of the future, Gavin decided it better that Lester trained me on the late shift. 'Late shift' was really a misnomer, running from eleven until seven; it really referred to the fact that the late man was the last to leave the office. I was relieved Gavin had changed the arrangements. It was not that I disliked him, more that I found his company tedious, his views outdated and stereotyped. I was also concerned my tobacco stocks, nearly all carefully hoarded duty free, were diminishing rapidly.

It was slightly disquieting arriving at eleven o'clock when some of the earliest of the earlybirds were preparing to go home. The welcome lie in was somewhat tempered by not having a great deal of time to achieve anything at home before I had to ride into work, but it was something I could become used to.

Lester quickly shattered my illusions. "We nearly always work overtime in the mornings. And as for having Saturdays off, you can forget it; we always work on Saturdays."

I was not so sure about that cosy agreement, but decided I would wait for a while before I asserted myself on this evidently tricky question of overtime.

The shift was easy, hardly necessitating any training, and Lester was relaxing company. It consisted of delivering parcels around the developments and to various other parts of Bramton, emptying all the post boxes within Bramton at around midday and taking their contents together with the mail from the main Bramton Post Office into Buddleshaw. After a break there was an afternoon collection on a rural route, followed by a repeat performance of the morning run to Buddleshaw.

The evening run was interesting. The main box at the Post Office could not be emptied before six o'clock. Lester and I waited in the van until the church clock chimed the hour, shot out of the van, emptied the box and roared off towards Buddleshaw. If the Church clock was known to be slow, we used our wristwatches instead, but if it was known to be fast we took that as the correct time, for a few minutes at that time in the evening were important. The trip to Buddleshaw was made with the accelerator flat to the floor, and with a bit of luck with the traffic, it was possible to travel the eight miles down the dual carriageway to Buddleshaw, dump the mail, have the registered letters signed for and return the eight miles to Bramton before half past six.

There was a little more to it than that. Before the last of the 'scheduled attendance' men who had been collecting from the rural rounds left, two of us had to lock the office with separate keys. This was before the days of electronic alarms. And I had to remember to bring my crash helmet, gloves and coat out before the dash to Buddleshaw. Once I forgot and in the pouring rain, helmetless, gloveless and coatless, I had an uncomfortable ride home: the water creeping up my legs and soaking my underpants, all the time hoping no police car was on patrol that evening. A quick phone call to Gavin ensured the delivery of my gear the following morning in time for the ride to work.

Lester also introduced me to the Buddleshaw office, where I had gone for my interview, and the garage, which was the workshop. The reception at Buddleshaw startled me on the first lunchtime run. There were still plenty of people working there at that time of day, and Lester and I were greeted with shouts of abuse as we entered the office. I thought at first it was some lingering antipathy left over from the strike, but Lester assured me they were always like that.

"They think we are ignorant country hicks at Bramton and it's their attempt at humour. Ignore them."

After leaving the mail on a large trolley we had wheeled into the main office for onward sorting we handed over the registered mail in the cage. The door at Buddleshaw was also left wide open just the same as Bramton, I noticed, making a mockery of security.

We drove the short distance to the workshop to collect some repaired tyres to return to Bramton. The workshop was large, airy and surprisingly well equipped. There were two jovial young mechanics, Jim and Dan, and their middle aged overseer, a man called Spratt who instantly reminded me of Murdoch by his dour demeanour. There must have been something about Royal Mail that either attracted this type of man or moulded them into disillusioned no-hopers, for that is what they were: they could advance no further within the organisation, nor would they readily find work outside it.

We loaded the tyres onto the van, and as we prepared to leave, Spratt came over and addressed Lester, completely ignoring me.

"Don't forget to bring your number six van in tomorrow. It's due for service."

I had noticed several new and nearly new vans in the workshop, so I asked Spratt, "Why is it we have such awful vans at Bramton while the other offices are given new ones? Some of our vans are barely driveable."

He bristled. "Are you suggesting your vans are unroadworthy?"

"No, no," I said hastily, aware I may have overstepped the mark, "I was merely saying most of our vans are old wrecks."

This inflamed Spratt. "I can assure you all the vans, which leave this garage, are in a roadworthy condition. You don't look after them at Bramton. You are always scratching them and denting them. No other office treats its vans like you do."

"Perhaps if we had some decent vans we might take some pride in them," I said boldly.

"You get the vans you deserve," thus Spratt brought the disagreement full circle and walked away.

Jim and Dan had been listening to the exchange with some amusement.

"You shouldn't have spoken to him like that," Lester said, "you don't know him. He's as bad as Murdoch."

"But it's true," I persisted.

"I know," Lester said with the hint of a smile, "but you won't win an argument with Spratt. He always knows best."

It was the lot of the late man to exchange vans, which required service or attention at the garage on the lunchtime run, occasionally with interesting results.

Sixteen

News travels quickly in rural communities. Shortly after I started on Gunners Castle, The Judge returned from his holiday. He was waiting for me. "I can't tell you how pleased I am to see you round here again," he said, enthusiastically shaking my hand. "Life has not always been easy since you left your farm. It is much better to meet people face to face than to telephone them, you know. Now you are back, in a manner of speaking, it will be much more like old times."

I did not entirely share The Judge's enthusiasm, but it was difficult not to be flattered by his greeting.

"Would you like to come and see the sheep?" He led me proudly out to one of his paddocks where twelve ewes, in remarkably good condition, were peacefully grazing. "I have bought two more, but I am slightly worried about one of them. There, that one on the extreme left. Do you think you could have a look at her?"

I sighed. This really was like old times. Since we had left our farm I had rather lost contact with The Judge, apart from shearing his sheep each year. But now, I thought, history really was about to repeat itself.

The Judge had been our most persistent, most frequent and most enthusiastic visitor. The trouble with him was, once installed in a chair by our Wellstood range, drinking his coffee, we couldn't get rid of him.

He was a man of generous proportions, shaped rather like an inverted pear. He was in his early sixties, and he thought he dressed the part of an English country gentleman. Watching him walk around the lanes in his green Wellingtons, expensive clothes and tweed cap, it was difficult to repress a smile; he reminded me of a geriatric Billy Bunter.

He really had been a judge, in London. And he had realised a lifetime ambition and retired to the country, to his dream house set in six acres of pasture. He had moved there at about the same time as we had taken over our farm, and he had watched our progress with great interest. As soon as he saw our sheep, he was converted; he wanted to have some of his own. He had his acreage expensively and expertly fenced and, with my help, procured ten Suffolk cross, two tooth ewes. He asked me if he could run them with our rams in the winter, and I agreed. This was a mistake, though I could hardly have known it at the time.

He doted on his ewes, and I became a slave to them. He bought all the equipment both necessary and unnecessary for their wellbeing and, worst of all, he bought himself a book on sheep husbandry. It was far too technical for a novice, and he constantly came over, clutching his precious book, the pages neatly annotatted with strips of paper indicating the passages he did not understand. And there were many of them. I spent hours explaining this and that to him, drank endless cups of coffee and fell far behind with the farm work. A day or two later he would return, with further pages marked for elucidation. I grew to hate that book, but it was The Judge's bible.

He was essentially such a nice man that it was impossible to become cross with him even when he had far outstayed his welcome, which was every visit. He possessed an almost schoolboyish, eager naiveté in his quest for knowledge. I often wondered how he fared in his court, and I suspected he was putty in his criminals' hands; if there was a sterner side to him, I never saw it.

He constantly invited me over to pare his ewes' feet with his brand new lambsfoot knife, drench them with his expensive worming gun and then help him run them through his footbath, set in his new concrete yards. He spared no expense.

"I hope he doesn't show an interest in cattle," said Matthew when I told him all this.

"I could mention it to him. It would share the load."

The look Matthew gave me rendered the proposition stillborn. The Judge was mine, and mine alone and I had to learn to accept this.

Like so many professional men, he was good on theory, but hopeless on practical matters. He took an active part in village life, and when a fund raising barbeque and dance was arranged he volunteered to move the upright piano from the village hall to the barn where the event was to take place. He had bought a low trailer to fit his estate car, and he asked my help to load the piano. We achieved this with comparative ease, and he secured the back flap of the trailer.

"I'll see you at the barn," he said, moving to the car door.

"Aren't you going to rope the piano?" I asked, aghast.

"Not necessary. It's only half a mile and I always drive slowly." He leapt into the driving seat with surprising agility for such a large man, and roared off, the piano cavorting from one end of the trailer to the other.

I followed at a respectful distance, and when the inevitable happened at the first bend it was unforgettably spectacular. The piano leaped out of The Judge's trailer as though determined to rid itself of such disrespectful treatment; it cartwheeled down the road, disintigrating with reverberating chords, and ended up in a thousand scattered pieces on the verge.

The dance proceeded with taped music. The village hall was presented with a new and extremely expensive piano and The Judge passed into local folklore.

The Judge's lambing was traumatic. He had put his ewes to our rams rather late and consequently our own lambing was nearly finished. I was enjoying one of my first unbroken sleeps for about a month, when the telephone rang. It was The Judge, and it was three o'clock in the morning.

He was clearly agitated. "I think one of my ewes is about to lamb. Can you come over?"

I groaned inwardly and asked him to explain the symptoms. There seemed nothing wrong, so I told him two tooths were longer in

The piano leaped out of the judge's trailer

146

lambing than older ewes, replaced the receiver and went back to sleep. Ten minutes later the phone rang again to report the next normal stage of lambing, and at four fifteen The Judge had his first ewe lamb.

"I know how a vet feels now," I said wearily to Sarah.

"And I know how a vet's wife feels. At least they can charge for their services. He's got nine more to lamb," she reminded me. "I think I'll go back to my mother for a while."

The remaining ewes happily obliged by lambing in the daytime, nevertheless, The Judge's lambing was one of the most exhausting I had ever experienced. He was loath to leave his ewes for a minute, and I could believe he sat up with them all night. He was becoming a shadow of his former self, looking haggard and tired. He was in constant touch with me by telephone and I spent more time with him than I did on our own farm. At least I could make my excuses and leave when I felt like it, but even this was difficult, and often no sooner had I arrived back than the telephone would ring again.

He had a bewildering array of lambing equipment that would have done credit to a farmer with five hundred sheep rather than his ten. It included patent devices that I had never seen before nor since. The local farm suppliers must have loved him.

His lambing could not last forever. One evening the telephone rang. It was The Judge, inviting me to view his last lamb. He was beaming and offered me a glass of sherry. As we sipped our drinks, leaning over the rail watching his last lamb, tail wriggling with pleasure as it suckled its mother, The Judge remarked, "I don't know that I could survive another lambing."

I knew how he felt.

He was thick skinned, was The Judge, doubtless a product of his calling. I was sitting on a stool in the kitchen reading a book, when I spied him walking through the farmyard. I waved and he waved back. I saw my young son run up and speak to him and he turned around and left. My son came into the kitchen and I asked him what he had said to despatch The Judge so rapidly. "I told him you were asleep."

He returned the next day. I was harrowing and it was almost dark. He was talking to my wife by the back door and never was a field harrowed so thoroughly. Eventually the darkness defeated me and I unhitched the harrows and drove back to the farm. He had come to show me his new foot paring secateurs, and could I help him trim his ewes' feet tomorrow? It was impossible to refuse him.

I was redecking our trailer, with Bert's help. He was quietly sucking on his pipe and passing me galvanised nails when The Judge, sitting astride his newly aquired mini-tractor, turned into the yard. He was dressed in his green Wellingtons, an outsize set of pristine bib and braces and his working hat - a woolly thing, with a large bobble on the top. Sitting on his tiny tractor he looked like some mobile, animated, prehistoric monolith.

"Just look at that," Bert said. "I ain't never seen nothing like it."

Neither had I, but, over the years we grew used to The Judge and his well meaning and often misguided efforts to help the community. His naivety and unconcious humour nearly mitigated the hours we spent trying to tactfully shift him out of his seat so we could get on with our work.

His rural idyll was entirely in his own mind, and he was not always sure how to manage it. In his first year he asked me if I would shear his sheep for him and I was happy to oblige. As I finished the last one he hesitantly asked me how much I was going to charge him. I had anticipated this question and I had decided to charge him nothing.

I was heartily fed up with coffee; I told him a bottle of scotch would suffice, it was about the going rate. He was horrified and I thought I had made a tremendous faux-pas. I held out and the next day he visited me with two large bottles of malt whisky. I will never know what would have happened had I asked for two in the first place.

We shook hands again as I left. "You will be able to shear them again this year?" The Judge asked anxiously.

I assured him that I would.

"I will see you right as usual," he said with a knowing smile.

Seventeen

One afternoon, when I was on the late shift, on my own as usual, Dave came into the office and he looked conspiratorial.

"Got something to show you," he said, producing a large envelope from behind his back. He lifted the flap and extracted some photo copied papers. "Read these," he thrust them into my hand. "I knew I'd find you on your own here this time of day, that's why I called in."

Dave was a strange, young man. He liked to know everything and he seemed to look on me as a friend. Probably because I was regarded as something of an outsider, someone who had a more detached view of the Post Office than most who worked at Bramton.

I started reading. They were private letters to Uncle John from a certain Colin Atkinson who was, apparently, the new Area Manager: the very same one whom Uncle John had described as 'tough'. I had never set eyes on the man, but it was clear from the correspondence that Uncle John had. 'Callous' or 'inhuman' would have better described him from what I was reading. I placed the photo copies on the table. "Where did you get these?"

Dave shuffled his feet, embarrassed. "From his drawers. He never locks 'em and I sometimes calls back to the Sorting Office when I knows there's no one here in the afternoons and goes through 'em to see what's going on. Never expected to find these, though."

I was shocked by Dave's deceit. I thought that he and Uncle John were friends together in the rough and tumble of the office, but an awful curiosity compelled me to read on.

'It is evident to me you are a weak manager,' one letter began. 'The incidence of overtime is beyond the parameters of Royal Mail acceptability. If you do not, or cannot, convert this into a downward spiral your position at Bramton could be seriously compromised.'

"Why are you showing them to me?" I asked Dave, holding the letters in my left hand. "'Cos I had to show them to someone," he replied lamely. "And I thought you'd be the best person, not being a real postman and all."

I ignored the insult. There were several letters, all written in a similar vein and all sent within a few weeks of each other. It was difficult to escape the conclusion that this Colin Atkinson was aiming to remove Uncle John from Bramton, though nothing gave a clue as to the reason.

Also, there was copious correspondence on some proposed renovations at the Bramton office. The Royal Mail in the late 1980's and early 1990's was awash with money, despite the huge amount the government took from it annually and, according to what I read, some of those funds were making their way to Bramton, the forgotten office.

I read on with a dreadful fascination. Apparently they were prepared to spend three quarters of a million pounds on alterations and refurbishments, and very shortly, too. There were even plans, which I studied with interest. Apart from knocking through a few walls, changing Uncle John's office into a Post Office shop and resiting him in a space little larger than a broom cupboard, it was difficult to see how the refurbishments could amount to such a large sum. Perhaps I had missed something.

I handed the letters back to Dave. "I still don't understand why you showed them to me. It's morally indefensible to do what you have done. If you are found out, at best you will be sacked and at worst you might be taken to court. You mustn't do it again."

Dave had the grace to blush. "I trusts you. I knows you won't tell no one - you won't, will you?"

"Only if you promise not to do it again, and I hope you can keep your mouth shut, too."

"Uncle John and I go back a long way," Dave said, "and I don't like to see him treated like this. I can keep my mouth shut when I wants to."

I believed him there. "What about not doing it again? These are private papers."

Dave thought for a moment. "I can't make no promises, I has to do what I thinks is best."

Every Tuesday, the quietest day of the week, Uncle John gave a team talk, reciting complete rubbish scripted by some semi-literate, politically correct, surplus middle manager from the excrutiatingly named Human Resources Department. These speechs were never listened to; we carried on sorting while poor Uncle John droned on in the background on such diverse subjects as the correct way to lift a mail bag, what to do if bullying was experienced in the office, including the correct procedure for complaint, and how to react to aggressive dogs. 'Look them in the eye and back off,' was the official advice one Tuesday, hastily followed by an addendum two days later at a specially convened team talk, 'Never look them in the eye, but still back off.'

The following week's talk was entitled, 'How to save Royal Mail money by more careful use of rubber bands.'

I settled happily into my new section, especially enjoying Gunners Castle.

"What did you think of the Brodies?" Mary asked me, well appraised that we enjoyed a coffee stop there.

"Proper skinflints," she went on before I could answer. "You'd think they were as poor as church mice, but they're among the richest people in the county. Won't spend a penny on anything, least of all on that dreadful house. They've got an old Morris Minor and they use it once a week to do their shopping and collect their pensions. As if they need them."

I asked Mary how they had made their money. She turned away from her baking and looked at me. "Not from fair means, from what I hear. He did very well at the end of the war. Never fought, but finished up with a packet. I lost a brother in the war." Mary was always eager to repeat gossip, whether it was about the drunken major who lived with a dubious wife in a large house in the village and was a churchwarden, or the new vicar who in her view was as dubious as the major's wife. I had met him once, one damp, drizzly morning.

"Good morning," I had greeted him affably. "Not a very nice morning."

"At least it's a morning," he had replied, continuing on his way.

I discovered I shared several mutual acquaintances with Mary and we spent many happy coffees tearing them to shreds. It was no more than they deserved. Mary was a staunch Christian, but she was also a pragmatic countrywoman whose advice I often asked and valued. She was as shrewd a judge of character of anyone I knew.

I met Ben, her husband, later on. He tended to emerge from his bed earlier when I was delivering and I gained the impression he did not think much of Gavin. Lester told me he was nearly always up when he was on the round, too. A spare man, he came into the kitchen, picked up his packet of cigarettes from the dresser and shook it.

"I see Gavin's left me a few," he said with a smile, offering me the packet. "Like one?"

I declined politely.

"One more for Gavin, one less for you," his wife said.

"More like two or three," Ben said resignedly, lighting up and drawing the smoke into his lungs with satisfaction.

Mary could never be described as a lonely person; she was far too involved with the various village committees and the church to have time for that, but as on most of the rounds there were lonely people and, as with the sadly uninformed Mrs. Compton, I tried to make time for them. There were some, however, who tried the patience and sometimes Barnacle Bill stretched mine to the limit.

154

Barnacle Bill lived in the centre of the village, and he had the advantage of me - the road separated by his house, running around the back of the village and rejoining the main road again by Barnacle Bill's cottage. It took ten minutes to deliver to the houses at the rear before emerging outside his cottage. This gave him plenty of time and, except in wet weather, he was waiting in the road for me. He did not receive a great deal of mail and most of what he did get was rubbish, but to him that was not the point at all.

On those days when I had nothing for him, I still felt obliged to stop and talk, and that was just what he wanted. He was a large man, well over six feet tall, heavily built, with craggy features and a fine nose, which was bent at a slight angle to his face. He had a full head of white hair and must have been over eighty. He was a widower; his wife had died about twenty years before.

Curiously, Gavin and Lester never attracted his attention - his real name was Bill Knowles, but I christened him Barnacle Bill from the first day I met him. It was not a particularly imaginative nickname, but apt nevertheless, for he attached himself, quite literally, to my van. The first time this happened, I was nonplussed. He ambled over to me from where he had been lying in wait by his garden gate, wished me good morning and, standing by the rear of the bonnet leant his right arm over the roof, looking down at me through the open window. He took the one letter I had for him and, without looking at it, thrust it deep into his trouser pocket with his left hand, never moving his right arm from the roof.

Casting around for something to say I came out with, 'Nice Morning.' For sheer banality it could scarcely have been bettered, but gazing up at the bulk of Barnacle Bill staring down unblinkingly at me through the window, had temporarily frozen my mind. It suited Barnacle Bill. If I had searched my mind for half an hour I could hardly have conjured a phrase more suitable for his needs.

"'Twern't like this back in '32," he began, "when we was sailing up from Lands End to Tilbury in a wool clipper, the Port Jackson, out of Australia. She were a fine ship, built in 1882, fast and well found. No, it were thick fog, thicker than any fog we gets nowadays. Course, I were only a nipper then …"

For the next twenty minutes I was forced to listen to a blow by blow account of how the Port Jackson beat up the channel, past the Goodwin Sands, with doubled lookouts, and eventually made fast in Tilbury docks. It was a fascinating story, and I listened to it with genuine interest, transported to a world I could only imagine, and Barnacle Bill told it from the heart, his eyes as misty as the conditions he was describing.

As soon as the Port Jackson was safely tied up and the gangplanks were in place he removed his right arm from the roof of my van and, without another word, sautered back to his garden gate, his hand searching in his pocket for the letter.

Unfortunately, Barnacle Bill's sea stories of the good old days - and his supply of them appeared inexhaustible - did not stand repetition. His favourite was the original one he had told me, but after the fourth telling, with minor variations, I practically knew it by heart, and trapped in my van there was no escape. I tried turning the engine off, giving the old boy about five minutes before switching it on again, but to no effect. Nothing would stop him and twenty minutes was quite a large slice out of the morning. It was quite impossible to drive off; there was no way to escape this purgatory. I once suggested he wrote these stories down, but he ridiculed the idea.

"No one would read them," he said emphatically. "They wouldn't interest the young of today."

Quite suddenly, he stopped coming out to see me. I wondered if he was ill, but I saw him digging in his garden, and with relief I was able to drive past his house unhindered. After a few months he was back with another batch of stories.

I asked Mary about him.

"He's never been to sea in his life," she told me. "He was a farm labourer, and I don't suppose he's been out of the village more than half a dozen times. But he does read a lot."

Eighteen

The vans we were given to drive at Bramton were awful, and if Spratt asserted they were roadworthy we had to take his word for it. The fact that the Royal Mail workshops were allowed to carry out their own M.O.T.'s did little for my confidence. None of the Bramton vans had a recorded mileage of less than one hundred thousand miles, some considerably more.

The trouble was we became so used to driving these wrecks that we considered them normal. They were a mixture of Ford Escorts and Morris Marinas, all petrol powered, all passed down the line to Bramton where they were driven into the ground. Because of the constant stop start nature of the job they were prematurely old, like overworked humans, old before their time. And they exhibited the same signs of crankiness and eccentricity as their irascible human counterparts.

As these vans were so aged, there was obviously a high mortality rate and, on the late shift, it was often my lot to affect the exchange; always supposing the van to be replaced had a sufficient reserve of energy to make the final eight miles down the dual carriageway to Buddleshaw. Some of them were in an advanced stage of decay and senility, with faltering engines, gears that had to be held firmly in place with the gear lever to prevent them languidly lapsing into neutral, binding brakes or brakes that were nearly non existent, and steering that caused the vehicle to wander all over the road.

Some of the replacements were not much better. Driving a Ford Escort back to Bramton, it was not until I went to change down to third for the roundabout at the end of the dual carriageway that I realised I had not changed into top gear in the first place. It had been a pleasant day, the sun was shining and I was in no hurry, lost in thought. It still seemed odd. Concentrating on the van, the reason became apparent. The thing had no power. In top gear it barely made headway; no wonder I had mistaken third gear for top. On a round it was diabolical and after a couple of days of constant gear changing I complained to Uncle John.

"It adds about half an hour to my round. Sometimes I wonder if it will reach the summit of some of those hills. And," I went on craftily, "I am having to claim that extra half hour as overtime."

Uncle John sighed. "You know how it is in this office. We just have to put up with what we are given."

I persisted. "It really is bad, even by Bramton standards. If it wasn't for the amount of mail, it would be quicker to use a bike. Why don't you have a test drive and see for yourself?"

He sighed again. "Very well, but it won't do any good."

Reluctantly he lowered himself into the driver's seat and carefully pulled on the seat belt. Dust rose from the belt as he plugged the end into the anchor point; it hadn't been used for years. Awkwardly squatting next to him on the floor space, which should have been occupied by the passenger seat, I directed him up some of the steeper hills within Bramton, and we struggled round the test drive. Fifteen minutes later we coasted down the Sorting Office slope and Uncle John climbed out. His verdict was entirely predictable and gave me enormous pleasure. "It goes all right downhill."

The test drive must have made some impression on him; the following day I was presented with another 'nearly new' van, which, whatever its other faults, at least had the saving grace of some power.

Lester had an even more unfortunate experience some days later. Collecting a van from the garage, he was half way along the dual carriageway when the temperature gauge moved into the red, and ominous grinding noises emmanated from the engine compartment. Gently easing back on the accelerator he coaxed the van into the Sorting Office yard where, with clouds of steam rising from under the bonnet and more noxious fumes mingling with the steam, we first thought it was on fire. It smelt terrible. Lester lifted the bonnet and discovered the black smoke came from the outside of the almost red hot engine, which was liberally covered with oil from numerous leaks. Sydney, attracted by the stench like a wasp to an open jar of jam, surveyed the smoking, steaming van and, reaching for the dipstick, pulled it out. It was bone dry, and Sydney hurled it to the ground as the heat seared his fingers.

"You're in trouble now," he said to Lester, gloating at his misfortune and taking pleasure that it was not he who was implicated for once. "Didn't you check the oil before you left the garage?"

Lester shook his head.

"You'll get the sack for this," Sydney told him. "It's laid down in the regulations. When you takes over a van, you has to check the oil, the tyres, the ..."

"Shut up, Sydney," Lester yelled. "You know no one does that. Let me think."

Offended, Sydney went back into the office, sucking his burnt fingers.

Lester looked at his watch. "Has Uncle John gone home yet?"

I checked in the office. He had left half an hour earlier.

"Right," said Lester. "I'll have a word with Jim. If I'm in trouble for not checking the oil, then the garage is as well for not ensuring the van had a full sump before I took it over."

Lester had a long conversation with Jim who, on a pretext, left the garage and drove out to Bramton with a large container of very old sump oil. He poured it into the still warm engine and tried it on the starter. The starter motor groaned, turning the engine over a few times before, in its turn, smoke emerged from it. Jim nodded with satisfaction.

"That should do it," he said, closing the bonnet with a clang. "When Spratt sees oil on the surfaces and oil in the sump, he'll never know how the engine seized.When that's completely cold it won't turn over again. You ring in tomorrow morning saying it won't start and Dan and me'll come and tow it away."

Spratt never smelt a whiff of a rat.

Sydney had been premature in taking pleasure from Lester's perceived misfortune.

The trouble with Sydney was that he could not resist the lure of money, undertaking work outside the Post Office in the form of gardening jobs, painting, carpentry - he was, surprisingly, a first class carpenter - and, sometimes, evening bar work. I admired his stamina; it was something I could never do, and I was a younger man. He maintained he needed little sleep, and the extra work kept him going.

The amount of mail was increasing at an alarming rate. In the few months I had been working for Royal Mail it was noticeable that gradually I was finishing later and later, to the extent I was averaging about half an hour a day in extra overtime. The office was hardly able to cope, and it only needed someone to phone in with a 'sickie' for rounds to be split up and more hours to be incurred. Sydney was always one of the first volunteers for this extra work. He who said the additional work kept him young was ageing as fast as the rest of us. Only he could not comprehend that.

It was a classic case of the spirit being willing and the flesh being weak and, I suspect to Sydney's horror, the flesh, weary with all the work imposed on it, won. Sydney went to sleep in his van on his round.

The first we heard about it was when a worried woman rang Uncle John to say Sydney had delivered her letters an hour and half before, returned to his van, closed the door, switched on the engine, but had not pulled away from outside her house.

"I think he might be dead," she had told Uncle John. "I can make out his shape in the van from the window, and he seems to be leaning back in his chair, with his head against the window. Should I call 999?"

162

Uncle John prevaricated on the question of the ambulance, instead electing to take Murdoch with him. When they arrived, they found the van, engine running, almost completely misted up on the inside and Sydney, head against the window just as the woman had described, fast asleep. They roused him and outraged he came out of the van with some alacrity and asked them what the bloody hell they were doing there. He refused to believe Uncle John and Murdoch when they told him he had been asleep for nearly two hours, despite the evidence of their watches.

"I always 'as forty winks here. No more, no less."

At that moment the woman of the house joined them. "Oh, Sydney, I'm so glad you're all right. You were parked there for such a long time that I thought you had passed away, and I've never seen a dead body before. If I had known you were only asleep, I'd have wakened you. "

Uncle John took the matter no further, probably wisely, but Sydney never lived it down.

The extra work not only imposed stress on the human aspect of Royal Mail, it also imposed a strain on the mechanical side, in other words the vans. At the rate we were getting through them, it was a wonder the garage could still find a supply of these ancient wrecks. But, unlike their vans, they never let us down.

"You'll enjoy this one," Lester told me as I started a stint on the late shift. He handed me the keys, but refused to elaborate.

It was an Escort, and it drove perfectly normally until I headed for Buddleshaw on the dual carriageway. Some of these vans, despite their inherent defects, could still manage a good turn of speed, but when the speedometer registered eighty five miles per hour the whole thing shook alarmingly. The box keys jingled a demented tune on the dashboard; the speedometer became an unreadable blur; the steering wheel vibrated so vigourously it made my fingers tingle, my whole body shaking in sympathy.

Suddenly, just as I was about to ease back on the accelerator, all was calm and serene, the speedometer registering ninety miles per hour and slowly rising. It was as if the van had broken the sound barrier and, true to the characteristics of that phenomenon, as I eased off for the roundabout, the shaking started again - vanishing at exactly eighty five miles per hour. What caused this effect I had no idea, but it was an exhilarating sensation, tempered with relief that the van had not actually disintigrated.

It caused Lester and me some amusement, but when I mentioned it to Gavin he was shocked. "I never drive at more than sixty on that dual carriageway in case a cow should wander across the road," he told me piously.

He would have been more shocked had he been a passenger in the old Morris Marina we were given some weeks later, when the sound barrier Escort went to the garage for service. It was my turn to sample its idiosyncrasy first: it went like a rocket.

The Morris Marina was never designed to travel at great speed. Its farmcart suspension, primitive steering and inadequate brakes were simply not up to even normal driving, let alone coping with, in motoring terms, supersonic speeds. But this one was fast, dangerously fast. At first I was disinclined to believe the speedometer which, at one stage on the return trip from Buddleshaw, registered one hundred and eight miles per hour, but the regularity with which I overtook the astonished drivers of allegedly far more powerful cars convinced me the Marina was far from ordinary, and even if the speedometer were ten per cent in error, it was still a very fast van.

On the evening run, the trick was to keep to the thirty miles per hour limit leading out of Buddleshaw, heading a queue of weary commuters returning home in their Volvos, Jaguars and Ford Sierras, until the roundabout heralding the start of the dual carriageway. Then, keeping to the left hand lane, one simply pressed the accelerator to the floor. All the queue behind pulled into the right hand lane to overtake what they considered to be a lumbering Royal Mail van, and remained there while the supercharged Marina surged forward like a thoroughbred racehorse, leaving the opposition foolishly in the fast lane pursuing a rapidly diminishing red dot.

Very occasionally an adventurous Jaguar might give the Marina a run for its money, but by the time other drivers had recovered from the shock of this rattling van's acceleration and given chase the Bramton roundabout would slow the proceedings down. The Marina, unfortunately, was not equipped for braking at high speed and, locked in combat with theoretically faster machines, I sometimes had to aver to their superior design and allow them a reluctant victory at the last minute - but the satisfaction lingered, a tradesman's revenge.

I briefly held the record at one hundred and ten miles per hour, but Lester beat this with one hundred and fourteen. Our Escort was returned after a week and we handed back the ton-up Marina, with some regret. I spoke to an engineer friend of mine about the magical Marina. He told me, without quite quantifying his theory, that sometimes if every component in an engine is completely in tune with the others it was just possible for an entirely ordinary engine to perform in such a way.

Weeks later, we had occasion to use the Marina again. It was a big disappointment, struggling to reach seventy five, with traffic overtaking it with metronomic regularity. Some components appeared to be out of harmony with the rest. It had had its brief moment of glory.

The most exciting and probably the most dangerous trip I made along that road to Buddleshaw was in Bramton's only Sherpa van, easily the oldest of the fleet. It consumed almost as much oil as diesel - it was the only diesel van we had at the time. About four miles out of Bramton I had an uncanny sensation something was wrong. It seemed to be going faster than normal, faster than the pressure of my foot on the accelerator justified. Furthermore, it appeared to be gaining speed of its own volition, without any help from my right foot.

Taking my foot off the accelerator made no difference, the van just kept going so, thinking the accelerator must have jammed I eased it into neutral, switched off the engine and pulled into a lay-by to investigate. The accelerator was normal, the linkage worked correctly, but the engine smelt hot and oily.

In addition, I had noticed more than the usual amount of blue smoke belching out of the exhaust pipe, but for such a decrepit vehicle this was hardly surprising. Assuming the trouble to be a temporary aberration on the part of the accelerator, I continued towards Bramton. Glancing in my mirror I saw the Sherpa was laying a blue smokescreen behind it, which was drifting lazily onto the opposite carriageway. There was evidently some problem. It would be easy enough to drop off the mail at the Sorting Office and continue to the garage. I had plenty of time.

Approaching the roundabout at the end of the dual carriageway, I changed down to third. The effect was startling. The Sherpa shuddered, faltered, emitted a noise that could only be described as a cross between a fart and a cough, recovered and slowed as I braked. Glancing in the mirror I was horrified to see a blue mushroom cloud, similar to that produced by the detonation of an atomic bomb, almost completely covering both carriageways behind me. Amazingly, the van continued to drive normally, but there was clearly something major amiss. There was a strong smell of hot oil pervading the interior.

Two hundred yards from the Sorting Office which was almost in the centre of Buddleshaw, there was a mini roundabout. With some trepidation, I carefully shifted into third gear, and then into second. The Sherpa gave a distinctive and clearly defined cough and stopped dead. Blue smoke enveloped the van, all the surrounding traffic and most of the pedestrians on the pavement. When the cloud thinned I found all traffic at a halt and the pedestrians who had not fled standing with their backs to the wall, some with handkerchiefs held over their faces, staring at the stranded Sherpa, which still had wisps of oil smoke rising from its engine compartment.

Unused to being the centre of attention, and slightly embarrassed, almost as an afterthought I turned the key in the ignition. The engine sprang to life as if nothing untoward had happened and I slowly completed the journey to the Sorting Office, backing the Sherpa up to the loading ramp.

"Bloody hell, that thing stinks," a passing postman informed me unnecessarily. "What's wrong with it?"

"It's a Bramton van," I replied inconsequentially.

"Oh," he said, continuing on his way, completely satisfied by my reply.

There was only a short distance to cover to the garage, and after I had unloaded I gingerly tried the starter. The engine caught immediately, and I eased out of the loading bay. But worse was to come.

Not a hundred yards from the garage the engine took over as though it was controlled by an evil alien surging ahead, unbidden by me, at a terrifying speed in a narrow street. Reaching for the key, I turned it off, but, to my horror, this had no effect. The engine revved wildly, completely out of control, and the Sherpa hurtling down the street, increasing its speed all the time. Leaving it in gear, I trod on the brake pedal as hard as I could, for good measure pulling up the handbrake and, to my enormous relief, it came to a juddering halt, stalled in the by now familiar cloud of blue smoke.

I crept the final twenty five yards into the garage in first gear, my right foot instantly ready to stamp on the brake.

"It's been feeding on its sump oil," Spratt announced. "You've overfilled it with oil and it's returned to the engine where it finds its way into the cylinders and acts as fuel. That's why it's been throwing out all that blue smoke."

167

Indignant at his accusation, I wiped the dip stick and tested the oil. It was half full. Knowing the Sherpa's thirst for oil, I had at least taken the precaution of checking it before I had departed from Bramton.

"That doesn't mean you hadn't overfilled it," Spratt said. "It's probably used all that up in combustion."

It was impossible to win an argument with this man.

In the event he was half right. The Sherpa had a cracked piston, which produced the same effect.

Two days later the Sherpa was returned to Bramton by Jim.

"We've fitted a new engine," he said with a smile. "Well, it's not that new. It has been on the workshop floor for a few years and no one can remember which van it came out of, or how many miles it had done, but it goes. You'll have to keep an eye on the oil, though."

Change was in the air. Two weeks later a brand new Ford Escort, diesel van was delivered to Bramton. It was given to Peter to drive, and we regarded it with awe, as though it was a new model unveiled before the world's press at a motor show. All that was missing was a half naked starlet draped over the bonnet.

"It ain't right Peter 'as it," Sydney complained petulantly. "I'm senior to 'im. It should be my van."

Within a few months the entire fleet of seven vans had been replaced, including the Sherpa, with brand new diesel vans.

Sometimes, in a wave of nostalgia, I rather missed the old wrecks.

Nineteen

Spring was heralding a new beginning. Hedgerows were tinged with green as the fragile leaves emerged from their winter dormancy. As the season progressed copper beech trees showed a delicate pink before the strengthening sun hardened their foliage to cast a gloomy darkness below. And the lambs gambolled in the fields, with an innocence and abandonment, which were as old as the fields where they played.

It was the lambs that depressed my spirits. This was the first spring for years I had missed a lambing. All the hard work. The sleepless nights. The weather, driving cold rain was the lambs' worst enemy. The snow. The obstinate ewes refusing to accept their own offspring, regarding them with astonishment and ultimately disdain. The frustration. And the other foes - the foxes. I missed it all.

Now I was driving a Post Office van through the very countryside I regarded as my own, the countryside I knew so well, delivering junk mail and bills to people who desired neither. Watching those lambs I felt all but an intruder. A traitor to my chosen way of life, which was now beyond me. I was experiencing a second hand lambing. Any feelings of relief that it was all over, forever, disappeared when I saw my first lambs unsteadily suckling their mother as she encouraged them to drink, with little nudges and maternal grunts, sounds only the lambs and the shepherd understood.

It was as if I were a town dweller on a day trip to the country on a Sunday afternoon, in the days when it was permitted to pick a posy of primroses and return home to place them in water. To wake in the morning to admire the delicate flowers in the alien suburban surroundings to which they had been so carefully brought. Savouring the memory of an idyllic excursion the previous day, before departing for a dreary time-dragging job. Lambing time had never been like this.

It was aggravating, watching farming from the outside, and the irritation was compounded by driving around the countryside nearly every day in a Post Office van.

Of course, there were annoyances in farming, especially at lambing time: from the weather and from meddling politicians. And on our farm there had been a particular frustration. I smiled …

We had acquired a sheep dog to help us with our small flock. She was five months old when we had her, a collie-cross bitch named, with startling unoriginality, Meg. There must be thousands of sheep dogs across the country called Meg, but at five months old we decided she was too old to be re-christened, so Meg she remained.

She was an odd mixture, both in temperament and breeding. She had inherited the true instincts of the collie, and to that extent she was a great help with the sheep, but she had also inherited an obstinate streak from some long deceased ancestor. And this stubborn ingredient was a constant cause of frustration to me.

The trouble with Meg was that she was unreliable. On her day she worked faultlessly, rounding up the sheep with barely a word of command necessary, knowing exactly what was required of her, and exactly what I wanted. At other times she started off full of enthusiasm, and at the vital moment when the sheep were beautifully poised to enter the yards, she would give up entirely and wander off. No amount of cajoling or shouting would change her mind, and the sheep, seizing the moment, would scatter to the furthest parts of the field. Sometimes she refused to even consider working from the outset, and rounding up the sheep was always something of a lottery.

When I was gathering the sheep one particularly morning, the owner of the travelling shop observed to our neighbour whom he was serving at the time, "I wonder who he's shouting at, the dog or the wife."

Meg had all the attributes of a prima donna.

Sarah - and it had been the dog I was shouting at - couldn't understand it. Although Meg was, in theory, my dog, she was happy to work on the odd occasion for my wife.

"I've never had any trouble with her," she informed me. "She's always worked perfectly for me. It must be something you do wrong. It doesn't help when you shout at her either."

I tried to explain shouting was the last resort, but she would have none of it.

I was due to be away from the farm when we had a lorry calling to collect some of our lambs.

"That's no problem," Sarah said. "I can manage with Meg."

When I returned, I was greeted by an extremely angry wife.

"I see what you mean about that bloody dog. She gave up on me and that poor lorry driver and I spent half the morning running after sheep."

It was with great difficulty that I repressed a smile.

If as a working dog Meg was an enigma, there were no such doubts as to her suitability as a family dog. She was friendly with everyone, excellent with young and old alike. The only time I heard her growl was when the Egg Man paid us a visit. The first time this genial old man called he bent to pat Meg on the head. "I loves dogs," he told me. "I gets on with them and they gets on with me."

Meg bared her teeth, top lip drawn back, hackles up, and growled ferociously. The Egg Man hastily backed away. It was the only time I saw her like it. Who can know what deeply hidden memories he had provoked?

Meg had been an outdoor dog when she came to us, and those first five months of her life had etched themselves too firmly in her mind ever to change, and even in her dotage she remained the same. If we took pity on her on cold winter evenings and brought her inside, she would sit by the door, shivering with nerves, whining to return to the corrugated shed that was her home. Only there was she happy.

Bert adored Meg. Whenever we went out for the day we dropped her off at Bert's home, and the two of them walked the lanes and fields for miles. "If you ever wants to get rid of 'er, you knows where to bring 'er," he used to tell me.

There were some mornings, working the sheep that his wish came close to being granted.

Meg loved cowpats, but she hated water. Whenever she came across a cowpat, she first tested it for edibility, and then comprehensively rolled in it. Progress through a field that had contained cattle could be tedious, but there was no breaking her of the habit. She never connected in her mind the link between cowpats and water. After rolling in ripe cowpats she was firmly bathed, something she hated above all else.

One night I let her off her chain to have a sniff around the garden, and walked the hundred yards or so up the hill to the old dairy where I had an ailing ewe to attend. I was with her for sometime, and when I left to return to the bungalow I had forgotten that Meg was loose. The dog, in her turn, had evidently forgotten I had gone to the dairy, and half way down the hill I heard frantic barking and crashings in the undergrowth followed by a resounding splash. I shone the torch on one of our large and deep ponds. A terrified and bewildered Meg was standing motionless, up to her neck in water, in the middle of it. It was the only time she voluntarily took a bath.

Meg hated lambing time. We had little use for her erratic services for the duration, and she was always looked after and exercised by my daughter and son, aged eight and six respectively.

Young children and farms are a mixture to be treated with caution. On the one hand there are the many dangers to consider, and on the other there are the rewards of responsibility and freedom that less fortunate children could only imagine. At lambing time my daughter had sole responsibility for the calves, and my son, under strict

172

supervision, helped in the lambing pens. He usually started lambing off with a disaster.

One year he fell out of a tree, escaping luckily, with only severe grazes and bruising. Another year, alerted by his screams we ran to the bungalow to find him hanging by his thumbs, trapped in the sash window, like a character in a cartoon. In general such accidents were rare.

In the summer the children filled the water troughs, fed the hens and collected the eggs, and carried out a host of other chores while I walked around the sheep and cattle with Meg. When they returned to school and all these chores fell back to me, I realised how much work they had saved. Their enthusiasm did not pass unrewarded and, as an occasional treat, we sometimes had a special Sunday lunch at an expensive and very good restaurant in Bramton.

It is not always easy to keep young children occupied and well behaved in unaccustomed surroundings where there was often a longish wait between courses and, in the manner of most families, we had devised a game to distract them. It was devastatingly simple. See a word, spell it backwards and let the children work out what it was. Sometimes these words passed into the family vocabulary. And so it was a large earthenware jar standing on a shelf in the restaurant proclaiming it contained tapioca, provided an alternative spelling and pronounciation of Meg's favourite delicacy.

We had a hogget that never thrived. We ran her through the winter, and she livened up a little in the spring, but never to the extent where she could be sent to market. We put her with the lambs in the summer, and she even grew slightly.

Sometimes, if one is not looking for the expected one misses the obvious. I sheared her in the summer - at least we had a fleece off her, I thought - and ran her on the following winter. But she deteriorated rapidly in the cold winter weather. I brought her in and, rather belatedly, gave her some tender loving care. It was almost too late, and one morning I found her lying on her side on the concrete by her pen, barely breathing, lashed by a cold rain. From time to time life provides a challenge, and for this reason I persevered with her.

I really could not understand why she was declining so quickly, but deteriorating she undoubtedly was. I brought her inside, dried her off with a towel and placed an appetising bowl of sheep nuts in front of her. She couldn't use her legs, but I was encouraged to see she nibbled at a few nuts. I gave her ivy, which she ate with some interest. If a sick sheep refuses ivy there is no hope at all for it. I was worried she could not use her legs, and in the morning she was again lying on her side, and again I tucked them under her and fed her some more nuts and ivy.

Gradually she improved and I improvised a sling, placing a sack under her and pulling her up on a rope attached to a rafter so her feet just touched the ground. This barbaric treatment worked well, and with her extra special diet she made a recovery, which exceeded all my expectations. As most sheep have an inherent death wish, I was especially pleased with her. She had instincts that I had never suspected, and a will to live that was far beyond the comprehension of a mere male.

In the early spring, before our main lambing, my wife came into the yards where I was feeding the hogget.

"Look at that dog, she's found another cowpat."

I looked, Meg was sniffing around the edge of a very large cowpat. To our amazement it suddenly moved and made a faint noise.

"You call yourself a sheherd," she said. "That's our hogget's lamb."

So it was, and I was mortified. I had overlooked every sign, and I had forgotten the rig lamb that had been running with the hogget the previous summer. She deserved a place in veterinary history for the rough treatment she had endured and still survived to produce a healthy lamb. I had to take a lot of leg pulling from my family that evening.

"They will have to have names," my daughter informed me. "I suggest coipat for the lamb and tapioca for the ewe."

174

Twenty

There appeared to be a new awakening at Bramton, not by an often benevolent, though sometimes treacherous, spring, but by a seldom benevolent and mostly treacherous servant of the Royal Mail in the diminutive form of Colin Atkinson.

I needed no calender to foretell his coming, Dave made sure of that. It was all there in poor Uncle John's unlocked drawers into which the deceitful Dave assidiously delved. From those dreary repositories emerged the information that the Area Manager, in person, was travelling to Bramton the following Monday to announce to the staff that the office was about to be refurbished.

Nothing I could do or say could dissuade Dave from his self appointed mission of reading Uncle John's private correspondence and nothing, for reasons I could not fathom, could discourage him from passing the information on to me.

"If you doesn't read it, I'll tell you anyway."

He showed me another letter from Colin Atkinson. I reluctantly read it. It gave a hint of his motive in the last paragraph. 'If you are incapable of reducing the hours of overtime worked I have a man on my staff who would prove more than capable of succeeding where you are so manifestly failing.'

It was more than evident this Atkinson was a thoroughly nasty piece of work. And it was perfectly clear to me he wanted Uncle John out of Bramton so he could install one of his acolytes. It meant nothing to him that Uncle John had reached the pinnacle of his career. His social standing with his friends immensely enhanced, his pride of achievement - and it was an achievement - giving him the satisfaction of having reached the dream of his lifetime, Sorting Office Manager at Bramton, where he hoped to finish his working days and enjoy an honourable

175

retirement. With a heavy heart I handed the photo copies back to Dave. Uncle John was fighting a lonely and losing battle.

When the great day of the visit arrived I looked at Colin Atkinson with interest. Unusually, no one in the office knew anything about him, nor did they at Buddleshaw, where he also ruled. The only information forthcoming was that he had been married several times and was now on his third wife. He was an insignificant little man, about five foot six inches tall, with dark hair, spectacles and a slightly flushed rounded face, which was adorned by a small moustache. I had heard men of short stature with moustaches encountered sexual problems; if that were true it explained a great deal.

He spoke in a series of clichés, which made little sense; they never quite connected with each other, as though he had not learned joined up writing. Donning a pair of glasses and using notes, he spoke. "The way forward to greater opportunities with Royal Mail starts with Bramton. The figures relating to the productivity schedules in place at this moment in time making a level playing field for all employees regardless of race, creed, colour or religious persuasion. All a part of the equal opportunities promulgated by Royal Mail in a volatile and changing world.

It made no sense to me, nor anyone else. He had probably been sent on a special course by Royal Mail so he could spout this rubbish to stupified employees. While he spoke Uncle John stood uneasily next to him, towering above him and scarcely helping his undoubted sense of inferiority.

When he turned to the refurbishments he was more specific, though the cliches continued to pour from his mouth like a stream of unchecked vomit. "The way forward (this was his favourite) is to be the market leader in a changing and uncertain world and the way to achieve this is by team work. And I have consulted with your manager to appoint team leaders, to lead Royal Mail forward into the twenty first century. To enable all of you to share in job satisfaction. And part of this exciting package is to bring the Bramton office into the forefront of our plans, steamrollering all before it with a secure and enjoyable refurbished workplace.

"We at Royal Mail are striving our utmost, straining at the leash of sound economic policy by investing in you and Bramton, over three quarters of a million pounds to make you one of the best small offices in the country. People come first in this business, and we fully appreciate here at Royal Mail, people are the key to a prosperous future. Any questions?"

There was one. It had to be Sydney, standing with his hand raised like an over eager schoolboy anxious to make an impression on the headmaster. It was always Sydney who asked the only questions after Uncle John's team talks. No one was interested, and nor was Sydney really, but he had to ask his question. He was the sort of person everyone dreaded on committies or at meetings, unnecessarily prolonging the proceedings with queries, which mostly missed the point or demonstrated he had not been listening.

Colin Atkinson looked inquiringly at Sydney who suddenly became tongue tied. He spluttered for a moment while we all watched with interest, then composed, came his question.

"This what's is name thing, you know, who appoints them?"

Atkinson, unused to Sydney's syntax, appeared puzzled. It was certainly turning out to be a bad morning for the English language.

"Team what d'yer call 'ems," Sydney elucidated helpfully.

"Ah," Atkinson said, suddenly aware of Sydney's meaning. "That will be the responsibility of your line manager."

Jangled by jargon, I groaned inwardly. I had never heard of a line manager before. It sounded like some sort of Fat Controller, but I assumed Atkinson was alluding to Uncle John. At this point I could have happily strangled Sydney. We all wanted to get out on our rounds and arrive home in reasonable time to make some sort of use of the day that was left to us.

He persisted. He had to. "Why do we have to 'ave these team what's 'is names when we've never 'ad 'em before? I mean, you know, we got by without 'em for years, so why now?"

"Because," Atkinson replied, "we are investing in people, people to lead us forward to a new era: a new era we will all share in, a new opportunity, a new beginning. It is the way forward."

This appeared to satisfy Sydney. There were no more questions. Exhausted, I returned to my sorting.

Uncle John, to his credit, courageously and sensibly never mentioned the subject of team leaders again.

That week I was on my town round, pushing my trolley around the streets of Bramton. This necessitated many returns to the office to deposit collected mail and replenish the trolley for the next section, and what worried me was that throughout the morning Atkinson remained closeted with Murdoch in his cage.

If those two colluded Uncle John did not stand a chance. It was doubtful Murdoch had a clue of Atkinson's intention, and I smiled to myself when I thought of him once again deluding himself that he would, at last, become manager at Bramton.

Much later, unasked Sydney joined them in the cage, bumbling in and - impervious to Atkinson's withering looks -' launching into some rambling speech, the content of which, though I could not hear it, I could accurately predict word for word. Sydney just could not help himself. Welcome or not, he had to be in on the centre of affairs whether they concerned him or not.

Throughout all this plotting Uncle John sat at his desk, desperately endeavouring to keep busy and cheerful. He knew he was being betrayed, but he had no one to whom he could turn.

The refurbishment started two weeks later. The builders' first task was to remove the perfectly sound and suitable old fashioned, porcelain urinals and replace them with a stainless steel trough, situated about two and a half feet from the floor. This horrible concession to modernity was highly unsatisfactory in use, splashing the hands, the trousers and that very part of the body it was supposed to serve.

But it was, I reflected gloomily, the way forward.

Twenty One

Lester was a fastidious man, particular in his dress and, he thought, correct in all he did. He seldom allowed the job to get to him, as it did with most of us from time to time. He was usually an example of calm when, as often happened, the office threatened to collapse into chaos as vast quantities of mail were unloaded from the Buddleshaw van in the early morning; and the phone rang with a repetitive persistence as people phoned in with real or, mostly, imagined sickness.

He, with his insatiable appetite for overtime, was happy to work until well into the afternoon cheerfully collecting as much of it as he could handle; it was almost a compulsion. He did have his aversions, and one of these was the coffin, a large contraption used for delivering parcels to the many small businesses in the main street of Bramton.

The fibreglass body was bolted onto a substantial metal chassis, with two wheels and two handles, rather like a wheelbarrow with a huge cabin trunk mounted on it. It was heavy, with noisy solid tyres that resonated through the fibreglass body, and awkward to propel along the busy pavements. It lacked any form of parking brake and had to be propped against a convenient wall whilst delivering the parcels to prevent it from running away.

Once, famously, it became detached from its parking spot, careering at high speed down the pavement, scattering startled pedestrians before it finished its involuntary journey embedded in the plate glass window of a greengrocer's shop, amongst shards of glass and vegetables that were scattered on the outside and interior of the shop. The entire stock was ruined. It had been an expensive experience for Royal Mail, but we still continued to use the coffin.

Lester hated it. It was all about his image. He said he felt like a coolie pushing it around, and I sympathised with him. Plenty of people made

181

many unflattering remarks about it and its attendant, as it made its erratic progress through the thronged pavements. I, too, felt like a coolie pushing the thing, but the difference between Lester and I was that I did not mind the contraption. Lester most certainly did, taking the parcels out on a much smaller four wheeled trolley, returning to the office many times to refill it.

Uncle John soon realised Lester was claiming dreaded overtime for these extra excursions and, confident at last he had found a concrete, if contrived, way of reducing the extra hours, which he could demonstrate to Atkinson, banned Lester from using a trolley and insisting he used the coffin.

In the finish, I made a deal with Lester. I would deliver his parcels in the coffin provided he undertook a reciprocal part of whichever round I was on. It was a satisfactory arrangement, which lasted until the offending means of transportation was retired, when Royal Mail invented Parcelforce and the burden of delivering parcels was removed. But that was someway in the future. In the manner of the passing of the awful vans, I missed the coffin. It had provided a good talking point among the mostly good humoured pedestrians who suffered the inconvenience of its passage.

As with any community, births, weddings and deaths were as regular a feature as the passing of the seasons, but it was only the last, which elicited any interest at the Post Office. We all knew which of our customers was ailing, had undergone complex surgery or were merely drinking themselves into an early grave. We knew when they had died simply by the amount of cards we delivered to the surviving family, and when we saw them we sympathised in a shallow way or, had we known them better, with genuine conviction.

Sudden death, unexpected and shocking, was always a source of morbid discussion, and Ted took a particular and peculiar interest in any deceased. It was as though he expected everyone to be immortal and, whether he knew the departed or not, was plunged into the depths of gloom whenever he heard the news. "I would never have thought it," he would mutter to himself as he sorted, "only forty. What a tragedy, what a tragedy." Then, turning to no one in particular would ask, "What was he really like?"

It was always a tragedy and all the secrets, and the postman was aware of most of them, were open for general discussion.

For a while, Lester had his own way of dealing with the loss of the customers on his rounds. He attended their funerals, often interrupting his round and parking his distinctive red van outside the church. It was difficult to understand why he did this. Many of the people, whose funerals he attended, we hardly saw from one week to another. It must have been somewhat disconcerting for the grieving family to find an unknown postman in his immaculate uniform prominent amongst the mourners. It was taking the duties of a postman to the extreme.

This aberration continued for a while over one December, January and February, always good months for undertakers, and suddenly ceased. I suspected Mary had had a quiet word with Lester, but she denied this firmly, confirming my suspicious. Lester always assured us he never claimed overtime for these reverential excesses.

Sometimes, though not often, the postman was incorrect in the conclusions he drew from customers' mail.

Peter had been going through a bad patch. Urgently in need of the loo, but finding himself in the depths of the country, he parked his van by a gateway, climbed over the gate and lowered his trousers, squatting behind the hedge well concealed from the road. It was during this very private moment that he felt a wet tongue licking his bottom: it was a black Labrador and behind was its owner, one of Peter's customers, on her morning constitutional. She called the dog, wished Peter a good morning and continued on her way, the curious dog casting backward looks at the mortified Peter who had been literally caught with his pants down.

That embarrassment withered into insignificance when he mistakenly interpreted the large number of cards addressed to an elderley woman as signifying the death of her husband. Handing her a large bundle he expressed his heartfelt condolences and sympathy, adding if there was anything he could do to help in such unhappy circumstances he would be more than happy to oblige.

The woman stared at him for a moment. "Unhappy? I don't know what you are talking about. I've never been happier. It's my eightieth birthday."

She slammed the door and Peter made his dejected and lonely way down her path to his van.

It was surprising how much we learnt about our customers from the mail they received. We knew who was on the dole claiming their benefit cheques whilst at the same time in some sort of renumerative employment. Who had won a premium bond. Received a summons from the county court. Failed to pay their rates on time. When they had holidays, and wedding anniversaries. And when they were cheating on their wives and husbands.

We followed their children's progress on their year out in various parts of the world, often from outlandish places, by reading their postcards with great interest. We felt almost part of the family, particularly if we had children who had undergone similar experiences.

We knew who was receiving pornographic literature, despite the plain envelopes. The number and quality of people who did was surprising. It was a source of endless amusement to me that they never suspected the postman was aware of the content. This sort of information was eagerly traded across the office, especially where risqué material was involved.

If it were one thing delivering doubtful videos, it was quite another delivering housing benefit cheques. These were designed to help the less well off with their rent and there were, like those receiving unemployment benefit, some people, generally the elderly, who had a genuine need of help. They were not many. By far the largest number of people claiming were young, crafty and fully employed, sometimes in the case of couples, either married or living together, holding down two jobs and running two cars. What made it all the more galling was that, unlike the dole cheques, which came from general taxation, the funding for the housing benefit came from local taxation, the hated council tax.

The charge could be made that we should have informed on these people, but it is not a trait inherent in the British people to act in such a way. That the local administrators so manifestly failed to check on the applicants was a source of anger to every postman and should have been a source of shame to these idle officials who dispensed our hard earned money with such reckless abandon. If they had to deliver their housing benefit cheques themselves they might have thought differently.

Twenty Two

Matthew looked tired when I drove my Post Office van into his farmyard one morning and I said as much when he came over to collect his letters. He gave me a wan smile that I knew so well from the years I had known him meant something had gone wrong again.

He leant wearily against the van, an arm on the door. "We were awakened at one o'clock this morning by a tremendous crashing and banging coming from the outbuildings by the dairy. We dressed and ran outside to see what was happening. It was our Friesian bull wandering around with the heavy gate from his pen hanging around his neck. Every time he moved the ends of the gate hit something, making him stop dead in his tracks."

I remembered this vast animal of uncertain temperament.

"He must have somehow slipped his head through it sideways and lifted it off its hinges. Florence took one end of the gate, I took the other and we slowly walked him backwards into his pen where I sawed the gate off him. He lay down, totally exhausted."

"I seem to remember you had trouble with another of your bulls some years ago," I reminded him.

"I remember that," he said, smiling with more animation now. "That was to do with your house cow ... what was her name?"

"Diamond."

We had been contemplating the acquisition of a cow for some time. We heard of an in-calf Jersey locally and went to look at her. I glanced at my wife and knew by her face we had our house cow.

Diamond arrived two days later, suffering the indignity of the cattle lorry with all the patience of an aristocrat, which indeed she was. She slowly came down the ramp, head lowered, sniffing out each step before placing her dainty feet between the rough wooden slats. Once installed in her pen adjacent to the old dairy she surveyed her surroundings with something approaching contempt. Evidently she had been used to better things.

"We'd better try and milk her," my wife said after we had given Diamond time to settle down. She certainly knew a bowl of cattle nuts, but as soon as I bent to milk her she kicked out and moved off. We haltered her and tried again, but there was nothing there apart from a few drops in the bottom of the bucket.

We were better organised the next morning, but she only yielded a tea cup of milk. "Don't cancel the milkman yet," I said as we ceremoniously drank a cup of tea made with Diamond's milk.

Gradually, as she became used to us, her yield crept up and up. We discovered later that she was an expert at holding back her milk. The slightest upset at milking time could make her clam up, and only an extra bowl of nuts and some soothing talk could make her let her milk down.

"You'll get fat on all that channel island milk," Matthew observed as he viewed our new acquisition with amusement.

"It's better than the chalk and water your Friesians produce," I answered.

But he was right, we did put on weight. We bought a churn and spent hours making butter and it was delicious and fattening. It was fortunate farming was no sedentary occupation, and the worst of Diamond's rich fare could at least be worked off.

Her milk started to become less and less, and we dried her off in preparation for her calving. We kept a close eye on her and one morning, with no fuss, she was standing in her stall quietly nuzzling and licking her new calf. There was no malice to Diamond and she was happy to allow us to examine her new arrival, standing back with a justifiable look of pride in her dark eyes.

Her calf presented us with a problem, for we had milk aplenty. We bought another calf for her to rear, but she would have none of it and despite every effort, she never accepted it. It was frustrating watching her own calf smugly suckling her whilst she was so thoroughly nasty to her foster calf. We were reduced to milking her out and feeding her foster calf from the bucket, which was patently ridiculous.

The problem resolved itself neatly. So many of our friends enjoyed Diamond's milk that we started a mini milk round with 'contributions' for her feed. This system worked well, and the bewildered foster calf was transferred to powdered milk, which it drank with the utmost reluctance, and was weaned as soon as was decently possible.

Diamond had a fatal flaw, inherent in Channel Island cattle: it was milk fever. She suffered a mild attack of it with her second calf, and I managed to control that easily enough with calcium, but it always returned when she calved.

We had always had her artificially inseminated, and sometime after her third calf Matthew casually mentioned his Hereford bull had nothing in particular to do at the moment. Would we like him to run with Diamond for a few weeks? We accepted with alacrity and I arrived on his farm the following morning to walk the bull the mile down the road to our field.

"He's very quiet," Matthew said. "We'll use the halter."

We walked him out of the farmyard, when Matthew suddenly said, "Hold him a minute, I'll be straight back."

He reappeared a minute later with a restraining stick, with a clip on the end, which snapped onto the ring in the bull's nose, giving effective control over the animal. He tucked the stick under his arm and we set off again.

We must have looked an incongrous sight, ambling slowly down the road, chatting animatedly - the massive Hereford bull plodding behind us, all but forgotten. A car came towards us and Matthew suddenly flung the end of the halter to me and, galvanised into action as though he had trodden barefoot on upturned tacks, took the stick from under his arm and firmly clipped it to the brass ring on the startled Hereford's nose. The car drove by and in it was Florence. We waved, but Florence remained poker faced.

Matthew was as red as a beetroot. "She won't let me move the bulls without the stick," he explained. "I don't think she saw me put it on, do you? I thought she had gone over to see her mother," he added lamely.

I was perfectly certain she had seen, and I was equally certain Matthew was in for a rough time when he returned home.

The result of this union was a heifer calf that my children mysteriously christened Jane. The birth was attended by Diamond's usual milk fever but, with veterinary assistance, she soon recovered. Eighteen months later Jane became 'John the bull'. Diamond had calved again, and again we had used Matthew's Hereford, but Jane had rediscovered the urge to suckle her mother, and Diamond was content to let her. It was an odd spectacle watching one large Hereford cross Jersey and one similar tiny calf suckling Diamond at the same time. Unfortunately Jane's urge for her mother's milk was stronger than our fences could stand.

"I'll come down and put a ring in her nose," Matthew said when I told him. "It's the only way to stop her." He was right, that ring did the trick; but it did more than that, and in the end made us some money as well.

We had a footpath running through our farm. I have nothing against footpaths used correctly for recreation - ours had its origins as a short cut to school for the village children years ago - but all too frequently walkers, ignorant of country ways, wreaked havoc. They left gates open, they strayed from the path into hay crops, and they tore up electric sheep fencing that I had carefully insulated to allow electric shock free passage to walkers.

'John the bull' solved all these problems. She was a friendly animal, but one look at the ring in her nose deterred all but the true countrymen from our footpath.

190

We kept 'John the bull' rather longer than we had intended, and at nearly two years old she was a beautiful animal. But heifers tend to run to fat and seldom achieve good prices at market.

"I doubt she'll make much," said the auctioneer, "but you never know."

She topped the market. A combination of alcohol (I suspected) and that shiny ring had done the trick.

"Some people have all the luck," said Matthew when I told him. "I must try ringing my heifers sometime." But he was far too honest for that.

Diamond had become part of our family more than just a part of the farm. She was tolerant yet firm with our children when they were young, and tolerant of them when we allowed them to learn to milk her. She was a prima donna, and if we were late milking her she was perfectly capable of showing her displeasure by flicking her tail around the face with a stinging, accurate blow, or planting a dirty foot firmly in our stainless steel milking bucket. I could tie her tail to a handy nail with a piece of baler twine, but I was never quick enough to remove the bucket out of the way of her foot.

There were magic moments. There was no electricity in her milking stall, and no door. In the winter we used a torch for light and, with Diamond contentedly eating her feed, the milk rhythmically hitting the sides of the bucket, the frosty fields illuminated brilliantly by the cold moon, there was a feeling of complete calm and peace. This was only broken when she had licked her bowl clean, and then she would shuffle back and forth, eager to return to her pasture.

She was intensely curious and loved human company. Whenever we had the sheep in the yards, Diamond was always there, supervising, eyes half closed chewing her cud.

But the years took their toll, and after each calf her bouts of milk fever became worse. After her seventh calf she had a really bad attack.

191

"She'll be all right in the morning," the vet assured me one evening after he had dosed her yet again with calcium.

He was wrong, and when I called him out in the early hours even his expertise could not save her.

She had been a part of our early farming days. Our children had grown up with her, and she had given us all immense pleasure.

As I drove off I said to Matthew, "I hope you have a better night tonight."

"Don't worry," he told me, "I have fixed that gate so he will never remove it again, however hard he tries.

The renovations progressed at a grindingly slow pace, raising much dust and acinine comments concerning the quality of the builders. Equipment went missing, including the trolley jack, so handy for changing flat tyres early in the morning; the tow rope, which, despite the new vans, was useful for starting those with flat batteries; and even the oil can we used for topping up thirsty engines with their vital life blood.

Instead of preparing Uncle John's new office first, they unnecessarily evicted him from his old one and started turning it into the Post Office shop. After wrecking the place for a couple of days, rendering it uninhabitable, they realised - or were told of - their mistake and belatedly started work on the new office, temporarily abandoning the old one, now little more than a pile of brick rubble. Poor Uncle John was forced to move into the cage with Murdoch, hardly a satisfactory move given Murdoch's antagonism towards him and the already cramped nature of the cage. The venture was doomed from the beginning and Uncle John eventually arranged for the telephone to be moved upstairs, taking up temporary residence in the tea room. The whole episode had been a masterpiece of mismanagement by the builders.

During his brief and unhappy tenure of the cage he used every excuse to escape from it, often spending his time pouring over the signing in and overtime sheets with a concentration and will he had seldom displayed before.

Uncle John was nothing if not unsubtle, and he let it slip he was intending to hold a fire drill one morning. When pressed as to which morning his standard reply was that if he told us the element of surprise would be lost and it would not constitute a proper fire drill.

It was perfectly clear to all of us a couple of days later that this was the morning of the fire drill. Uncle John furtively emerged, from the cage and, casting glances left and right, walked through the office, pausing on his journey to pass inane comments to those in his path. His air of assumed nonchalance was transparent; we knew exactly where he was going. The fire bell, a manual affair operated by a handle, was situated in the locker room at the rear of the Sorting Office. Twice he sauntered into it and twice he came out again to resume his prowl around the office. He could hardly keep up the pretence for much longer, and the third time he entered the locker room he rang the bell loud and long.

He left the locker room and charged through the office yelling "Fire, fire, everybody out, everybody out," pausing only at the signing in desk to collect the precious sheets before hurrying up the slope to the main gate, which carried a faded, barely readable sign that proclaimed it was the fire assembly point.

Collectively sighing, we ambled after him, many of us taking the opportunity to put the excercise to good use by treating it as a cigarette break, pausing to light up as we left the office. Uncle John was not amused, waiting patiently by the gate, the signing in sheets in one hand, a pencil poised in the other. Curbing his impatience, he asked if we were all present. Sydney, standing next to him, facing us, assured him we all were there with no possible basis for this assumption. No one had been deputed to check the supposedly blazing Sorting Office.

Uncle John read off the names from the signing in sheets, carefully ticking off our names as we answered. When he had finished there was a brief silence, broken by Gavin asking Uncle John, "What about Lester? You didn't call his name."

"He's on overtime," Uncle John replied. "He doesn't have to sign in until his duty starts at eleven o'clock."

"But he still has to be accounted for," Gavin persisted, "whether he's on overtime or not."

Uncle John looked at him with pity. "You don't understand. He's on overtime. He doesn't have to sign in, so his name is not on the signing in sheet so I can't call it."

"But surely, if you know he's here, you must call his name whether it's on the sheet or not. He could be burning to death in there and because you haven't called his name, we might assume he didn't come in on overtime."

"If his name doesn't appear on the sheet, how can I call it?" Uncle John replied with devastating logic.

"He's right," Sydney said, worried at not making himself heard. "If 'ee not on the sheet, 'ee can't be called. And if any of you forgets to sign, you won't be called neither. It's regulations, same regulations what says them signing in sheets is used to call the roll. It makes sense, see."

With some relief Uncle John told us we were free to return to the office. I asked Lester on the way down the slope why he had not said anything.

"Well," he said, "I thought as I was not officially here, I might as well keep quiet."

Jack greeted us with his tray of tea and coffee, which he had evidently been making during the fire drill. I asked him why he had not attended.

He smiled. "Because I am employed by a different branch of Royal Mail and have a different boss. I record my own hours and send them in each week. I am not required to sign in here."

Twenty Three

We had a friend who had recently retired. Casting around for a means to fill the empty days he discovered the extraordinary hobby of making concrete garden ornaments. His industry was as extraordinary as his new found mission in life, and soon his house and garden were filled with these monstrous creations, some carefully painted, others naked concrete. The quantity of the different models he cast was impressive, ranging from ordinary garden gnomes to foxes, dogs, peacocks, cats, sheep, giraffes and a whole lot more. The company, which made the moulds and supplied the ingredients, must have gone onto overtime to have met his demands. After a while his garden resembled a still life concrete zoo; mowing the lawn must have taken him nearly all day.

At first, his wife was indulgent towards his hobby, pleased he was able to fill his time without becoming a nuisance to her. But as these grotesque creatures cluttered the garden, the garage, and eventually started creeping into the house, she rebelled. If he made any more, she told him, he would have to give them away to his friends; she had had enough of his hobby and this invasion of concrete icons.

Undaunted, he continued production unchecked, and it was for this reason we acquired a peacock with no head, a peacock with one leg, half a dozen fully painted garden gnomes, which we hid in the garage and brought out and arranged around the garden when a visit was imminent, an unpainted dog and several other concrete edifices.

Fortunately for his wife and to the relief of his friends, he discovered the delights of painting by numbers and the supply of unwanted garden ornaments abruptly ceased.

It was the concrete dog which gave me the idea. I saw it on the garage floor one morning when I was wheeling my Puch out for another day at the Post Office. It was about one foot high and sat on a substantial base. One of its ears and a back leg had suffered slightly when it had emerged from the mould, but otherwise it was intact. It looked sad, gazing into the middle distance with unpainted eyes and a mournful expression on its rough cast face. It was also a considerable weight.

For some reason I thought of Sydney. Some days later, when I was on the late shift, I loaded the dog into the Puch, with some difficulty, and smuggled it into my van, unseen. I had made up a label, which I had attached around the sad dog's neck with a rubber band, addressed to the lady of the manor where Sydney had partaken of his fateful breakfast.

The message on the obverse was simple: "Thank you for a wonderful night, Royston." I placed the concrete dog in one of the post boxes Sydney would have to empty in the morning.

Sydney was not amused. In fact he was furious. It never occured to him that the unfortunate creature, whose concrete eyes would have wept from the banality of the joke had they been capable, was placed in the box by one of his colleagues. He assumed some unauthorised person had a key.

"There'll be repercussions," he muttered darkly, "I'll see 'Iggings about this, and there'll be repercussions. And that's another thing. There weren't no bloody stamps on it."

The concrete dog, quite literally, did the rounds, appearing in post boxes all around Bramton, even on the bicycle rounds where weary postmen brought the heavy thing back on their Pashleys.

Eventually, the joke wore thin and Peter, writing a fresh label to an address in Buddleshaw, dropped it into a bag and the dog was despatched to its new area. Months later, it reappeared at Bramton, slightly chipped, with part of its tail missing and was retired to a windowsill where it mournfully and unseeingly sat as a sort of mascot, until the annual health and safety inspection, when Sydney consigned it to the dustbin.

"I 'ates that bloody thing, and it might fall off that what's 'is name and break someone's toes, so it goes in the bin and good riddance."

There was a man on the Topleys who was a partner in a private bank, Alexander Brownrigg. He was so rich he regarded millions of pounds as an ordinary person would regard tens. He lived, mostly, in the capital close to his work. But somewhere in his unreal, monetarily orientated world there was a simple man, yearning for the rural basics of life, provided those fundamentals were not too rudimentary.

He owned the ideal country retreat, Charcoal Burners Cottage, a beautiful two bedroomed home set deep in the woods, a mile down a rough track that led from a little used B road. It had been lavishly restored, with every modern convenience. The original charcoal burners would never have recognised it, nor had a clue how to use the modern equipment contained within. Mr. Brownrigg seldom used this rural haven, perhaps one weekend in four, and he paid a local woman to look after it. I had met him when I did the Topleys. He was a short man of about five foot ten inches, completely bald, with large ears.

Looking at the collection of garden gnomes on the garage floor, the connection was obvious and difficult to resist. I selected the gaudiest - a fat little fellow about nine inches high - and wrote a label with a message on the back addressed to the banker, and attached it to the gnome's neck with a rubber band. The message read, "Thank you for a wonderful dinner. We must see more of each other. Yours in delicious anticipation, Ursula."

Remembering Sydney's complaint, I stuck a one penny stamp on the label and placed the cheerful character in a box one morning and it was duly collected by Peter in the afternoon.

Lester had been making a rare appearance on the Topleys that week as Duncan was on holiday, and it had been my intention that the gnome would be placed on his sorting frame where he would discover it the

I placed the cheerful character in a box

following morning. But Peter took the joke a stage further. He found some registered letter stickers in Murdoch's cage - Murdoch seldom appeared in the afternoons - stuck one on the label next to the stamp, entered it on the registered sheet and despatched the gnome to Buddleshaw.

The next morning it arrived back at Bramton, with the rest of the secure registered mail, now officially registered itself. No one mentioned anything to Lester and it was not until he entered the cage to collect his registered mail from Murdoch that he saw it, standing, grinning out of the Topleys pigeon hole, its label around its neck, the registered sticker and the hand franked one penny stamp facing the front. In addition, Murdoch had made out a demand for the deficient postage, some three pounds and eighty pence.

Lester was not amused. "I'm not taking that bloody thing out, especially with that message on the label. It's a joke. Why don't you throw it in the bin?"

"Can't do that," Murdoch replied, perfectly aware of the identity of the perpetrator, "it's officially registered. It's got to be delivered."

"If you won't throw the bloody thing in the bin, I will."

"I wouldn't if I was you. It's an official item of registered mail. You'll be in big trouble if you does."

Murdoch could easily have killed off the garden gnome had he wished, but as usual he was milking the maximum unpleasantness from the situation. A furious argument ensued, but Murdoch refused to give way and Lester stormed out of the cage clutching the fat little garden gnome in one hand and his box keys in the other.

"He won't be there," he told Murdoch as his parting shot, "I'll have to leave a docket."

"Then leave one. At least you've covered yourself."

Alexander Brownrigg was not at home, as expected, and Lester left an official Royal Mail docket stating there was a registered item of mail for him awaiting collection at Bramton, with a surcharge of three pounds and eighty pence to pay on it.

Returning to the office with the gnome, he handed it to Murdoch who carefully placed it in the safe, with the other undelivered registered mail and locked the door.

Fully aware there could be trouble brewing for me, I kept an anxious eye on the thing, as far as I was able; the safe was normally closed, the combination known only to Murdoch and Uncle John.

The following Saturday, as I was handing in my box keys to Murdoch, I noticed the safe door was open and there was no sign of any garden ornaments, "What happened to the gnome?" I asked Murdoch innocently.

He swivelled his chair round to face me, fixing his expressionless eyes on mine. "It were very strange, very strange indeed. Brownrigg came to collect it about an hour ago. 'Ee presented his docket, and I took the gnome out of the safe and give it to him. 'Ee read the label, and give it back to me, saying 'ee didn't want it. Then, 'alfways up the slope 'ee stopped, turned round and come back. 'Ee said 'ee'd changed his mind and would 'ave it after all. 'Ee paid the surcharge and took it away. It were all very strange."

I was relieved. There would not be any trouble after all, to Murdoch's great disappointment. I wondered why Alexander Brownrigg had changed his mind.

The fat little gnome took up residence in the porch of Charcoal Burners Cottage, minus his label, where his mission in life was to prevent the occasional notes to the milkman, placed under him, from blowing away.

He had truly found his home.

Twenty Four

Working the late shift brought more problems than merely adjusting to the unusual hours. Although Gavin and Lester were happy enough to work the overtime in the mornings and continue, almost without a break, into the late shift itself, I was not always so happy to oblige. While I did not particularly mind working the whole day through, provided I had advance notice, I objected strongly to the telephone ringing at five o'clock in the morning summonsing me to work when I had been expecting a leisurely lie-in. Absenteeism was the usual reason, and the usual reason for absenteeism was Dave, who worked the system of sick leave to perfection. He knew exactly how many days he could take off before incurring the official wrath of Royal Mail, and he took them all. If the symptoms were spotted in time, it was possible to prevent him taking his sickies; for all his craftiness, he was unable to stop himself from giving advance warning of his latest ailment.

If he admitted to a headache, it was a sure sign he would not be coming in the following day. The same was true of stomach pains, mysterious pains in the legs and other parts of the body. The trick was to sympathise wholeheartedly with him in a voice of sufficient volume to alert the office and inform Uncle John, in Dave's hearing, he was not at all well and would probably have to retire to his sick bed for a few days to recover. This usually solved the problem, somehow shaming Dave into abandoning his plans for a day or two at the seaside, and ensuring I enjoyed my lie in.

Unfortunately, it was not always possible to spot Dave's symptoms as they developed. It depended entirely on whether I was in the office at the time of their onset, and this could not always be arranged. The result was a call at five o'clock, five minutes after his preferred time of announcing his sickies, usually to Murdoch, before returning to bed to continue his slumbers, devoid of concience.

Unplugging the telephone was no use. The first time I tried this Neville was despatched in a van to wake me. Never one to whisper when he could shout, he announced his arrival on the driveway with loud honking of the horn and the blare of classical guitar music issuing from the radio of the van at full volume, his usual choice of music. This was followed by a thunderous banging on the door accompanied by shouts of, "Wake up, you lazy sod."

It took much patient talk later in the day to pacify the irate neighbours, trying to explain if a postman rose from his bed at four o'clock in the morning he expected the whole world to wake at the same time.

It did not make for easy lie-ins on the mornings I supposedly had off. If Dave appeared in good health the previous day, it was still no guarantee he would remain so through the night. And it was easier on the nerves to leave the telephone plugged in rather than risk the wrath of the neighbours by the racous arrival of Neville in the early hours.

The result was I awoke at four o'clock, spending the next two hours in fitful sleep, constantly looking at the alarm clock until about six, when I reckoned any crisis was past; and then finding sleep impossible, I would get up exhausted, trying to come to terms with the day. It would have been more restful to have gone into the office at the normal time.

There was a small measure of revenge when Dave, normally a fit individual, having expended all his sick leave, fell genuinely ill, arriving for work pale and evidently unwell. I took a malicious delight in enquiring after his wellbeing, advising him loudly to return home to bed, or take a seaside cure for the sake of his health. It was all a wonderful illustration of the fable of the boy who cried wolf.

There was also an unconcious, but nevertheless, satisfying revenge to be taken on James Macbride, the dour Scot who had interviewed me and whose type of negative, but all knowing personality appeared to be rife within Royal Mail.

Uncle John, desperate to comply with Atkinson's orders, had decided we were claiming too much on the overtime round we worked on some of the newer developments in Bramton, and just as anxious to appease the little dictator had hit on the idea of having the round investigated. And it was my misfortune to suffer this indignity.

Both the postman's speed of delivery and sorting were calculated. It involved the counting of the letters, the packets and any other items of mail, and timing the letters sorted by means of a stopwatch. It was like a kindergarten assessment, in reality, more of a test of the postman than of the round, as I thought it was supposed to be. The tester had to be an impartial outsider, hence the arrival of James Macbride. But, as is the way of the Post Office, no one had thought to inform me and I approached it in a lighthearted manner, pausing for cigarette breaks and tea whilst James Macbride clicked his tongue and his stopwatch alternately. It was not until a few hours later that Macbride informed me of the full implications.

Out on the delivery, on a bitterly cold, late spring day, James Macbride had to accompany me on a bicycle and it soon became obvious he had not been astride a Pashley for years. He was tremendously unfit, far more so than I had been when I had first started at Bramton. He puffed and panted up the hills, ultimately having to dismount and push his heavy machine up the steeper gradients, which I, now much fitter, barely noticed.

About one hour into the round there was a school where the friendly caretaker allowed us to use his lavatories; we delivered there long before the children arrived. Without this stop it would have been impossible to complete the round without having to find alternative arrangements. Coming out of the door, it occured to me I had quite forgotten to mention this relief stop to James Macbride who was waiting for me outside, his breath condensing in the unusually cold air, his face red either from the effort of propelling his machine up the hills or the bitter wind. I decided to keep him in ignorance. We continued pedalling in silence, James Macbride angry and missing the comforts of his office on such a day. I was hardly on his wavelength to conduct an interesting conversation.

After a further hour the inevitable occured.

"Where does one go for a pee round here?" he asked.

With a certain sadistic delight I replied, "Nowhere."

We were in the middle of what the estate agents would describe as an area of high density housing. I indicated with my arm. "There's nowhere you can go here. Your best bet is to pedal back to the school."

"There must be somewhere. I'm desperate."

I shrugged. I didn't much care about James Macbride and his bursting bladder.

"There are some bushes, you could try there, but they're a bit sparse."

A few minutes later I showed him the shrubbery, not ten feet from the road and footpath. They were even sparser than I remembered, not much more than waist high, and there were only about half a dozen. And they were, I noticed, hawthorn. I politely offered to hold his Pashley.

The cover might as well have been non existent, for Macbride was visible to all. At that moment a car passed, tooting loudly, its young occupants laughing.

Looking down the road I saw two elderly women walking up the footpath. I urgently relayed this information to him.

"How far away are they?" he asked through clenched teeth, half turning his head towards me.

"About twenty five yards."

"Go and stop them," he said in panic, "I can't cut off now. They mustn't see me."

"By the time I've put the bikes down, they'll be here," I replied.

"Can't you try kneeling? They might think you are praying."

"Don't you be funny with me," he said, furious. "I'm not a bloody contortionist."

"Then keep very still," I advised him, "and they might not notice you."

They did notice him, hurrying by with their eyes averted. "Disgusting," one remarked. "He should learn to control himself. No standards any more, that's the trouble, and Royal Mail, too."

She glared at me as they passed.

A thoroughly shaken James Macbride emerged from his inadequate lair shortly afterwards. He was a wreck, his grey trousers streaked with damp, trailing loose threads where the hawthorn had snagged them - middle management did not wear a uniform - and his previously beautifully shining black shoes covered in mud.

"You ..., you ...," he said, shaking with anger. "I suppose you went at that bloody school. You might have told me."

"It never crossed my mind," I said innocently.

His bulging eyes goggled at me. We finished the round in silence. The dour Scot had a few words with Uncle John before returning to Buddleshaw and what James MacBride presumably thought was civilisation.

Uncle John called me into his office and informed me I had passed my test. "I don't know what you did to James, but he was in a terrible mood. He asked me to tell you he didn't think much of your sense of humour."

It had been a thoroughly satisfying morning.

I had never considered the Buddleshaw office as civilised. It struck me as more akin to a lunatic asylum than a place where supposedly sane men were earning a living sorting mail, shouting continual insults at each other and especially the Bramton man when he brought the mail in, but I had become completely used to it, ignoring the abuse, which I soon came to accept as normal.

There was no franking machine at Bramton. All the bulk mail had to be taken to Buddleshaw where there was a man whose sole occupation was running this mail through his huge machine. Bringing in a large quantity one day, I loaded it onto a trolley and wheeled it over to him. Screaming obscenities at me, he took hold of it, pushing it half way up the office before giving it an almighty shove, causing it to crash into a wall. Smiling at him, I said I would see him the following day, and swiftly left the office to the sound of his curses and threats.

It was all quite normal Buddleshaw behaviour, and I thought no more of it. The following day I had a further load for him, and this time I was genuinely startled by his reaction. He came up to me, placed an arm round my shoulder, "I'm really sorry I was upset with you yesterday. I wanted to go home early, and I was having a bad day. The stuff you brought in was the last straw."

I would never have guessed.

As Matthew took his letters from me, one morning in June, I could tell by his face that he was going to ask me something, and I knew what it was.

"I know you have a full time job at the Post Office, and you must be pretty tired when you finish at half past twelve or so, but I was wondering whether you could give me a hand with haymaking in the afternoons? It would only be tractor driving – tedding, wind-rowing and that sort of thing."

I knew the difficulties of haymaking and had helped Matthew many times in the past, as he had helped me. He only had one full time employee, Joe, and he had the milking to do. Matthew gazed at me anxiously.

"Yes, I'll give you a hand." It was impossible to refuse him.

He beamed at me, his face lighting up. "The weather's set fair, can you start this afternoon? We should be finished in a week if it stays like this."

I loved haymaking. It is one of its delights to gather up armfuls of dried grasses, bury one's nose in it and savour the delicious aroma. "Take a little sunshine into the barn," is an old saying, and there had been an abundance of it that year. And that sunshine would be released on dark winter days when the string on the bales was cut and the sweet smelling hay was shaken out.

Quite how I would manage, rising at four o'clock in the morning, working for Royal Mail until half past twelve and continue the day with Matthew, I was not sure. I knew I would not just be tractor driving; there was the small matter of carting the bales to the barn as well.

Before I left I asked Matthew, "Have you still got your old baler or have you bought a new one yet as you kept promising yourself?"

"I've still got the old one. This really is its last season."

I groaned to myself. It was the most diabolical machine, obstinate, stubborn, cantankerous, temperamental and plain bloody minded. It hardly ever completed one line without a breakdown of sorts; how Matthew put up with it I never knew. Matthew was a man of strong religious beliefs and he never swore, but if he was tempted to swear the Good Lord must have provided that baler as the ultimate temptation. I remembered one year, after about the tenth breakdown of the day, Matthew had dropped a vital spring into the hay.

"Oh," he had paused and looked at me. "Bother," he finished and smiled wearily.

I started work at one o'clock, windrowing hay for Matthew to bale. Matthew had already baled about a quarter of his crop before he had asked for my help and Joe had started loading bales onto a trailer on his own before he went to start the milking later on in the afternoon.

We worked well, and, as if it was trying to win a reprieve for the following year, the old baler performed perfectly. When the dew started to dampen the hay and it 'went back' we carted bales to the barn. It was undeniably hard work loading the trailer by means of the two grain prong, work I had taken in my stride before I worked for the Royal Mail. I became dreadfully tired and, to my wife's disgust, took to retiring to bed at nine o'clock.

"It's only for a week," I told her.

"With that old baler of Matthew's it'll probably take a month or more."

It did take more than a week - I knew it would. The weather broke temporarily after a few days, and one evening, as we headed for the barn, it started to spit with rain. We were using two tractors and trailers; we hurled the bales off the trailers in disarray and had just finished when the heavens opened. Matthew and I sat on a bale in a coma of fatigue, watching the curtain of rain soaking all before it.

Suddenly, there was a loud crack, like the crack of a whip, followed by a sharp rumble of thunder. Beth, Matthew's dog, disappeared and there was a strong electrical smell. The barn had been struck by lightning; presumably the steel framework had acted as a lightning conductor. Beth, Matthew told me later, did not reappear until the following morning.

The rain at least gave me a day's welcome respite and the following week we made steady progress.

One of Matthew's further fields necessitated quite a long journey back to the barn. I was driving his 'best' tractor, a relatively modern Ford, while he came on behind in an old David Brown of uncertain vintage. I had driven it before and it had terrible steering. At anything over threequarter throttle it became unmanageable, weaving involuntraily from one side of the road to the other.

Driving back with the last load of bales for the day, I settled into a pleasant dream, watching the fields and scattered houses slowly passing by; it was a time to savour, the cooling breeze drying the sweat on my face. Smelling hay I looked to my left. I was in estate country now and a field close to the road was having its last windrows baled. The tractor driver leant out of his cab and waved his hat at me. I happily waved back and continued my peaceful drive.

Rounding a corner, about a mile from the field, I encountered an elderly woman cyclist pedalling towards me. She raised her hand, halfway between a wave and a salute, wobbling dangerously as I passed her, a look of horror on her face. I returned the greeting, thankful she had retained her balance.

I backed up to the barn, switched off the engine and, still savouring the peace, sat in the cab, waiting for Matthew. He was surprisingly close behind me, considering the dreadful condition of his tractor's steering and, red in the face from the effort of wrestling with it, he jumped off the tractor and ran towards me.

"Come away from the barn," he shouted, "you're on fire. You'll set all the hay alight."

Startled, I pulled forward and climbed off the tractor. I walked round the trailer; there was no sign of fire. I looked questioningly at Matthew.

"You were on fire, all the way down the road until I lost sight of you. Clouds of smoke were coming from the left hand side of your trailer."

There was certainly nothing there now. We looked closely at the wheel and I felt the tyre. It was hot to the touch and the woodwork of the rickety trailer bed was charred and burnt into a semi circle above the tyre. A bolt on one of the stringers had snapped, allowing the trailer bed to drop, but only so far. The tyre had burnt its way into the woodwork and the fire had miraculously extinguished itself once the semi circle had formed.

"It would appear the Good Lord even looks after the unrighteous," Matthew said with a smile. "Let's throw those bales off before he changes his mind."

We finished Matthew's haymaking at the end of the second week. Apart from minor breakdowns the old baler had performed as though it was a new model. At the end of the last field it was making alarming noises, creaking and groaning and threatening to scatter its innards all over the field. But it didn't, and finally it triumphantly spat out its last bale.

"You looks tired," Sydney said to me. "What 'ave you been up to?"

"Haymaking," I replied,

"'Aymaking? At your time of life? And doing this job? You must be mad."

I thought that was rich coming from Sydney.

Twenty Five

Ivan Sitwell was a tall man, well built, his black hair balding in the manner of a monk. He had a ruddy face, a pointed, slightly retroussé nose, soft brown eyes, and on his ruddy face he always wore a half sardonic smile, as if he were looking down on the world and its follies from a loftier perch than most. He lived with his wife and two children in a tiny council estate in the village of Ruston, and he survived entirely on state benefits. Indeed, apart from the odd bill, the only mail I delivered to his house was official, the inevitable dole cheque and copicus correspondence from the D.H.S.S.

His wife was a short, plain, severe looking woman of barely five foot in height, but his children, two girls aged eleven and thirteen, were pretty, lively and intelligent in appearance. The family travelled everywhere on their bicycles, forsaking them once a week when they caught the bus to Buddleshaw for their weekly shopping expedition. Even then, they rode them the half mile to the bus stop, parking them behind the bus shelter, to return much later burdened with shopping. Wobbling and lurching astride their dangerously overloaded machines they pedalled the half mile of gentle uphill gradient to Ruston.

I asked Mary about Ivan. She knew most of the happenings in the surrounding area, but for once she couldn't help.

"They're an enigma, that family. They arrived out of the blue from goodness knows where about two years ago. Ivan's never worked in his entire life that I know of, neither has his wife. They keep themselves to themselves, are always polite, but no one really knows a thing about them. And those lovely girls ..."

I suggested to Mary they might be adopted.

"No, I don't think so," she said. "Who would let a pair like that adopt children?" She had a point.

For once I was able to tell Mary something she didn't know, for I had come across Ivan before, in another life, a life before Royal Mail.

Ivan had a weakness, perhaps even two. He had an overfond partiality for alcohol; it was in my local pub I had first set eyes on him, shortly after he had moved with his family to Ruston. To say I had met him was too strong a phrase, for he spoke to no one, sitting in a corner with his pint of bitter, surveying all that passed with that fixed, half sardonic smile. All attempts to engage him in conversation failed. He was quite content with his own company and the comfort of his pint. He visited the pub usually once, but sometimes twice a week.

His routine was unfailing; he drank three pints of bitter, and then departed to indulge his second failing - and it was perhaps a failing more than a weakness - a visit to the Rectory, which was a short walk from the pub.

The Rector, normally a patient if slightly morose man, had his good nature sorely tried by Ivan Sitwell who wished to be confirmed into the Church of England. The Rector, for reasons of his own, was reluctant to accept him.

This was revealed one evening when an unusually belligerent and, for once, loquatious Ivan returned from an unsuccessful foray to the Rectory. After loudly telling the landlady his views on the Rector, he drank his pint and left. The Rector, knowing Ivan's routine, visited the pub three quarters of an hour later for a well earned pint or two, but would not be drawn. Whatever it was, he refused to divulge, and it was never discovered.

Mary was as interested as anyone by Ivan's aberrations and promised to solve the mystery for me, but she never managed to uncover it.

"He's always so polite," she said, "but neither he nor his wife gives anything away, and the only person who knows anything about him is that Rector, and he won't tell. Those two girls are just the same from what I hear. They've no friends at school and keep themselves to themselves, fiercely protecting their parents if a word is said against them. The strange thing is that their house is spotless, not a speck of dust to be seen anywhere."

I had more of a first hand experience of Ivan's eccentricities one dark night at about ten o'clock. Hearing a tremendous noise on our driveway accompanied by a string of expletives clearly audible above the sound of the television, I picked up a torch and went to investigate.

The cause of the commotion was a very drunk Ivan. He was kicking something around on the ground, and each time he made contact with it he howled with pain as he hurt his toes, the thin leather of his shoes providing inadequate protection for the purpose. Fortunately for Ivan most of his wild kicks missed, and I retrieved a badly dented, large can of peas. I handed it to him and he took it gratefully, remembering his manners, forgetting his temper and thanking me politely. Shining the torch around I discovered his bicycle in the hedge, where he had evidently thrown it, the pannier at the rear spilling its contents of provisions.

It was not difficult to work out what had happened. Becoming low on supplies, Ivan had been despatched to Bramton, a distance of some five miles, to purchase more. He had then spent the remainder of the day and most of his money in the pub, returning far later than he intended.

I pulled his bicycle from the hedge, stood it up, picked up the spilled provisions and re-packed them. Ivan lurched over, still clutching the dented tin of peas. I took it from him, placing it firmly in the pannier and passed the machine to him. It appeared undamaged.

Suddenly he spoke, surprisingly clearly.

"You know what?" he asked rhetorically, 'some blighter shouted at me from his car, just back there. Said I was a danger to him and myself 'cos I didn't show a rear light. Makes me wild these do gooders." He paused for a moment, gathering his scrambled thoughts. Then he continued, with all the logic of Uncle John at the fire drill. "If I haven't got a rear light, how can I show one?"

With that, the well lit up Ivan unsteadily mounted his bicycle and wobbled off into the darkness. The Rector, I reckoned, was in for a bad evening.

In my Post Office van, I often passed Ivan and his family cycling in single file down the narrow country lanes. They always heard it coming and unfailingly dismounted, waving to me as I went by. I doubted Ivan remembered the time he had been playing a painful form of football on our driveway.

Suddenly, they were gone. One day a removal van arrived outside their council house and the crew loaded up their furniture, their bicycles and all the household gadgetry donated to them by the council, and departed to an unknown destination. No one in Ruston knew where they went, nor particularly cared, but in a curious way the village was the poorer for their passing. Ivan, with his sardonic smile, took his family and his mystery elsewhere. The Rector did not know where they went, nor did they avail themselves of the Royal Mail re-direction service. For once, even the postman did not know.

Twenty Six

It is scarcely news that postmen and dogs do not, nor ever have, enjoyed each other's company, but no convincing reason has been advanced which explains this phenomenon. Invasion of their property, the sight of the uniform, the colour of the van, protection of their owners, children, relatives, and the family cat are all theories put forward by 'experts'. But none of them, collectively or singly really solves the conundrum. It could just be that decades before a rogue dog bit a postman, his colleagues became fearful they, too, might suffer a similar fate, the fear spreading like a virus throughout the postmen in the whole country, resulting in dogs smelling this fear and atavistically reacting to the scent.

Whatever the reason, there can hardly be a postman in the land who has escaped nips, bites, or savagings from delinquent dogs, though the strange thing was that most dogs were docile and well behaved. The general attitude was to treat all dogs with grave suspicion until proven friendly, and then never to trust then completely. There is no greater truism that dogs are like their owners, though there are rare exceptions. Mostly, we knew our dogs and we knew their owners, treading carefully up the garden paths of those we did not trust.

The tiny village of Ashley housed a rogue Alsation, but, Gavin assured me, the owners were aware of the animal's temperament, never letting it out until the mail had been delivered. But one could not always be certain of its whereabouts and it was always a relief to see it barking at the window, safely confined to the house. Gradually I relaxed, confident I would not encounter the beast in the garden, and nor I did.

I encountered one of the Postman's worst nightmares one day in that same village. I had seldom met the owners of this particular Alsation, but I did know they had two young children of about five and six. It seemed a dangerous mix, but they appeared responsible and aware of a duty to keep the dog inside until after the postman had called, so I had no qualms about knocking on their door one morning to deliver a registered letter, which required a signature. Indeed, I had done so before, and the dog had been shut in a side room before the mother of the children had opened the door to me.

Confident, I knocked on the door, expecting the same routine. It was a big mistake. The door was opened almost immediately, not by the mother, but by one of the children. For an instant I had a vision of the two children standing in the doorway, the Alsation just behind and between them, its mouth open, barking ferociously, its hackles raised all over its neck, back and tail, the upper lip pulled back revealing its terrible teeth. It was like that brief moment between striking a finger with a hammer and the onset of pain.

So it was with the Alsation. Launching itself at me, knocking the children aside, it made a charge straight for my throat, its intention never in doubt. Hurling the mail to the ground, in a desperate act of self preservation, I grabbed it by the muzzle with both hands, wrestling with it on the doorstep while the terrified children fled up the stairs. It was like grappling with a snake, the maddened dog twisting its head and body, trying to free itself from my inadequate grip. I had not a hope. Writhing and pushing back with its front feet it broke free, immediately lunging forward and biting me right through my left hand. Grabbing the beast by its collar with my right hand, we waltzed around the path by the front door in a macabre parody of a dance, blood pouring liberally from my bitten hand.

The mother, thoroughly alerted by her by now screaming children, ran down the stairs, took hold of the collar and heaved the dog away, my blood still running from its jaws, shutting it in the side room by the front door. It instantly reappeared at the window, barking and slavering, its breath condensing on the glass. I hoped the glass would hold.

216

What followed was bizarre, though from other postmen's experiences, not uncommon. There was a total lack of sympathy, almost as if the attack had been my fault. The children, having seen the dog pulled off me from their sanctuary upstairs, descended and watched the blood still pouring from my hand with interest. Their mother, apparantly disinterested in the damage her dog had inflicted upon her postman, bent and retrieved the blood splattered registered letter from the doorstep, holding it by a corner with some distaste. "Where do I have to sign?" she asked.

I goggled at her in disbelief, holding my by now throbbing left hand up in the air in a vain attempt to staunch the flow of blood; there appeared nothing broken, though the Alsation's teeth had met through the flesh between my thumb and index finger. Ignoring her question, I asked whether I might be allowed to rinse my hand under a cold tap.

"I suppose so," she said reluctantly, walking back into the house.

Dripping blood over her kitchen floor as I followed her, she indicated the sink, and I ran the cold water, holding my bleeding hand under it, the diluted blood swirling down the plughole like thin red paint. The mother, meanwhile, mopped up my bloody trail with paper from a kitchen roll. The children, wide eyed, watched every move with an economy of speech they could only have inherited from their mother. The bleeding slightly staunched, I tore off some of the kitchen roll which she had left, by habit, near the sink, twisting it around my hand. Disapprovingly, she followed me to the door where, remembering, I asked her to sign for her letter. Regarding the blood soaked slip of blue paper with horror she asked if I could do it for her. I assured her I would and with some relief she closed the door behind me without apology.

Changing gear was a nightmare, blood spurted from my left hand with renewed vigour, drenching all around it. There was only one thing to do; I drove to the surgery in Bramton where a doctor saw me straight away, taped up the wounds and administered an undignified injection into my backside. Feeling better, the bleeding finished, the throbbing easing, I decided to continue my round, but the constant changing of gear re-opened the wounds, which dripped and seeped for the rest of the morning. Mary provided me with sympathy and plenty of kitchen roll, but when I returned to the office I encountered a different attitude from Sydney, who was drinking his inevitable cup of tea, sitting on his garden chair by the wicker table.

"Dog get you?" he asked, observing my hand swaddled in red kitchen roll. "Let's 'ave a look."

I reluctantly unwrapped the sodden mess from my hand and showed him. It was a measure of my demoralisation that I submitted so weakly.

He studied it with interest. "You'll 'ave to go to the hospital an' get that seen to."

I explained I had already been to the surgery.

"That's no good," he told me, "'Ealth and safety says you 'as to go to casualty. Regulations, see, in case anything goes wrong otherwise you 'as no comeback."

Convinced he was talking nonsense, I told him so. I had no intention of spending the rest of the day sitting in casualty. Crestfallen, he said, "Well, you'll 'ave to get a dog bite form from 'Iggings. That's standard."

Ted was due to take over the van in the afternoon, so I borrowed a bowl and some washing up liquid from Jack and started cleaning the congealed blood from the van. Sydney came over to watch. He was in his element. "Who 'as this van next?" he inquired.

"Ted," I replied briefly.

"Well, 'ee can't drive it. That van's got to be professionally valeted by professionals an' completely sterilised and what's 'is named. It's regulations."

I had had a bad morning, and I had heard quite enough of Sydney's rubbish. I told him so in no uncertain terms and, offended, he walked away muttering some twaddle about regulations being regulations and

218

health and safety overriding everything.

I did obtain a dog bite form from Uncle John. It was, surprisingly, quite straightforward, and contained an interesting question. "What recommendation or action do you think Royal Mail should take concerning this incident?"

That, I thought, gave a pretty free rein, so I answered the question comprehensively, suggesting that, in view of the young children and the dog's proven record of aggression, it should be destroyed. And should Royal Mail fail in its duty to bring this recommendation to the notice of the owners it could be held liable should a further incident occur. Smiling grimly, I sealed the envelope and handed it to Uncle John.

Sydney was not the only one who could play the official game.

Of course I never heard another word.

Sometimes the biter was bitten. There was one farm I visited where I did not dare set foot outside the van, the owner nearly always walking across the yard to collect his mail accompanied by his particularly vicious looking dog, some sort of ugly hybrid cross between an Alsation and a rottweiler. "Don't you never get out your van if I ain't here," he told me, "else 'ee'll 'ave yer."

I didn't doubt his word for a minute.

One day he walked across the yard with no dog at his heel. I asked where he was. The old farmer replied, with the hint of a tear in his eye, "Ee got bit by an adder, an' 'ee died within the hour. Real sad it were. I misses him dreadfully."

Cynicism had never been one of my traits before I joined Royal Mail, but it was difficult not to applaud the adder.

Davina Harcourt also dwelt in Ashley, in an expensively converted, sixteenth century farmhouse close to the little lane, which threaded its way through the village like a randomly discarded piece of string. She lived there with her seldomly seen husband who worked in the city, her young daughter, her ancient mother, and to complete the country idyll, her dog.

Davina was a strong minded, attractive woman of about thirty five who eschewed convention and petty rules. I once saw her sitting, waiting, in the bank at Bramton smoking a cigarette, the sign above her chair condescendingly reading 'Thank you for not smoking'. I admired her spirit, but I did not admire her dog.

Quite in keeping with her character there was no traditional Labrador or spaniel for her: she was the owner of a pyranean mountain dog. This massive beast, quite the largest dog I had ever seen, must have weighed eight or nine stone. It was called Rupert, and was entirely placid. But Rupert suffered from one serious flaw. He adored human beings, but not, perhaps, for all the right reasons.

Rupert would wait for my red Post Office van to arrive, leap the high rails of the front garden, which were supposed to keep him confined, and saunter up to the window, his tongue hanging out, a certain glint showing in his eyes. Usually a whack across the muzzle with Davina's mail was sufficient warning, but not always.

One particular morning, pulling up as usual outside Davina's house, Rupert sailed over the railings, clearing them by a couple of feet, remarkable even by his standards. He required two firm hits on the muzzle before he quietened down and I walked up the path as usual with the slightly battered letters. As I pushed them through the tiny letter box I felt a tremendous weight on my shoulders, pinning me to the door. It was Rupert. Half turning and straightening at the same time made him lose his grip for a moment but, with a turn of speed I would not have thought possible in such a large animal, he lunged forward, firmly planting those giant paws on my shoulders, pinning me again to the door with a crash. Empty milk bottles scattered as I fought back, but it was hopeless Rupert was far too heavy to shift and it was impossible to twist away from him as the doorway was too narrow to offer the opportunity for manoeuvre.

Unexpected salvation came from within. Davina, hearing the racket, opened the door. The result was spectacular. Propelled by Rupert I was hurled into Davina who was thrust backwards into her daughter, standing behind. The four of us collapsed in a heap on the floor, Rupert with his feet planted on my chest. Davina recovered first and, with a turn of phrase and a strength that surprised me, pulled her giant dog off and, quite literally, booted him out of the door. Judging from the high pitched yelping from outside she had found a tender spot.

"You won't have any more trouble from him today," she said. "I think we had better have a drink."

There was an aged crone sitting in a chair in a corner, a rug over her knees. She was Davina's mother.

"He, he he," she cackled, "First the paper boy and now the postman. He, he, he." I stared at her, wondering if she was completely sane.

Davina thrust a large whisky into my hand, offering me a cigarette, which I gratefully accepted. She smiled ruefully. "Yes, we have to collect our papers now. The paper boy is terrified of Rupert. I hope we won't have to collect our mail."

I never had any more trouble from Rupert. In his mind he must have associated his painful ejection with me. As soon as he saw the van coming, he disappeared behind the house, peering round the corner when the van departed, before taking up residence by the front door again.

Several months later the Harcourts sold their farmhouse, moving into a flat in town. How Rupert and the old crone would cope with that was anyone's guess.

Twenty Seven

The refurbishments were all but completed. Uncle John was installed in his new - if cramped - office and the old fashioned rather characterful furniture removed, replaced with bland plastic chairs and tables, which anonymously and seamlessly blended in with the unimaginative gloomy beige décor. The coat and hat stand had been consigned to the builder's skip; there was no replacement, Uncle John having to carefully fold his jacket and place it on a beige plastic chair. On a plastic topped table adjacent to his desk was a brand new computer, yet to be connected: there was a similar one in Murdoch's cage.

Months later, when these monstrous machines were set up, Uncle John and Murdoch, seperately, were sent on courses, which were supposed to induct them into the mode of their use. Uncle John, naturally, had not a clue how to operate one, nor did the studies he attended improve matters. Murdoch, on the other hand, grasped the basics and Uncle John was content to allow him sole use of the computers.

I could never quite understand the need for them at Bramton. Apart from sending daily reports, which used to be sent more easily by telephone, the overtime and holiday entitlements were stored on them. When I wanted to check my holidays with Murdoch he got himself in such a tangle - jabbing at the thing with his fat fingers, revealing meaningless irelevant information on the screen - I suggested he looked it up in the holiday book. Reaching into a drawer, he flicked over the pages giving me the information in an instant. It was probably the way forward, but that was not the way I viewed it.

The Post Office shop, in Uncle John's old office, was fitted out, stocked, and staffed with a rota of part time fat Bramton women from the estates. Jack's kitchen now boasted a brand new cooker, microwave and toaster (none of which was ever used) and the tea room had gained, ominously, a combined television set and videotape recorder.

There was also an outbreak of plastic signs, which some tidy minded, politically correct person had decided were necessary to catalogue everything. Four of them appeared outside, proclaiming the obvious warning 'Beware of Wheeled Containers' presumably referring to the trolleys we used for loading the vans. The gents became 'The Male Rest Room'; the little area where we drank our tea and indulged the occasional cigarette became the highly important 'Designated Smoking Area'; and the space next to it was named 'Motor Cycles and Mopeds Only'. As I was the only person to arrive on two wheels I was pleased the little Puch Maxi at last had an officially designated parking area. More mysteriously, the tea room was re-named the 'Welfare Suite'. I puzzled over that for a long time, but couldn't work out why. Perhaps it was envisaged as a place where traumatised postmen could be counselled. And the Sorting Office became the 'Sorting Hall'. It was all very grand.

There were a few more minor alterations, but it seemed to me Royal Mail had a poor deal for the expenditure of three quarters of a million pounds.

There were changes other than the refurbishment in the air, I learnt from Dave. I was becoming weary of his lack of moral values as the sordid little tale unfolded and wondered if he had done this before to other managers, particularly at Buddleshaw. It would not have surprised me, and would certainly explain how he appeared to know so much of the workings of Royal Mail almost before they had happened.

"I'll tell you the first bits," he said. "I knows you doesn't like reading them letters. We're getting a night shift, at the earliest opportunity."

That would be a good thing. The mail sorted each morning was growing almost daily as the Royal Mail salesmen were discounting rubbish mail so heavily that eager firms were sending it out in vast quantities for virtually nothing. 'At the earliest opportunity' was Royal Mail parlance for sometime in the distant future.

"And Jack's going," Dave said. "Atkinson don't think we warrants a full time cleaner at Bramton, so he's making him part time. He won't work here part time, it wouldn't be worth his while driving out here."

Dave was probably right. Jack would go. It would be a shame to lose him; he was a beacon of common sense in an often haywire office.

He thrust a letter at me that he had been hiding behind his back. "You'll have to read this, whether you wants to or not."

It was from Atkinson. It was one of the most breathtakingly nasty documents it has been my misfortune to read. It concerned Uncle John's heart attack and reading it made me think there must have been some awful scenes behind his closed office door on Atkinson's weekly visits.

'I can make no allowance for your medical condition,' it read, 'nor can I accept any responsibility for a recurrence as you suggested. You have been declared fit to resume your position at Royal Mail by the medical profession and as that is the case I see no reason to relax any much needed pressure on you. It is not the fault of your superior officer, myself, that your incompernce has caused the overtime in this office to escalate to unacceptable levels and I shall continue to pursue a relentless campaign against you until you have achieved the results I require. In consequence, as I see it, any recurrence of your condition would be entirely the fault of yourself and not of any third party.

'Finally, I should like to remind you I have a younger and significantly more competent member of my staff available to take over the Bramton office should you fail to achieve these results.'

There were two results from this, one surprising, the other less so. The latter was the Jack's departure, rather as I thought. I had not told him I had an idea he would leave, but when he told me he was going at the end of the week I saw no harm in divulging the information Dave had given me. Perhaps Dave had a point when he had said he had to share his information. He was shocked, but not disbelieving.

"I always knew that man was a complete toe-rag," he said, "but I didn't realise he was that bad. He's the sort of person that's so heartless that if he didn't kill Higgings first he would, and probably will, shove him out anyway. And if the poor blighter died in the meantime he'd probably think he had done a good job."

Jack did leave at the end of the week. Interviews for a new cleaner started two weeks later.

The surprising news was that the night shift was to start the following week. There must have been much manoeuvering behind the scenes: no one at Bramton had shown any interest in working at night, but there was a younger man who lived close to Buddleshaw, working in the office there, who had expressed a willingness to take on the shift. His name was Dennis. We all knew him, for in the many moments of crisis when we were short staffed Uncle John would borrow him from Buddleshsw to help out. He was about thirty five, short, fat, always carrying a faint aroma of stale sweat about him, and he was a phenomenally fast sorter. I had always considered Peter the fastest sorter in the office, but Dennis made him look like an amateur.

We were not allowed to take our vans home at night. So, the idea was that Dennis should drive to Bramton at about a quarter to ten, leave his car at the Sorting Office, and collect the Sherpa van and drive to Buddleshaw. There he would spend the night sorting as much of the Bramton mail as he could. He would then load the van for the return journey, arriving at Bramton at five o'clock in the morning.

The new system worked well. Obviously, Dennis could not sort all the Bramton mail overnight - there was far too much for that to have been possible - but he made considerable headway with it. There was also mail arriving throughout the night from other offices, some for Buddleshaw and Bramton, other for the outlying offices in the area. It often did not arrive until shortly before Dennis started loading his van for his trip to Bramton. The Buddleshaw van arrived at Bramton as usual each morning with our share of this mail and the residue Dennis had not had time to sort during the night shift.

It was pleasant, and less depressing, to see a smaller heap hauled in from the first van followed by Dennis's neatly and correctly sorted mail, which arrived a little later. It had the added bonus that we finished earlier, claimed less overtime and Uncle John was at last able to show a reduction in his figures to the inhuman Atkinson. But I doubted that would be enough to save him.

It was one of my duties every morning when on Gunners Castle to walk round to the front of the main Post Office and empty the main post box. There was seldom much mail posted between six o'clock in the evening when it was last emptied and five a.m., but the idea was any local mail could be extracted, franked by hand, and delivered that morning. It was what was once called service.

Opposite the main Post Office was a hotel, and between the two was a pedestrian crossing controlled by traffic lights. The road to Buddleshaw stretched dead straight into the distance, sloping downwards to a cross roads before rising and disappearing out of town over the brow of a hill where it joined the infamous dual carriageway.

Bramton was known to be a quiet town. To the casual visitor who stayed within the confines of the centre without straying onto the awful estates or, in a different way, the equally awful developments, this was undoubtedly true. It was situated in an area rich in history, making it an attractive proposition for a place where wealthy tourists could stay and gently explore the beautiful rolling countryside, with its picturesque villages complete with ancient churches, and the battlefields of the civil war, that we took so much for granted.

The majority of these tourists originated from the New World; most of them stayed at the George Hotel, opposite the main post office.

When I was emptying the main box on the first morning of the night shift I could clearly hear Dennis's van approaching, the still air as yet uncontaminated by the daily awakening of thousands of noisy, polluting, internal combustion engines. Turning away from my task, I could see the approaching headlights illuminating the trees as it started its descent into Bramton, and soon it was possible to make out the familiar box shape of the approaching Sherpa.

Shutting the door to the box, a mail sack with the few letters it contained in my left hand, I noticed the Sherpa was by the cross roads at the bottom of the hill, accelerating for the final gradient to the Sorting Office. On impulse I pressed the button, which controlled the pedestrian lights: there was a pause and when Dennis was about fifty yards away the lights changed to amber, then red, and a dreadful electronic beeping shattering the relative peace indicated it was safe to cross. Out of the corner of my eye I saw Peter coming from the opposite direction, riding to work on his bicycle.

With a squeal of brakes Dennis brought the Sherpa to a halt, and spying me standing by the crossing slid the driver's van door back. "What the hell did you press that button for? The Sorting Office is your side of the road. Where do you think you are going? To the George over the road for an early drink?" Dennis was very literal.

"Why did you stop?" I asked him.

"Because you pushed the bloody button and the lights changed red. I had to stop, you might have crossed the road and I would have killed you."

The little, green, flashing man ceased flashing and was replaced by a red man. My finger went back to the button.

"Don't you press that again," he shouted, "I'm bloody going now."

But he was too late. Peter, sensing a chance to further enrage Dennis, pulled up on his bicycle and started pushing it across towards the hotel.

"You can't do that," Dennis yelled, "the man's turned red. Get back

228

before I run you over." He revved the engine impatiently. Peter continued his sedate progress towards the George, pausing in front of the van. The deafening beeping stopped and the lights began to change back to green. I kept my finger on the button, the lights changed back to red and the beeping started once more.

"Now look what you've done," Dennis screamed, almost beside himself with frustration. "I'll have to wait all over again."

Peter continued his leisurely progress over the crossing and turned to come back, propping his bicycle against the front of Dennis's van while he searched his pockets for his cigarettes. I kept my finger on the button, and the lights changed yet again. Later, I asked Dennis why he had stopped for pedestrian traffic lights at five o'clock in the morning when there was no traffic about and the person who had activated the lights was unlikely to use the crossing.

"Because it's the law," he said. "If you see a red light, you have to stop."

Dennis was normally the most placid and easy going of men, but his patience was sorely tried during the coming weeks, for the traffic light fiasco became an office joke, with quite a number of postmen suddenly eager to cross to the George at five o'clock in the morning.

What it did for the tolerance of the American tourists staying there one could only imagine. Perhaps they thought it was a quaint English custom specially enacted for their benefit.

Peter often cut a lonely figure. He participated in the crude office humour and banter as much as anyone else, but there was a certain unreachable remoteness to him. It was rumoured he had wife trouble. I had met her once and she did not strike me as a woman to fall out with, and my suspicions were further increased when I chanced upon him in a country lane on a week he was supposed to be on holiday. He was carrying a black plastic bin bag and, the altruism strong within him, collecting litter from the verges and hedgerows. I stopped my van and we had a brief chat, but it was a curious way to spend a holiday. He also encountered the greatest number of what can only be described as revealing moments of any postman working at Bramton. To listen to him recount them one would draw the conclusion there were more ravishing beauties in a permanent state of undress on his round than adorned the pages of a top shelf magazine in a newsagent. For myself, a fleeting flash of the left nipple of an attractive radio presenter as she bent, unfettered, to sign for a letter was the best I ever achieved.

Peter and Dennis were great friends. They had been to school together and Peter had been Dennis's best man at his wedding, so it was natural that on the night of the robbery Dennis turned to Peter for help.

Dennis had arrived for work at about a quarter to ten. He parked his car at the top of the yard and walked down to where the Sherpa had been left ready for him and unlocked the door. Before sliding it open, he paused. There was a noise coming from within the Post Office building, high pitched, like the whine of a dentist's drill. Leaving the van he went to the rear door and listened. It was definitely a drilling sound he had heard and he also thought he could discern muffled voices.

The Sorting Office and the main Post Office were seperated by a single locked door and Dennis did not have keys for either office. He had no need and, besides, it required two people each with different keys to open them. He hovered by the door, undecided, then his mind made up he walked to the telephone box and phoned Peter. He was not amused to hear the telephone ring at ten o'clock. He had already been asleep for two hours.

Dennis asked him whether there should be anyone in the office that night. Peter replied that, as far as he knew, both offices should have been empty. He told Dennis if he was worried he should ring the police, replaced the receiver and resumed his slumbers.

Dennis was both worried and undecided. Returning to the yard he quietly walked down to the door, listening again. He could still hear noises. Making up his mind and with sudden resolve he made his way back to the telephone box, dialled 999, explaining to the duty constable at Buddleshaw he suspected there was some dirty business afoot at the Bramton Post Office. The constable told him a car would be despatched at once, and advised Dennis to remain by the telephone box until it arrived.

But there must have been a lingering doubt in Dennis's mind. Maybe, he thought, he was mistaken; he had to make sure, so once again he returned to the door and listened. There was now no doubt. He could clearly hear voices. Looking around he saw a brick left over from the refurbishments. Picking it up, he hurled it at the door with all his might then, as fast as his fat little legs could carry him, ran to his car, started it up and fled to Peter's house. The robbers - and they were robbers - also fled, in the opposite direction, leaving their expensive safe breaking equipment behind.

The police car, with two policemen, arrived three minutes too late. The birds had well and truly flown. They checked the telephone box, but Dennis was not there.

Peter was once again roused from his sleep by Dennis's frantic banging on his door. It was now ten thirty. When Dennis had explained what had taken place, he abandoned any further attempts to sleep, returning with Dennis to the office. There the policemen, their numbers now reinforced by two further patrol cars, were wondering why the burglars had disappeared so precipitately. Dennis was able to explain why.

There is no record of the policemen's replies.

The object of the robbers' attentions had been the safe containing the pension money for Bramton's senior citizens, a considerable sum of money. The gang, identified by their equipment and other objects they had abandoned in their haste to leave, had been hunted by the police for months. Their frustration was understandable.

The first I learnt of the night's events was when I arrived in the yard at five o'clock in the morning to be greeted by the sight of three police cars and Dennis, overcome with excitement, hopping around like a demented gnome, telling his story to anyone who was prepared to listen.

He rushed over to me and started gabbling his version of the night's events almost before I had taken off my helmet, finishing with, "Not everyone would have thought of throwing a brick at the door."

Sydney's usual garden chair was occupied by a fatigued and fed up Peter who, deprived of his sleep, was not looking forward to the day. The Buddleshaw van and its bemused driver were parked by the open door as usual, but no attempt had been made to unload it. A few people were standing talking or aimlessly strolling around the yard smoking cigarettes, and Sydney, his arms akimbo, stood in the centre of the doorway. He was enjoying himself.

Breaking free from the still gabbling Dennis, I made my way over to the Sorting Office.

"You can't come in 'ere," Sydney said officiously.

"Why not?" I asked.

"Because of the what d'yer call its and things," he replied. "The police ain't finished in 'ere yet. There's intimidating evidence there, and you mustn't disturb it. They've got to put what's 'is name powder all over the office for fingers and things. You can't go in. Not even 'Iggings can go in there when 'ee arrives."

It didn't look to me as if the police had started whatever they were supposed to do in Sydney's vivid imagination. One of them came over to us; he must have been acquainted with Sydney, there were few who were not. "It's perfectly all right, Mr. Tuck. They never went near your side of the building. You may go in there if you wish."

Deflated, Sydney stepped aside while we entered to start the day's work. Sydney joined the throng, his moment of glory over. I almost felt sorry for him.

Later, I gloomily surveyed the mountain of mail lying on the floor. There had, of course, been no night sorting. It was going to be a long day.

I overheard Gavin say to Lester, "Dennis did well. He saved the Post Office a bundle of money when he threw that brick."

"He wants that brick thrown up his backside," Lester replied.

Unfortunately Dennis, who regarded himself as a hero, took the former view, while the Post Office, more pragmatically, took the latter. Dennis, primed by Sydney, thought he ought to be given a reward for his bravery, his estimates ranging wildly from several thousand pounds to some mysterious percentage of the money. Heaven knows what Sydney had told him. The Post Office took a less generous view, remaining silent about their vociferous hero, and it was not until Sydney contacted a more senior union official that they relented.

Dennis was presented with a cheap, engraved, quartz watch and a cheque for thirty pounds. He was outraged.

Twenty Eight

"Have you renewed your friendship with Mike yet?" Matthew asked me one day with a wicked grin.

"No," I replied cautiously, "not yet. I've seen him sitting in his caravan and he's seen me, so he knows I am his new postman, but he hasn't spoken."

"How are you getting on with his dog? You could claim danger money from the Royal Mail delivering there, I should think." Matthew was still smiling.

"Fortunately he's put a post box of sorts by his gate. Probably the only sensible thing he has ever done."

Matthew's farm, Upper Castle Farm, bounded our farm, Lower Castle Farm. And Mike's farm, Castle Farm, shared our bottom boundary. We were sandwiched between the two. In Matthew it would have been difficult to have found a better neighbour; in Mike it would have been difficult to have found a worse one. When we had taken over our farm I went to see Matthew about Mike. I had a problem that was bothering me.

Mike was a livestock dealer, the sort who gives all the others a collective bad name. He was a powerful man in his early forties. His farm was a disgrace: almost bereft of fencing, littered with rusting cars, evidence of a failed attempt to break into the scrap metal market, and heaps of rubble where - for a fee - he allowed builders to tip their waste. He had a temper to match his physique, and on more than one occasion had been in trouble with the law.

His skeletal stock was in pitiful condition, freely wandering around the area - unimpeded by fences, grazing the verges and other farmers' pastures, spreading their diseases and worms with impunity. It was an eternal mystery to me how he managed to make a living. That one felt sorry for his emaciated, uncared for stock went without saying, especially when they were knocked over by cars and the carcasses were left uncollected by the roadside for all to see; this man had no shame, no care. But, like all my neighbours, I had no desire to have these animals mingling with my stock. His sheep were so starved they had little difficulty in wriggling their way through my tightly stranded barbed wire fences, and I was constantly rounding up my sheep, drafting Mike's out, and returning them to his furtherest pastures in the vain hope that they would not reappear - a singularly time wasting and increasingly futile exercise.

This was the problem I was discussing with Matthew. "It beats me how he gets away with running animals in such terrible condition," I said. "He ought to he reported."

"He is, frequently," replied Matthew, "there are often inspectors around his farm, but Mike has a gift for soft talking and he's full of unkept promises. I think his size and reputation intimidate the inspectors and they take the easy option. But it doesn't exactly help your problem." He thought for a moment. "You could try charging him rent," he said with a smile, but I doubt you'll get any. He still owes me for some baling I did for him last year. He owes money all round the place, but you're new. It's worth a try."

I left, pondering Matthew's last somewhat illogical remark, but he was right. It was worth a try.

The following week I drafted out five of Mike's sheep and shut them in the yard. Full of trepidation I squelched through the thick cloying mixture of mud, dung and rubble of Mike's farmyard to the caravan, which was his home. A ferocious mud caked mongrel, leaping at the end of its chain, barked inanely at me. I didn't like the look in its wall eyes and hoped the chain would hold.

I knocked on the door and it was flung open by an unshaven and bleary eyed Mike. "What d'yer want?" he asked, and I explained my errand. "I'll be down directly and get 'em," he said and slammed the door.

Within half an hour, to my surprise, Mike pulled into the yard in his truck. We loaded the sheep in silence. As Mike was climbing into the cab, I cleared my throat and said nervously, "That will be ten pounds."

He turned and came off the step, facing me. "What for?" he enquired.

"Rent, and my time," I replied, wondering what would happen next. He stared at me for a moment, and then pulled out a greasy wallet from his back pocket. He extracted a five pound note and fished around in his other pockets, finding two pound coins. He handed them to me. "That's all I got at the moment, I'll owe you the rest."

Slightly bemused, clutching seven pounds in my hand, I watched him go with a mixture of relief and disbelief.

Matthew laughed when I related the story. "You must be the only person around here who has ever had a penny from him. I doubt he'll fall for it again."

But he did. The next time he handed me a grubby five pound note in return for my request for ten pounds rent. I thought it unwise to mention the three pounds he owed me for the previous lot, but the third time he said he had no money on him. "I'll drop it in the next time I passes," he said. But I knew he wouldn't.

Whether it was coincidence or he took the hint I shall never know, for shortly afterwards he moved all his sheep away from our boundary. All save one, a wether lamb, which had found its way in with our sheep, and it hardly seemed worth rounding up the flock to remove it. The next time I had the sheep in for routine worming I did Mike's stray, too. I really intended to return it, but at the same time I didn't wish to face Mike again. I suppose I could have dropped it over the fence onto Mike's land, but it scarcely seemed worth the effort. There were no sheep there now and it would only work his way back in. Somehow, it stayed with us; I never quite seemed to find the time to hand it back.

Winter came, and I put it in a small paddock with half a dozen or so crock lambs and ewes that required special attention and feed for the colder weather. Mike - for that is what my children had christened the lamb - became tame and flourished on its extra rations in a way that none of Mike's original sheep could have hoped. It wintered well, and by the spring it was a nice healthy wether.

"What are you going to do with Mike?" my wife asked me one day. The morality of this question had been bothering me for some time. I admitted as much. "With all the money we've spent feeding it in the winter, together with the money its namesake owes us I think we should keep it," she said. "He doesn't know how many he has anyway."

My concience was clear. It, I decided, was officially ours. Together with our tail end lambs, I sent Mike to market. There were ten lambs in all, two pens of five. Mike rather spoilt the appearance of one pen, as he was somewhat larger than the other four. That couldn't be helped. They were two nice pens of lambs, nevertheless.

Walking around the market I saw the original Mike, or Mike's 'father' as my children, sworn to secrecy, called him. "That's two good pens of lambs you got there," he said to me. "I likes that 'un there, with the big feller in it."

I swallowed hard. I was about to say I thought he only bought rubbish, but rapidly discounted making such a rash statement.

"They wintered well," I replied lamely.

The bidding was keen; it was going to be a good day. When our two pens came under the hammer I watched Mike closely. He seemed uninterested.

The first pen sold well, and the auctioneer moved to the second. "Another good pen of lambs here. A little uneven, but all good lambs." Again Mike appeared uninterested. "All done, all done?" the auctioneer intoned, raising his hand to slap his catalogue to close the deal.

Mike raised his hand. He had topped the bidding. The lambs were his. He had bought his own lamb.

Twenty Nine

Bonus schemes seldom made for harmonious industrial relations, but Royal Mail, always eager to aggravate the already troubled relationship with the union worked out a scheme, surprisingly with their agreement, of such staggering complexity that no one had the remotest idea how it worked or how the bonus was calculated, though part of it was related to productivity. Uncle John, when pressed, had to admit he could not understand it and when Gavin asked Atkinson, on his weekly visit to harass Uncle John, he, too, was forced to admit his ignorance of the scheme's workings. Only Sydney, as union representative, claimed to have a thorough working knowledge of it. With much what's 'is naming and what d'yer call its he explained the mysteries to a bemused Lester one day, at great length. It was a masterpiece of obfuscation and at the conclusion Lester was as confused as Sidney.

What was perfectly clear, though, was that the more mail we sorted the larger was the bonus, which was ridiculous, because we could only sort the mail that came into the office. We could scarcely generate more genuine mail to increase our pay.

The solution was simple, and Royal Mail became hoist by its own petard at Bramton and, probably, by every office in the country. Royal Mail, like many businesses, was addicted to statistics and it was of paramount importance to them that the amount of mail coming into the office was counted. Obviously it was impossible to count each individual item, so they devised a system of averaging the mail received each day.

This was achieved by counting the contents of every sixth or seventh trolley into which we tipped the mail. These trollies were really waist high skips about five feet long and eighteen inches deep. They were numbered, and Uncle John had to prepare daily sheets onto which

239

these figures had to be entered and, underlined in red ink, the spaces where we entered and recorded the number of items in the selected trolley. A similar system was used for counting the letters, involving specially designed boxes, and Dennis used the same system on his night shift.

When the sorting was completed, Uncle John collected the sheets, averaged the amount of mail we had sorted and sent the results to Buddleshaw.

It was a simple method, and wide open to abuse. We all knew roughly how many items were contained in a skip, and it was easy to add a few more to the total and enter the figure onto the all important sheet. We seldom actually bothered to count the items at all. We estimated: Uncle John averaged. It was also easy to add in mythical skips to inflate the total, and it was the same story with the letters. Everyone was happy. Uncle John was pleased with the amount of mail sorted, Atkinson was impressed by the industry of the Bramton office, Royal Mail was delighted with its productivity and, naturally, we were pleased when we received our bonus.

Of course, we had to be careful when we received official visits. We had, at least, to go through the motions of counting before inflating and entering the figures, and it was surprising how much they varied from the true count, but most of the visiting Royal Mail dignitaries had not a clue what we were doing anyway. Nor had poor Uncle John. He was far too preoccupied with his troubles with Atkinson to realise what was going on, though on one particular occasion we were, completely by chance, able to convince him of the accuracy of our counting.

In a fit of concience I decided to count one of the trollies, having slightly overdone the entering of non existent ones onto Uncle John's sheet. It so happened the trolley my troubled concience dictated I count was filled with what we referred to as biscuits: small tightly packed cellophane wrapped biscuit shaped advertising leaflets measuring about four inches by three. Slightly daunted, I applied myself to the task without enthusiasm and entered the total on the sheet. It was an incredible number, far above any of the usual over estimates we entered. By chance that morning, Uncle John glanced at the sheet after the trolley was sorted. Refusing to believe what he read he ordered a recount, watching while I reluctantly carried it out. To his amazement and my relief the recount produced the same astonishing figure. I was completely vindicated. Never again did he query the counting.

Later on, out of curiosity, I did count the contents of a less extremely loaded trolley to compare them with our usual estimates. Our estimates were consistently far higher than the actual contents, and our happy system continued, secure in the knowledge that Uncle John was unlikely to challenge the figures again.

All this cutting and tipping of bags made a tremendous mess. Each bag was secured, with either string or plastic ties, and carried a label indicating its origin and destination. These were snipped off with the special curved scissors and fell to the floor where they joined the other detritus of the morning's work. Snapped rubber bands, small slips of paper, which identified the bundles of letters, torn packaging and sometimes pieces of polystyrene that had somehow escaped from the inadequately wrapped parcels, the contents of which they were supposed to protect.

It had been Jack's job to sweep all this rubbish away after the office was clear, but since his departure the standard of cleaning had declined. Although Gavin and Lester, always on the lookout for overtime, were supposed to dispose of the worst of this mess the whole office was never cleaned as well as it had been by Jack who had all day to accomplish the task.

With surprising speed the cleaner's job was advertised and interviews arranged. There was no shortage of applicants, despite the position only being part time. Unemployment was on the increase and there were mortgages to be paid; some of the applicants came from the developments in Bramton, well educated and well qualified people who were the victims of ruthless job cutting as the economic climate worsened; others were no-hopers forced into having an interview by their dole office, with thinly veiled threats of withdrawal of benefits if they failed to do so.

The appointment of a part time cleaner was not deemed of sufficient importance to merit an interview at Buddleshaw, and they were conducted at Bramton, in the curiously named Welfare Suite, by Uncle John and Murdoch. After much deliberation and, presumably, argument they chose an unemployed, forty year old man called Billy Shiner.

Maybe it was his surname which clinched his appointment, but it was probably more of a case of Murdoch browbeating Uncle John into agreement in order to impose a particularly nasty, unnecessary and pungent hardship on the office. It was not as if Murdoch would have pressed for the inappropriately named Billy Shiner's appointment from a malicious sense of humour - he was devoid of that human virtue - rather he swayed Uncle John to agree out of a sense of pure malice.

It was difficult to understand the workings of Murdoch's mind, but it was perfectly clear when Billy Shiner started work the following Monday that Uncle John, a man of integrity, but no match for Murdoch's wiles, would never have appointed him had he alone conducted the interview.

Billy Shiner reported for work at half past five in the morning and made an immediate impression. He stank. He did not smell of mere body odour. That was a sweet perfume compared to the horrible stink he carried through the Sorting Office as he made his way to the stairs leading to the kitchen. His particular smell could only be described as a mixture of rotting vegetables blended with decomposing meat, which had been left in the sun for days, spiced with an overpowering lavatorial mixture of stale urine and dung, topped by such a smell of dirty feet that one could only conclude they were in a terminal state of green, putrid decay. This appalling aroma surrounded him like a cloud of invisible, noxious gas, which seeping insidiously crept unseen into every corner of the office where it lingered, contaminating and polluting, for hours.

The stench of Billy Shiner made several of us, including myself, feel physically sick. It was not as if he suffered from a medical condition: he did not. He was, quite simply, the most unhygienic, unwashed human being I had ever encountered. He had been unemployed for years, which in view of his attitude to personal hygiene was hardly surprising. He was short, about five feet five inches, fat, with a pronounced squint; and came from one of the poorer parts of the estates, living in an overcrowded council house with his elderly parents, three brothers and a sister. It was almost impossible to imagine the conditions within that house. He was also illiterate.

Dave, who knew most of what went on in the estates, reckoned he was known as the dirtiest man in Bramton living in the dirtiest house on the estates. It was a wonder health and safety had not closed it down. He was, unsurprisingly, banned from every pub in town on account of his personal habits rather than his behaviour, which was just as well for the addition of stale beer oozing from his pores was too much to contemplate. It was entirely typical of Royal Mail to employ the filthiest man in the area as their office cleaner. I could only think he had partaken of his biennial bath before his interview and the demoralised Uncle John's better judgement had been squashed by Murdoch's preference for a man from Bramton whose social standing was inferior to his own, and Billy Shiner fitted that requirement admirably.

In a whimsical moment it occured to me his employment might have resulted from a brainwave from Uncle John, a masterstroke of genius for reducing the overtime, for with that dreadful smell we sorted faster than ever before, fleeing the office for the freedom of fresh, clear, reviving air.

Inevitably, Billy Shiner acquire the sobriquet 'Stinking Billy', which clung to him as his distinctive smell clung to our memories and our clothing long after we had left the office.

There were complaints, bitter complaints. The onset of the warm summer months only served to emphasise the problem. Once, when returning with my trolley from my town round on a hot summer's day, I could actually smell Stinking Billy's by now familiar odour before I reached the corner to enter the yard and there, at the bottom of the yard, was Stinking Billy pouring sweat, sweeping the parking area, about fifty yards distant.

"I'll speak to him," said Uncle John with a sigh. There was a lot of sighing in this office. "But it's difficult, because it's such a personal and sensitive issue. We will have to give him a chance. After all he has only been here a short time. He might improve. We shall have to give him the benefit of the doubt."

There was no doubt in my mind and I forcibly said so.

"You are not the only one to complain," Uncle John said. "Just be patient and I will speak to him." He suddenly leant forward. "What did you call him?"

"Stinking Billy."

"You will have to be careful. If he gets to hear of it he might just sue Royal Mail for discrimination."

"Then let him. If he does it will result in the quickest judgement in history. No sensible person could endure that smell for more than five minutes in the confines of a court. At least we can open the doors to disperse the worst of Stinking Billy's excesses."

Uncle John did have a word with him. He must have found it difficult for he was a sensitive man. And for a short time the smell abated slightly, returning to full power after a few days. It was an endless exercise: complaining to Uncle John, experiencing an improvement before Stinking Billy, tiring of the task of unaccustomed attempts at hygiene, reverted to his normal disgusting self.

Then we complained again …

We complained to Sydney, as union representative, but he responded with such a spiel of nonsensical rhetoric, which concluded with the words, "Not a union what's 'is name," that we realised there was no salvation from that corner. There was little anyone could do, other than grimly wait for the winter months, hoping the colder weather might mitigate the unwelcome assault on our olfactory senses.

One of Stinking Billy's tasks was to make the morning tea and coffee for us, but I could not bring myself to drink a cup of tea made by him, nor could I bring myself to enter his kitchen to make one for myself, for he had so impregnated the room with his smell that it had assumed a permanence that I doubted any cleaning product devised by mankind would ever shift.

There was little humour to be found from having a cleaner of the calibre of Stinking Billy working at Bramton. Quite apart from his physical attributes his cleaning left much to be desired. The basins in the gents soon took on an overall brownish tinge and Lester started spraying disinfectant and air freshener around. The same was true of his other cleaning duties; the Sorting Office was barely swept, the corridor and stairs were left filthy; and the kitchen itself, when I finally plucked up the courage to enter it one day, was disgusting.

Uncle John could only utter meaningless, politically correct phrases he barely comprehended, like 'social deprivation' and 'community concience', so it seemed we were stuck with Stinking Billy and his total lack of understanding of the basic principals of human hygiene for evermore.

There was a crisis in the middle of summer - the usual crisis, which was so common at Bramton - lack of manpower. Quite simply, holidays had overstretched our already thin resources, and there were not enough people to cover all the rounds. Uncle John had arranged for two Buddleshaw postmen to fill the gaps and they arrived at five o'clock to start work on sorting the easy town rounds, which were second nature to an experienced postman. With eager anticipation we awaited the arrival of Stinking Billy, half an hour later, with bated and, later, held breath.

He made his grand entrance on cue - he was never late unfortunately - walking past the two borrowed postmen with the mincing walk that was as individual to him as his smell. We watched, and a second later they both spontaneously rose to their feet as the impact of Stinking Billy's presence assaulted their nostrils.

"What is that dreadful smell?" they asked in unison. We laughed united, for once, in the hardship of what we had to endure.

The last word came from Murdoch. Almost. Complaining to him one day about Stinking Billy, and knowing he would not hear a word against anyone coming from Bramton, his reply was entirely predictable.

"I 'ave no problem with him," he said, his watery pale blue eyes fixing mine for a brief moment. "I doesn't know why you all keeps on whingeing."

"Then you must be nasally moribund," I told him and left the office.

Thirty

The largest house in the exclusive village of Ashley was inhabited by the Walker family, Elizabeth and James Walker. It was a beautiful Georgian mansion, set in about seven acres of landscaped gardens and paddocks, which were tended by two full time and one part time gardeners. The grounds were perfection and their creation, evolvement and maintenance were the lifetime's work of Elizabeth. James Walker was known locally as being 'something in the city', though exactly what was unclear, but his job required him to make many flights on Concorde to New York each year.

The house was vast, with a large number of bedrooms and an elaborate orangery built onto the south side. It was approached by a long, sweeping drive, which wandered its way through parkland planted with specimen trees, crossed the river on an ornate bridge before terminating in front of the grand entrance steps leading to the front door.

The Walker children - a boy and a girl - were often home at the weekends, bringing some of their many friends to fill the empty bedrooms. In the winter there were several formal balls and once a year it was the venue for the hunt ball.

Elizabeth and James Walker were of a similar age to me, and I admired James's energy, working in such a high profile job and playing the perfect host to large house parties most weekends.

Elizabeth was very much a lady of the country, riding to hounds, and adoring her dogs - the inevitable Labradors. But above everything she prized her gardens, which she opened to the public on several weekends during the year. When he had the time James hunted, too, and was a keen and, by all accounts, excellent shot, barely missing a pheasant shoot throughout the season.

They were entirely typical, country gentry. Every village in the area had a family like the Walkers, living in large houses, devoted to country sports, their dogs and often their drink. The Walker residence was grander than most. The house had belonged to Elizabeth's family who had lived in it for generations.

In my youth I had known Elizabeth slightly and had even attended the odd hunt ball, which then had been held under the auspices of her parents. She had been quite a pretty girl - if a little on the well built side - and now, nearly thirty years later, had matured into a statuesque, somewhat formidable woman. I had never met her husband, James, before. It is difficult to forget the friends and acquaintances of one's youth. However slight the acquaintance may have been and the years may have changed people, decades later there is usually a glimmer of recognition of lost looks.

Elizabeth Walker was one of those who set a lot of store by her mail; she was one of a dying breed that kept in touch with her friends by writing and receiving letters. As soon as she heard the approaching Post Office van disturbing the neat lines of the freshly raked gravel in front of the house she opened the front door, descending the stone steps to collect her usually considerable bundle.

On the very first morning I delivered her letters I recognised her. Her married name had confused me: I had assumed the Georgian mansion had been sold and she had moved elsewhere. I was also perfectly certain she had recognised me, but there was something indefinable in the look she gave me, which discouraged me from re-introducing myself. In any case, I had not known her that well and if our particular positions in life were now that of mistress of the house and tradesman that was perfectly all right with me, and that was the way our relationship stood.

She was always polite and civil to me, as befitted a woman of her standing, and when she had cause for complaint - usually when the mail was late - she was never rude or condescending as those of lesser breeding with comparable wealth often were. She treated me, I imagined, in exactly the same way she treated her gardeners, with fairness and courtesy she might well not afford to those she considered her social equals. And all the time she knew who I was, remembered I had attended hunt balls at her house and that I was aware she had recognised me. But neither of us said a word about the past.

Her husband James was a much more outgoing character, a heavily built man, almost a caricature of the country gentleman. I liked him. We often had a chat when he collected the mail, usually on a Saturday, and there was never the feeling that one must not cross the invisible boundary his wife had placed before her.

I asked Mary about the Walkers. She thought for a moment, absent mindedly wiping her flour encrusted hands on her apron, causing a cascade to fall to the kitchen floor like a light dusting of snow.

"They're nice, good, Godfearing people, without malice. Their children are well brought up and well mannered. James is a churchwarden and is well liked locally, though when they married some thought it odd he came to live in her family home. They are a typical, country, gentry family, unpretentious and always doing their bit for the community."

I told Mary I had known Elizabeth before and wondered why she had not acknowledged it.

"Well," she said practically, "perhaps she has forgotten you and, in any case, why didn't you mention it to her? She won't eat you."

But I knew I never could, as surely as I knew she had recognised me. There was something in that first warning look, which made me hold my counsel.

I had a friend from the past - a friend rather than an acquaintance – called Adrian, with whom I had lost touch for more than twenty years.

We had moved in the same social circles, drunk in the same pubs and attended the same parties. But, as happens, he had moved away, and I had moved overseas for a few years and contact had been lost. Then quite unexpectedly he phoned me one day.

He had met a mutual friend who had told him I was still in the area. We caught up on twenty years of almost forgotten news. He had married, had children, divorced and re-married. He worked in the wine trade, but when his parents had died he had transferred back to the area he knew so well and lived in the old family house, with his new wife, Sally. He had found that many of his friends from the old days had moved away, died or vanished without trace and he was endeavouring to re-establish contact with the few who still remained.

In my turn, I brought him up to date with my news, told him of my wife and children and told him what I now did to meet the always increasing bills. He laughed, saying at least it must be an interesting job. I did not comment on that.

It transpired the purpose of his phone call was to invite my wife and me to dinner, an invitation which I readily accepted.

After twenty years I was pleased I remembered the way to his house, never easy to find in a network of lanes, which followed no logical direction, doubling back on themselves with a diabolical ingenuity designed to confuse the casual interloper. His house was exactly as I remembered it, unchanged, any temptation to extend and destroy resisted.

My friend was instantly recognisable despite the ravages of twenty years in the wine trade, and we introduced our wives. Passing through to the sitting room for drinks, I glanced at the dining room. The table was laid for six. Wondering who else he might have discovered from the past I enquired who the other guests would be.

"The Walkers, Elizabeth and James. She used to be Elizabeth Jackson before she married James. They still live in her parents' old house in Ashley, that huge house. Surely you remember her?"

For a moment I was stunned, then I laughed. "I remember her well, and now I am her postman." I went on to tell Adrian and Sally the story and they shared the funny side of it.

"If she cannot accept someone she once knew is now her postman," Sally said, "then let's play along with it and not say a word."

So it was agreed.

Elizabeth and James arrived twenty minutes later, apologising for their lateness. They had become lost.

"Surely you remember each other?" Adrian asked mischievously. Elizabeth never broke her stride.

"I thought your face looked familiar as soon as I came in," she said sweetly, "and now I know your name, of course I remember you. You used to come to our hunt balls in the old days and most of the parties we all went to."

We made small talk until dinner was ready. I was seated next to Elizabeth, my wife next to James. She was charming company and we chatted about our many mutual friends, her prized garden and grounds, her horses and dogs. Anything except the Post Office. I could guarantee with a perfect certainty she would never ask me what I did for a living, so I told her about my farming days, my travels and our tiny garden, not saying a word about the Post Office either.

My wife found James easy to talk to and, relaxing, encouraged him to draw on his formidable fund of anecdotes. At the conclusion of the meal Adrian, always a great traditionalist, ushered the ladies into the sitting room whilst he, James and I indulged in our port at the dinner table, discussing politics, the coming recession and the state of farming.

Much later, the Walkers took their leave and after a few more drinks we, too, departed. It had been a delightful evening and as we finally left I told our hostess so with perfect sincerity.

"Well, at least Elizabeth is in no doubt now who you are," she said.

But I had my doubts. Monday morning might reveal that.

I drove my Royal Mail van up their drive, bringing it to a halt on the immaculately raked gravel as usual that Monday morning, but with some trepidation, unsure how to respond to Elizabeth after the dinner party, unsure whether to mention it first or leave that to her. I decided to take the latter option, leaving the initiative to her, remembering that barely perceived warning look.

I need not have worried. Everything was exactly as before. She courteously bade me good morning, took the bundle of letters I gave her, flicking through them as she walked back to the stone steps leading to her front door, all interest in the postman lost after he had discharged the duty for which he was paid.

I was not surprised, but I was puzzled. In a modern world it was a little extreme to separate a tradesman from the customers he served, whatever their status, but it appeared in Elizabeth's mind everyone had their place and should be aware of it.

I did wonder, perhaps, if Elizabeth had not recognised me when I was wearing Royal Mail uniform. It had been known that when wearing ordinary clothes in unfamiliar surroundings postmen had gone unrecognised by their customers, but only briefly. So I discounted that theory.

It was James who gave the game away. When I met him on Saturdays delivering their mail he started calling me by my Christian name, something he could not possibly have known before. Elizabeth would never have divulged it.

Sometimes I wondered whether Elizabeth and James dined out on the story of the dinner party they had attended where the only other guests had been their postman and his wife.

But I rather doubted it.

Thirty One

I enjoyed my town round, the only true 'walk' in the office. Pushing a Royal Mail trolley around the streets of Bramton required little effort and gave plenty of opportunity for gentle reflection. It was also a welcome break from the often frenzied driving we did on the other two rounds when time was always the greatest enemy. There was a particular style of driving adopted when in charge of a Post Office van, an aggressive style, dashing up to a house, halting abruptly, delivering, roaring off again and showing little regard for other road users. It had to be so, for other people were often reluctant to let a Post Office van into a traffic queue, or to pull off a country lane to let one by, so a different driving technique had to be developed. A special irritant was the enormous, four wheel drive vehicles, never driven off road in their lives, and usually employed as outrageously thirsty conveyances for school runs. They were mostly driven by women who had no idea how to drive them properly, and meeting one of these on a country road it was, ironically, the Ford Escort standard Post Office van, which was forced to make a detour off the road.

My wife often complained that I "drove like a postman" when I drove our car. It took a surprisingly long time to re-adjust to normal driving after hurtling around in a red van. And there was a further hazard: one could get away with murder in a Post Office van, but not in a car. Other drivers respected and probably feared the former, but once in the latter one became just another driver.

I came across Neville one day on my town round. He had parked his Pashley against a lamp post and was running from house to house pushing what appeared to be leaflets through the letterboxes. Wondering what he was doing on my round, I watched him for a while. He really was the most extraordinary sight, half running, his head held low like a charging bull, his arms pumping as he belted between the houses and his breath coming in short panting gasps. After a while he saw me.

"What are you looking at?" he asked brusquely.

"I was looking at you, thinking it odd you should be delivering something on my round. What are those things?" I asked, walking over to him and making as if to take whatever it was he was holding in his hand. He thrust his hand behind his back like a naughty child.

"Never you mind. It's none of your business anyway."

"I think it is," I said officially. "It is, after all, my round and you are trespassing on it."

"I can deliver what I like, when I like," he said defiantly. One thing I had learnt about Neville was that he had a limited sense of humour. He was far too intense for that, and he could never tell when he was having his leg pulled. I persisted.

"Not in Post Office time. Uncle John wouldn't think much of you doing that and claiming overtime on top. What are those things?"

He reluctantly brought his hand round to his front, proffering a fistful of yellow leaflets.

"They're Liberal party leaflets if you must know, and I'm delivering them in my own time."

I laughed. "I am sure you are, Neville, but you're wasting your time round here. They're all staunch Conservatives."

He leant towards me, his eyes intense. "But that's just it, don't you see? That's exactly why I am delivering them, because …"

I was in no mood to listen to one of Neville's political discourses. Cutting him off abruptly, I continued on my way leaving him to his leaflets.

I had once asked Neville what he intended to do if he obtained his degree.

"When I get it," he had corrected me, "I am going to become a schoolteacher."

I was aghast. To my mind there was nobody more temperamentally unsuited to teaching unruly children. Remembering his performance in the cage at Christmas and his futile attempts to handle postmen, some of whom were little more than overgrown schoolboys, I knew for certain the real article would make mincemeat of him.

Bishop Harry Vaughan was a charming man who lived on the round. He was in his seventies, retired from the church in as much as anyone can retire from Holy Orders, still taking the odd services when the local incumbents were unwell or on their holidays. He was a tall, thin man, with a full head of grey hair and a ready laugh. I liked the old Bishop and his sense of humour. His wife was nice, too, a large jolly woman. Both the Bishop and his wife were addicted to their aviary, which they had built in their small garden and contained many rare and exotic species. They were two completely contented people, living in a modest home, devoted to their birds and each other.

It was the Bishop I came to know the better, for, in his retirement, he was still active with the probation service. I never discovered in exactly what capacity, but whatever it was it involved a large amount of mail, all of which arrived by recorded delivery. Whenever I knocked on his door I always found him in some disarray. He was either half way through his morning shave, answering my knocking covered with lather, or in the middle of his breakfast when he would absent mindedly come to the door with a half-eaten piece of toast in his hand, dripping drops of Marmalade onto his wife's spotless carpet. At other times, receiving no reply, I would have to make my way down to his aviary where he was tending his birds. When I gave him his mail and the little book to sign, his comment was always the same, "Ah, my boys again," after which he would laugh and raise his eyes heavenwards.

I never asked him about 'his boys'. It was none of my business. But it struck me that no probationer could wish to have a better man than Bishop Harry to oversee their interests.

Some years later Royal Mail decided to 'absorb' - an euphemism for cost cutting - my town round with several others. I wondered, sadly, if I would see the charming old Bishop again.

At the same time the round was absorbed Neville passed his Open University course, as he had so confidently predicted, immediately resigning from the Post Office to pursue his new career as a teacher. I was sure I would see Neville again, and I told him so. But he was over confident, even elated if he understood that emotion, so much so he gave me his old Post Office jacket. Mine had fallen to pieces.

As it happened, I saw both the Bishop and Neville again, Neville somewhat sooner than the Bishop.

Neville re-applied for his old job at Bramton ten months after leaving. He was accepted and returned, all the elation and confidence with which he had left dissipated. He had become dispirited and morose and had developed a significant twitch in his left eye. He refused to talk to anyone about his abortive teaching career. He had lost all his seniority at the Post Office, and when he angrily demanded the return of his coat, I refused.

It was years before I saw the Bishop again. I attended a funeral in our local church of a much loved village character, and the old boy took the service. He must have been well into his eighties, but he conducted a beautiful service, never faltering or hesitating. He looked exactly the same as I remembered him; extreme old age had not altered him at all.

At the end of the service he stood by the church door in all his regalia, shaking hands and murmuring condolences where it was appropriate. When my turn came, he shook my hand firmly, looking me in the eye. "I know you," he said, "but I cannot quite place you. Wait a minute … you weren't one of my boys were you?"

I assured him I was not nor ever had been one of his boys, reminding him I had once been his postman. His eyes twinkled with amusement and he started laughing. "Of course, of course. I remember you now. I never forget a face."

256

There was a small cul-de-sac on that town round, which contained two houses both with quite large gardens. The first house, at the top, boasted a small orchard and was occupied by a man of about fifty called Mr. Barnes. He was a rather florid man with the slightly dissipated look of a bon vivant, which, indeed, he proved to be. He made frequent wine raids on France, returning with his car laden to the limits of its suspension with fine wine. He was a generous man and often presented me with some of his booty in the form of a bottle or two of the cheaper plonk, with the advice to drink it quickly. That was never a problem.

He must have been extraordinarily wealthy, for, as far as I could ascertain, he did not work and he lived in his rather grand house with his extremely attractive girl friend who was about twenty years younger than him. He was one of those people who assumed everyone had an intimate knowledge of his family. He would discuss his mother's ailments quite frankly with me and often talked about Janice and Colin, their financial affairs and their love lives. I had not the faintest idea who Janice and Colin were, and did not like to ask, until a chance remark revealed they were his sister and brother.

I liked Mr. Barnes - call me Bob - and I liked his young girl friend even more, but I knew my position.

The house at the end of the cul-de-sac was inhabited by an elderly retired major and his wife. The house exuded an air of genteel shabbiness, the garden was neglected and they drove an ancient Volvo, which had evidently like them seen better times. Bramton and the surrounding area was home to many retired service-people, but most were in a better state of financial health than this major and his wife.

Quite what had gone awry I never established, but the contrast between the top house and the bottom house in that cul-de-sac was stark. Bob was aware of this and went out of his way to help with small plumbing and electrical problems such as changing washers and mending fuses, and supplying them with bottles of wine.

When I met them I found them correctly polite and formal to the point of self parody; they lived in a world that had passed them by, but without the money to sustain the old way of life they had so cherished. Knocking on their door to deliver a parcel I always expected a maid to open it - as doubtless would have happened in the past - but it was usually opened by the Major's wife, with an apologetic look. In a strange way, I knew how she felt.

The little I was able to see of the interior of the house complimented the genteel shabbiness of the exterior: dusty relics collected from long years serving overseas, tribal shields on the walls and stone Buddhas on the floor in the hallway, which had a leather covered sofa standing next to an ornate but badly faded umbrella stand.

The Major who was tall and thin to the point of emaciation, dressed himself in old threadbare clothes, moth eaten sweaters or cardigans and ancient trousers held in place by a thick leather belt. His shoes were dulled and worn; he was the complete antithesis of Colonel Mackinnon. Whatever the season he wore a thick woollen scarf knotted around his neck, even in the middle of summer, when his only concession to the heat was to drape it around his shoulders. His wife made much more effort with her appearance. She was always correctly made up, neither over nor under done, and she wore the clothes that she must have kept from their service days, carefully preserved over the years, but hopelessly out of fashion.

In their way, they were perfectly happy, reminiscing to themselves about the better days of the past, discreetly appalled at the way the modern world was progressing. The way forward, as Royal Mail would have it.

I liked the old couple, slowly fading away together as their previous way of life had faded before them.

An exasperated Bob greeted me one morning at his front door. "Sometimes I just do not believe those two down there," he said, indicating the bottom end of the cul-de-sac. "I took them down a bucket of apples yesterday afternoon. And do you know what she said to me? She said, 'I would love them, but I have no one to peel them for me.' No one to peel them for me. Can you believe it? Sometimes you can't help people even if you try."

Bill and Ben

Thirty Two

I had first met Bill and Ben when I had fallen behind with my fencing schedule in the first year we had our farm. The problem was the clearing of the hedges, which had encroached considerably into the pasture. I could not get it done quickly enough and finish the fencing before the start of the autumn sheep fairs, and we could start stocking the farm. Matthew solved the problem for me. "You need Bill and Ben to help you."

I must have looked puzzled, for he continued hastily. "They're not their real names. They're really called Les and Frank Jackson. They're a pair of bachelor brothers who have lived in the area all their lives doing odd jobs, and they've been known as Bill and Ben for as long as I can remember."

They were not on the telephone and Matthew gave me directions to their house. I went to see them that evening.

They lived in a ramshackle, 'colonial', corrugated iron bungalow, complete with a dilapidated verandah. The garden was a jungle and here and there the remnants of once proudly tended herbaceous flowers bravely thrust their heads through the undergrowth providing unexpected splashes of colour. The bungalow had once been painted green and flakes of old green paint were hanging off the iron, some twirling in the breeze on the end of broken spider webs. Some of the windows were blanked off with hardboard where they had been broken, and there was an all pervading smell of paraffin, for in addition to the lack of a telephone there was no electricity. A faded sign by the door proclaimed the name of the property as The Nest.

I knocked on the shabby door and it was immediately flung open. Evidently my progress up the garden path had been noted. I was greeted by a small man of about sixty dressed in a collarless shirt

261

fastened at the neck by a stud, worn and well patched trousers, old slippers and wearing a cap. Peering over his shoulder, similarly clad and of similar stature was a younger version; he was about fifty five. They both had half smoked, unlit, soggy, roll-up cigarettes hanging from the corner of their mouths. They were Bill and Ben and somehow I could not think of more appropriate names for them.

The brother who had opened the door was, in fact, Les and he was the boss. He was also the spokesman, which was unfortunate as he had a bad stutter. Frank had developed the habit over the years of completing his sentences for him, and carrying on a conversation with Bill and Ben was no easy matter. Les spluttering incoherently and Frank, knowing exactly what he was trying to say, finishing off for him. Not having grasped the first part, I had to try and guess the beginning from Frank's ending.

With some difficulty, I understood they would be happy to help me and would start the next morning. They drove into the field in a Morris Minor pick-up of incredible decrepitude. They assured me it had an M.O.T. in answer to my inquiry, but I wondered for which year. Frank was the driver and, having witnessed his antics on the road, I always gave him a wide berth when I met him in the lanes. Les had never driven, which was probably as well, but he proudly told me Frank had passed his test at the eighth attempt. Frank shuffled from foot to foot, head down, looking as though he deserved his brother's praise.

"Made a big difference when 'ee passed," spluttered Les. It must have been a brave examiner who had ridden with him, and it was my guess he passed the persistent Frank to avoid the terror of riding with him again.

As Matthew had predicted, Bill and Ben's help made a big difference to my progress. They were slow, methodical workers and soon I was fencing the areas we had all cleared, leaving them to clear ahead of me. On the stroke of twelve o'clock they knocked off for lunch, which they took at the local pub, not the Gunners Castle - no locals frequented that opulent establishment - but a much more appealing and less salubrious hostelry a few miles down the road. I joined them there sometimes and they always observed the same ritual: two halves of bitter and a cheese sandwich each.

Frank usually tried his luck for a third half pint, and Les invariably refused to allow it. The only exception being when they were offered a drink, when Frank would have a pint and a thoroughly disapproving Les a further half.

The day came when their work was done and I gratefully paid them off, well up on my schedule, and I often employed them on a casual basis in future years.

I frequently met them in the pub, and when I came through the door Frank drained his half pint at a swallow, anticipating my offer of a drink. They were incorrigible, those two. There was a hedge partially obscuring vision to the right on leaving the pub car park, but this never bothered Frank; he never looked right anyway, blithely turning out left, Les sitting ramrod straight beside him. It was fortunate it was a quiet country lane, but one lunchtime he made the mistake of pulling out in front of the local policeman's panda car.

We heard the rest of the story from the policeman who was enjoying an off duty drink in the bar one evening. "Frank, as usual, hadn't looked right, and never saw me, so I decided to switch on my blue flashing light to give him a bit of a fright. Still he didn't see me. But in the end Les, in the passenger seat, looked round and saw it. I could see him tell Frank who caught me completely by surprise by performing an emergency stop. It frightened the living daylights out of me and I came to rest about half an inch off their rear bumper. Les leapt from his seat, ran round to me and came out with some story that he knew the tyres were worn and they were just on their way to the garage to have some new ones fitted, and after that they were having the M.O.T. done. By the time I had deciphered all this I was past caring, besides being thoroughly shaken, so I let them go."

Frank, apparently, had never budged from the driving seat, staring steadfastly ahead, content to let Les sort matters out.

One lunchtime Frank was on his own in the pub, drinking pints and more than a little merry. "Where's Les?" I asked him, for I had never seen them apart before.

"'Ee's in 'ospital," beamed Frank. When pressed as to the reason, he said, "I doesn't rightly know. 'Ee were bleeding or something so doc said 'ee 'ad to go in."

Frank had a ball for a few days until several lunchtimes later the phone rang. The landlady placed it on the bar in front of Frank and handed him the receiver. He took it with grave suspicion. There was total silence in the bar and we all listened, enthralled.

"'OO's THAT?" he shouted. There was a pause, and he held the receiver away from his ear. We could clearly hear Les stammering loudly at the other end of the line though we couldn't understand what he was saying.

There was another pause and Frank yelled, "RIGHT," and slammed down the receiver with a mighty crash. He turned to face his audience and shrugged helplessly.

"'Ee's coming 'ome," he said almost tearfully. "'Ee's discharged 'eeself and 'ee's coming 'ome."

The party was over, but I felt so sorry for Frank that I offered him a beer. He looked at me in amazement. "I can't 'ave no drink now. 'Ee'll be 'ome in an hour, and if I doesn't get the place cleaned up 'ee'll kill me."

They were a curious pair, Bill and Ben, surviving on their gardening, odd jobs and native wit. Frank had a habit, when speaking, of shifting his weight from one foot to the other, conveying the impression of standing on the deck of a ship in a moderate sea, with Les nodding vigourously as he spoke as if to make up for his own unfortunate inadequacies.

Les's bouts of 'bleeding' and his consequent visits to hospital became more frequent. I suspected he had cancer, but Frank seemed neither to know nor understand. Some weeks later when I saw Frank I enquired after Les. "'Ee passed on yesterday," he said, his eyes brimming with genuine tears.

For all Frank's bravado and apparant lack of compassion for Les's ill health, he was a lost man when his brother died. There was never any spare flesh on him at the best of times, and he slowly wasted away, his will to live extinguished. His clothes barely hung on him, he became gaunt and ill and despite good hearted folk cooking for him and helping with his housework he joined his brother within the year.

I never discovered who was Bill and who was Ben.

Now I was delivering mail to The Nest. It still retained its name, but little else. The original Nest had been razed and a modern monstrosity, a five bedroomed town-style house, complete with swimming pool and two double garages, occupied the site. It was, as Royal Mail managers would have pointed out, the way forward.

Thirty Three

Jack had been wrong when he had predicted that I would have to watch out for Murdoch when I joined Gavin's and Lester's section. He left me alone, indeed with the exception of Ted, he left nearly everybody alone. But he could not resist taunting the unfortunate Ted, who was quite incapable of standing up to him, with his crude mixture of sarcasm and invective. He was destroying the young man's confidence and there was little that could be done about it. Uncle John was far too preoccupied with his own problems to notice and, in the way of the Post Office, no one else cared.

The general mind-set was that if you couldn't help yourself, no one else would bother: if you could not take it that was your hard luck. Even the normally altruistic Peter adopted this attitude - perhaps he had been a postman for too long - and my own inadequate attempts to help Ted were of little use, so demoralised had he become. He was always talking about looking for another job, but somehow I knew he never would, for he had become so drawn into the cogs of the machinery of Royal Mail that he was enmeshed there for life, like a moth attracted irresistibly to a light without quite knowing why.

But if Uncle John had become distant, so had Murdoch, and in his preoccupation he could only cope with one target at a time, and that target, the easiest one in the office from his point of view, was the hapless Ted.

His fixation centred on Atkinson, the plotting to get rid of Uncle John and the near certainty in his mind that he would finally be given the office. From reading Uncle John's latest missives from Atkinson it was perfectly clear to me that he would not, and it gave me a certain malicious delight when, in the re-named tearoom where we were alone briefly, he lowered his mug to the table, raised his weak eyes to fix mine

267

and said, "There are changes on the way here. This office will be mine sooner than you might think, like it always should've been. Just you wait and see."

He suddenly rose to his feet and left, and I watched him. I wondered how he would react when Atkinson informed him once again that the managership of Bramton had eluded him. I could guess. He would sit in his cage, brooding and withdrawn, plotting his revenge.

Uncle John's preoccupation was based on a more realistic premise, which was also centred on Atkinson. There were now references to 'The advisability of taking early retirement,' coupled to a revealing passage that read, 'In my opinion you should not have been appointed manager of Bramton. You display no managerial skills whatsoever and it is clear the appointment was a mistake. Regarding the reduction in the overtime figures you mentioned at our meeting last week, while I agree there has been a certain drop in the hours, nevertheless it falls far short of the figures I mentioned I would consider acceptable. There is more work to be carried out in this direction and I feel you are not the man to achieve the figures I require.' In his own cliché ridden jargon, he had moved the goalposts.

It was perhaps unfortunate that about then Lester and I had split a week on the late shift. It was at the time of the local elections, and we were allowed a certain amount of overtime for delivering political leaflets, which had been carried over from the previous week. In addition, Lester had discovered the Buddleshaw office had been granted two hours extra overtime in lieu of their bonus falling short of expectation and, deciding this would also apply to Bramton, we claimed it as well, keeping the information to ourselves.

Lester had as much sympathy for Uncle John as I had, and it would not help him if the whole office claimed it. This brought us to an amount of overtime which allowed us to claim an extra extended meal break of three quarters of an hour, and with the overtime we had already worked during the week, brought the figures to a point where we could claim yet another extended meal break. This was all within agreed Royal Mail working practices, but when we added the figures up we found it supposed we had been working until twelve fifteen in the night, which, of course, meant we could claim an extra payment for night duty allowance. (According to Royal Mail the morning did not officially start until half past five and the week did start until Monday.)

It was all a bit complicated, because the system was unclear as to how the overtime was carried over from one weekday to the next. So we spread the overtime around a little, finishing at eleven fifty five on two nights of the week.

The fact we were home by half past six on those evenings, in my case enjoying a well earned pint of homebrew, was immaterial: we had claimed what was due to us under Royal Mail regulations.

But it was all too much for Uncle John to swallow. He must have very nearly had a fit when he looked at Lester's and my overtime sheets. We were summonsed to his office to explain.

"I can't sign these," he said, fingering the sheets. "No one from this office has worked these hours before. What did people say when you delivered letters at five minutes before midnight?"

Lester patiently explained we were not delivering letters that time and how we had arrived at the figures, pointing out it was all within accepted agreements between the union and Royal Mail. He took Uncle John through our calculations step by step, and Uncle John could not disagree.

"Were you delivering at that time?" he asked.

"No," we said. "It was the various allowances which made the hours that long."

It would have been tactless to have mentioned we were home at half past six and tucked up in bed with our wives at least an hour before we were supposed to have finished work.

"But if you weren't delivering letters, how could you claim all this overtime?" Uncle John asked.

Once again we patiently explained the reasoning. "I understand all that," he said, "but what I cannot understand is how you can claim these hours when you were not actually delivering letters."

The argument continued for an age, always returning to Uncle John's stubborn belief that if we were not delivering letters we could not claim the overtime. I even pointed out, in a mild form of blackmail, we had not told the rest of the office about the two extra hours awarded to Buddleshaw in lieu of their bonus. It was the weakest part of the argument: Buddleshaw's bonus was quite separate from our own, but the horrible spectre of the whole office claiming the two hours was enough.

"I am not happy about this," he said as he reluctantly signed them, "and I still can't understand how you can claim overtime when you were not delivering letters."

Uncle John unwittingly sealed his own fate when he took on Denise as our first postwoman. We were having one of our usual staffing crises when Denise Shaw quite literally walked in from the street and inquired whether there was a vacancy, rather in the same way I had started work at Bramton. Uncle John took her on immediately and she started work the following day.

Uncle John was evidently worried about having a woman working in what had been, until then, an all male office, and he took the unusual step of introducing her to us formally. Adding, as we now had a woman in our midst, we must accord her the respect she deserved and, at all times, remember the courtesies that should be shown to her as the only representative of the gentler sex at Bramton.

What he was trying to say, but could not quite bring himself to put into words in front of her, was that he did not want any swearing in her hearing nor any lewd comments. He need not have worried. Denise Shaw was as foul mouthed as the worst postman Royal Mail could boast, and as far as sexual innuendo was concerned she was the equal of anyone. Denise Shaw was the product of modern ideas, modern schooling and modern attitudes. She was a short, chubby girl and she was only eighteen. It was her surname which bothered me. I had heard it somewhere before and I could not quite remember where or in what context.

Uncle John put her with Dave on the Topleys. Dave was welcome; she had only recently passed her driving test. It was not, perhaps, the best round to start her on and Dave, wisely, decided to do the driving. She was a fast and wildly inaccurate sorter and the same applied to her driving. In her first week she was involved in an accident with the school bus, and the week after she collided with a tractor. Old Colonel Mackinnon must have loved her, ringing his postmaster daily to complain. Uncle John promptly gave her a town round where he mistakenly thought she could inflict no further damage, keeping her on it for two months continuously.

Denise was not liked in the office. Her language offended the most hard bitten of postmen - it was not what anyone expected from a girl as young as Denise - and her general attitude was one of could not care less. She was aggressively rude to Uncle John and she was a fine actress, once bursting into floods of tears when he mildly rebuked her for some misdemeanour. He had not a clue how to handle her, taking the easy way out by letting her get away with anything she chose. The tears had worked their trick.

We were all wary of her, avoiding her wherever possible, knowing she was trouble, hoping she would leave. She was always first back from her town round, taking her second delivery out in her car so she could finish and go straight home, a practise Royal Mail condoned.

Belatedly, I made the connection I had been seeking with the name Shaw. It had cropped up some time ago when Dave had shown me some of Uncle John's correspondence and I remembered some reference to a Ray Shaw, a higher grade postman at an office outside the area. It was a long shot, but I asked Dave if he knew of any relationship.

"Why don't you ask your friend at Buddleshaw?" he asked sarcastically: "he seems to know most things that go on in the Post Office."

I had to admit, for once, my source had failed me.

"I'll see what I can find out," he said, pleased to be ahead of me at last.

Some days later he came back to me.

"I've found out about Denise and Ray Shaw," he said triumphantly. "They are brother and sister."

Sydney, overhearing, walked up to us.

"I knew that," he said. "Ray's a postman at Buddleshaw and lives local. I could 'ave told you that."

"Sod off, Sydney," Dave said. "He don't work at Buddleshaw and he don't live local. Sod off and mind your own business."

Sydney walked away, muttering to himself. Lowering his voice, Dave continued, "He works directly under Atkinson who thinks a lot of him, but the family's crap, all wrong 'uns. There's bad blood there, and Ray's the best of a bad bunch. That's all I could find out. What made you think they might be related?"

"My source at Buddleshaw," I lied. "He thought there might be a connection, but couldn't be sure."

There were vague whisperings on the Post Office grapevine about Denise. We heard that Buddleshaw had come across large amounts of mail over the weekends that all came from Denise's round, which were re-sorted and returned to Bramton on the Monday for delivery. The inference was obvious. She was dumping her mail in the boxes she was supposed to empty on Saturday mornings so she could go home early. The Saturday late man, also in a hurry to return home, emptied these boxes without looking at the mail and drove it to Buddleshaw. Dennis confirmed this.

"They keep bringing this mail to me on my night shift," he said, "saying there's a lot for Bramton there, all for the same round. I can't be certain but there does seem to be a lot for her on Sunday nights."

There were more sinister whisperings, mutterings about missing mail, important mail, and visits from irate customers to Uncle John demanding to know what was going on; all customers from Denise's round. Matters came to a head when a customer demanded to know what had become of his holiday tickets, which had failed to arrive, and the duplicate set that had been sent out and had yet to be delivered.

Uncle John could prevaricate no longer. He called Denise to his office and, behind closed doors, demanded an explanation. Tears could not save her now, for Uncle John realised he was in as much trouble as she. He boldly, but reluctantly suspended her from work and called in the investigation branch of Royal Mail. In the event their work was done for them by Denise's landlady; she lived in rented accommodation some five miles from Bramton. The landlady had discovered some black bin liners, which appeared to be full of mail in an alleyway behind Denise's ground floor flat, was it important?

The investigation men retrieved the bin bags and returned them to Bramton. Spread around the sorting benches the amount of mail was impressive. No wonder Denise had returned to the office so early, she could hardly have delivered any of her mail, secreting it in her car either before she went out on her delivery or, more likely, on her return when there were few people around. Her second delivery simply had not been delivered at all, but taken straight home. There was even mail from the Topleys there, and I shuddered when I saw a letter addressed to Colonel Mackinnon in the pile. The overwhelming amount of mail was, of course, junk, but interspersed with that were bank statements, duplicate bank statements, cheque books, duplicate cheque books, holiday tickets, premium bond cheques and personal letters. We re-sorted the lot, on overtime, and delivered it, also on overtime.

Uncle John had the look of someone who had been condemned to the gallows. Denise, her brief career with Royal Mail at an end, was taken to court, remanded for psychiatric reports and eventually placed on probation.

We never saw her again, but the damage had been done.

Thirty Four

Sydney, one morning, was at his officious worst. We were having our annual health and safety inspection that day and Sydney, as health and safety officer, took his duties seriously once a year. He bullishly swept all the debris from the tops of our frames, dumping it on the benches below and started pushing the trollies from the office into the yard. We sorted through the debris he had dumped with interest: pieces of paper we had intended to do something about and promptly forgotten; forms we had been supposed to sign and return to Uncle John as soon as possible, but had similarly forgotten. There were various items we had picked up from our rounds of no particular importance, such as the odd bent screwdriver or broken spanners that we had found on the road, intending to take them home, but somehow never getting round to doing so. Discarding some of this rubbish and returning the remainder to the frame top, we continued our sorting.

Frantic, Sydney rushed around the frames, once again clearing the tops. "You must keep them clear," he shouted. "It's a legal requirement. That rubbish shouldn't never 'ave been put there in the first place."

"Why not?" Lester asked reasonably. "There's nowhere else to put it."

"Because it's regulations, and besides, it might fall down and 'it you on the 'ead."

"But it's only paper, mostly," Lester said.

"It's regulations," Sydney persisted stubbornly. "It must come off."

We retrieved the trollies from the yard.

Sydney was nearly beside himself. "Take them bloody things back out," he yelled. "They're blocking the alleyways. What if there's a fire?"

"What time does the inspector arrive, Sydney?" Lester asked.

"About ten thirty."

"That's not for four hours," Lester said. "We'll leave the trollies outside when we've finished with them."

Sydney gave up the unequal battle, returning to his sorting frame, sulking and refusing to talk to anyone. After we left the office he cleared the frame tops and pushed the trollies outside once more. The health and safety inspector was impressed, rewarding Sydney's efforts with a safety award and a ball pointed pen for everyone in the office bearing the curious legend, 'A safe workplace is a healthy environment'.

Sydney proudly presented us with our pens, emphasising it was entirely through his own efforts we had won the award. He was probably right, but nobody cared, and at least we were free from the health and safety inspector for another year. We returned all the junk to the tops of the frames and wheeled the trollies back into the Sorting Office.

The pens were rather nice, well balanced and refillable. I scrubbed the slogan off mine and used it for years.

The Bracewell family were relative newcomers to Gunners Castle. They were in their middle thirties, very wealthy and devoted their energies to breeding children. When they arrived there were four of them aged between two and seven, with another one very evidently on the way. They lived in an expensively converted barn on the outskirts of the village and they were not country people. Mary was able to tell me he worked for a large computer company and she took little interest in the village. I was able to tell her more: they were both exceedingly bad tempered and, to the postman, exceedingly rude.

She was a large woman with the build of a shire horse, he an insignificant man, undoubtedly dominated by his ample wife. Doubtless the number of children they had produced contributed to their ill humour, but that was not the postman's fault.

What they did perceive as the postman's fault was the manner of delivery of the numerous parcels and packages they appeared to order almost daily from the pages of the glossy catalogues, which arrived with depressing regularity.

The problem lay with the particular design of their converted barn, their hallway and, in particular, their heavy brass doorknocker. It was a problem that only affected me, probably because it was my misfortune to be on duty the week they arrived. And, in the way of human nature, the first perpetrator of a crime is always the worst offender. Gavin and Lester were unaffected.

The first parcel turned up two days after they had moved in. Lifting the heavy knocker I gave the door a couple of sharp taps, which echoed into the house. Rapidly the door was flung open and an extremely angry Mrs. Bracewell confronted me. I could clearly hear a baby crying upstairs.

"Didn't you know there was a baby asleep upstairs?" she shouted at me, "You've woken it up, banging that door so hard. There's no need for it."

I was surprised by the outburst, for I was unaware I had knocked particularly violently, but a glance into the hallway explained the echoing. The floor was stone flagged, bereft on any covering, furnished in a trendy minimalist style and the front door was a flimsy affair. The hall had acted as a sounding box. Incautiously, I pointed this out to her, adding that as I was only a postman I could scarcely be expected to know there was a baby sleeping upstairs. It was not a good start.

She snatched the parcel from my hands, slamming the door, and renewing the pitiful wails from the baby's bedroom.

The following day there was another parcel for the Bracewells and I worked out my strategy for delivering it with some thought. Tapping lightly on her door would amount to an admission that I had deliberately knocked too hard before, which had not been the case; leaving the parcel on the doorstep would be cowardly, so I decided to knock in exactly the same way, without making any concession to her.

The strategy did not work. Furious, she hurled the door back, her tribe of children wide eyed behind her, some sucking on dummies, and shouted, "I told you yesterday about banging so hard on my door. I shall complain to your manager unless you knock more gently."

Patiently, I explained it was the acoustics of her hall that was the cause of the trouble, not my knocking too loudly, suggesting, perhaps, she fitted an electric bell which could ring discreetly somewhere inside the house where it could not wake the baby. Red with anger she grabbed the parcel and slammed the flimsy door in my face without saying another word.

It was stalemate. There would be no Christmas tips from the Bracewells. She did complain to Uncle John.

I tried leaving official Royal Mail notes telling her to collect her parcels from the Sorting Office, but these gave the recipient the option of a re-delivery, and she merely rang the office requesting the parcel be delivered the next day. I resolutely refused to moderate the intensity of my knock with the heavy brass knocker, which I considered perfectly reasonable, and she, just as resolutely, refused to moderate her attitude.

I was due for a week's holiday shortly afterwards, and Dave was to take over from me. It just happened to be the week I was on Gunners Castle. On the Saturday morning before my holiday he came over to me and asked if there was anything new he should know about since he had last covered the round.

I thought for a moment. "There is one thing. You remember that new barn conversion that was under construction last time you were on Gunners Castle?" Dave nodded. "It's occupied now," I continued, "by a charming family called the Bracewells. They order lots of parcels, but, and it's really sad for they are only a young couple, they're both nearly stone deaf and you'll really have to pound the door as hard as you can to make them hear.

"Right," Dave said, "I'll remember that. Anything else?"

"Not that I can think of."

There was no harm in killing two birds with one stone. I still remembered my humiliation with the gear lever on the Topleys.

On my return I asked Dave if he had encountered any problems.

He turned on his heel and walked away without a word. There was no further trouble from the Bracewells.

Refreshed by our holiday in France and well re-stocked with tobacco and wine I resolved to tackle one of the problems, which had been bothering me for some time - Gavin's blatant cadging of cigarettes. It had started with a few, but, bolstered by the knowledge mine were nearly always duty free, it had almost reached the stage where I was supporting nearly all his smoking habit during working hours. It was not as if I was his only victim, Lester ran me a close second in the tobacco cadging stakes. I was becoming increasingly irritated by his bohemian attitude, which demanded the world owed him, amongst other things, a constant supply of free cigarettes.

The first time he asked, 'If I might cadge a cigarette?' on my return from holiday, I replied innocently, "It's not my turn."

Startled by the unexpected reply, he said, "I don't understand. What do you mean, 'It's not your turn?'"

"Lester, Ted, Peter and myself have started a rota system to supply you with cigarettes, a weekly rota," I told him. "It's Lester's turn this week, followed by Peter." Grumbling to himself he wandered across to Lester's bench and I watched while he gave him a cigarette, looking over at me. Later he asked me what I meant by a cigarette rota - I had neglected to tell him of my brilliant idea - and I explained.

"That's good," he said. "It's about time he bought his own smokes,"

The rota idea spread through the office, right down to the more itinerant postmen, most of who smoked. Desperate, Gavin even asked them for a cigarette, but their reply was always the same. "It's not my week on the rota."

In fact, it was never anyone's turn on the rota and after a while the

279

message filtered through to his nicotine starved brain that there was no such thing as a free cigarette, and he started buying some cheap, foul smelling, thin cigars, the smell of which clung to the interior of our van in the same way Stinking Billy's odour permeated the kitchen, but it was a price worth paying.

I told Mary of the cigarette rota and its success. "It hasn't stopped him taking Ben's cigarettes. I think perhaps I'll hide the packets and tell him Ben's given up smoking."

Thirty Five

We soon discovered the purpose of the combined television and video machine in the Welfare Suite. Uncle John's weekly team talks had been replaced by 'team briefs'. These were a nightmare both for us and for him, comprising stultifyingly boring videos followed by a question and answer session. Unfortunately, there was no way of avoiding them. At least with the old talks we could shut ourselves off from Uncle John's monotonous drone and carry on working.

But not any more. We had to troop up the stairs, sit in front of the television set watching politically correct garbage, which was of no interest to anybody except Sydney. And then have whatever ridiculous message the video was trying to put across rammed home by means of a flip board onto which Uncle John had carefully written all the points we had just digested, going through them one by one all over again. The question and answer session afterwards was dominated by Sydney, only Sydney, and at that point we drifted out of the door, dazed by the tedium and the insult to our intellects.

Several, wisely, went to sleep. Fatigue and sleep were seldom far away at the Post Office, but I could not manage the trick of falling asleep in front of that television and found the slow, measured tones of the narrators irritating and condescending, as if they were addressing a class of backward children.

The titles of these videos were as banal as their content. The Way Forward, Team Working, the daringly entitled Manoeuvering Wheeled Containers in Confined Spaces, and Royal Mail as a Caring Employer. The last title was greeted with hoots of derision, which would have baffled its producer, but woke some of the sleeping postmen.

Uncle John's heart was not with these team briefs. He was unused to the flipboard, frequently flipping over several sheets at once, becoming lost, and then turning back to ones he had already dealt with. No one cared. All we wanted was to go out on our rounds, get home and be free from this futile attempt at indoctrination.

I do not think Uncle John cared much either. He had lost all appetite for his job, which was scarcely surprising as Atkinson now had the lever to remove him, something of which Uncle John was well aware. Bramton was one of those little offices where the manager was either someone who had been shunted into a dead end, as in Uncle John's case, or where a young manager could learn the business, making his inevitable mistakes, which would pass almost unnoticed - unlike learning in a large office. It had been clear for a long time Atkinson wanted to install one of his bright young acolytes at Bramton, but he had been unsuccessful, lacking a real reason for ousting Uncle John from his seat. The threats about the overtime figures were a red herring, probably designed to undermine Uncle John to such an extent he would tender his resignation, for there must have been many offices in the country in a similar position. But the Denise incident had provided him with the ideal excuse to remove him.

Atkinson had not paused to consider Uncle John's feelings; that he was content and proud to be the manager at Bramton; nor had he given a second thought to the sense of shame and disgrace Uncle John would undoubtedly feel when he was finally ousted. As far as Atkinson was concerned it gave him power to have one of his men in charge at Bramton, using the office as a stepping stone in his turn to force his way up the ladder of promotion. It was all a form of small time politics with no regard to human feelings, rather like politics in the real world.

Dave informed me that there was a new tactic from Atkinson. He showed me a letter to Uncle John, which I read with some misgiving. It appeared he was now prepared to overlook the Denise incident provided Uncle John, 'In view of his ongoing medical condition would consider early retirement,'- a neat reversal of his previous reasoning. He went on to state, 'The terms would be generous,' and urged him to think through the proposal, 'as a matter of some expediency'.

At the conclusion of his letter he wrote, "I shall be visiting you as usual on Friday and I shall be bringing with me Ray Shaw, who has expressed an interest in managing the office after your departure. He is an ambitious young man and I trust you will afford him all the help he requires during the transitional period of takeover, should he decide to take the position.'

It was no less than I had expected. Uncle John had been left with little option other than to accept his early retirement. I failed to discover the generous terms Atkinson referred to, for he must have taken that particular letter home with him. It also occured to me it was typical of Atkinson to visit on a Friday, leaving Uncle John the weekend to worry about his future - like the classroom psychology of a headmaster telling an errant pupil he would deal with him the following day.

The entire office was now aware that Uncle John would be taking early retirement, though most were not aware of the reason. And Murdoch must have suspected he would not become the next manager of Bramton Sorting Office, but he merely brooded in his cage, crouched over his paperwork like a frustrated vulture.

Ray Shaw was a surley looking lout, thickset, beetlebrowed, aged twenty six, but correctly dressed as the occasion of his introduction as manager-in-waiting demanded. He would have been more at home dressed in jeans, a tea shirt with a lewd slogan printed on the front, and an American baseball cap worn reversed on his head. Colin Atkinson certainly had a strange taste in bedfellows.

They closeted themselves with Uncle John in his office and were still there when we returned from our rounds some five hours later.

On the following Monday Uncle John formally announced he was taking early retirement and Ray Shaw would be the next manager of Bramton Sorting Office. He wished him luck and hoped we would give him our support in the transitional period. It was we who needed the luck by the look of Ray Shaw.

The transitional period proved shorter than we expected, just two weeks. In that time we held a collection for Uncle John and, with the proceeds, bought him a whisky decanter, four glasses and a bottle of whisky to complete the set.

On the day of his departure Colin Atkinson, Ray Shaw and Lennie Murdoch assembled in front of us for the farewell speeches. They were rapidly joined by Sydney, determined not to be left out of the proceedings.

Atkinson's words were worthy of a demonic politician who had just stabbed a rival firmly in the back. He made the presentation and Uncle John, without guile or bitterness, gave a reply, which was both honest and heartfelt, telling us how he had enjoyed his time at Bramton and how it had always been his ambition to have managed a small office in a country area. He took his enforced early retirement with honour and dignity.

Later, sitting with Lester on the white plastic chairs in front of the wicker table, enjoying our cigarettes, I said, "It's a bitter irony that the brother of the girl who brought about Uncle John's downfall is to be our next manager. A callow youth who can barely construct a sentence. But it's entirely typical of Royal Mail to appoint him, in the same way as they employed the dirtiest man in Bramton as our cleaner."

Lester thought for a moment, exhaling his tobacco smoke with some pleasure. "I do believe," he said, "you have become a cynical old postman."

Other Autobiographies published by Red'n'Ritten Ltd.

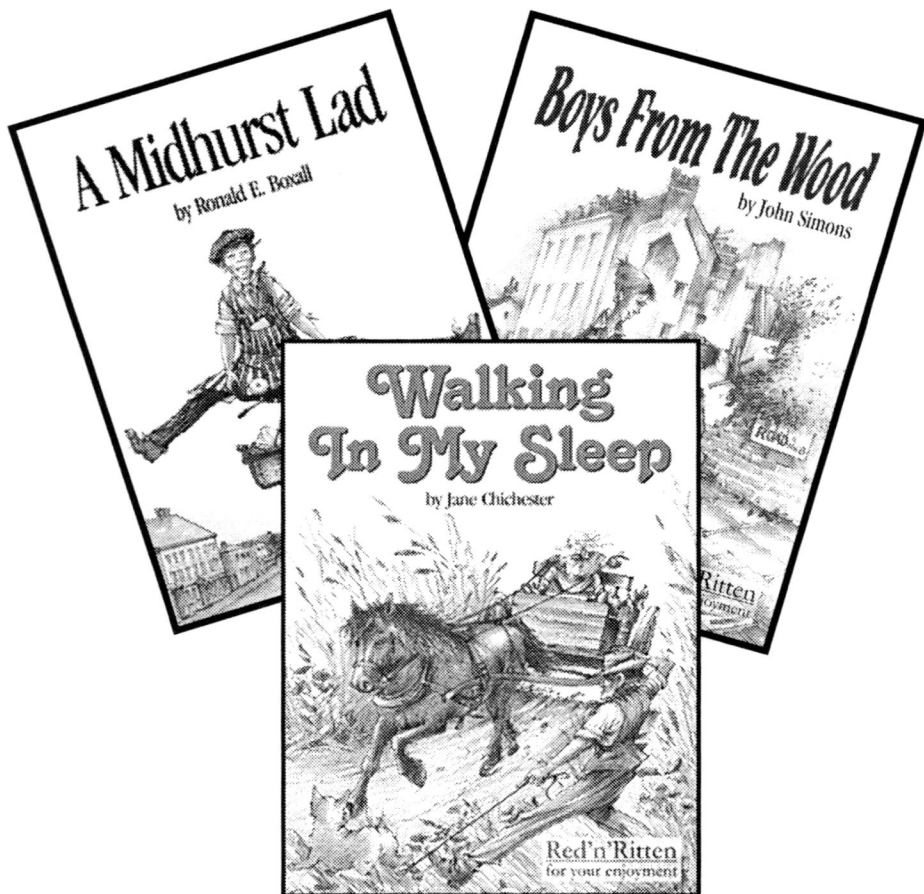

A Midhurst Lad
by Ronald E. Boxall

Boys From The Wood
by John Simons

Walking In My Sleep
by Jane Chichester

Red'n'Ritten
for your enjoyment

Three delightful childhood memoirs
set in Sussex, London
& Hampshire

Autobiography:

The story of an RAF Armourer, 1939-1946.

ISBN 1904278329

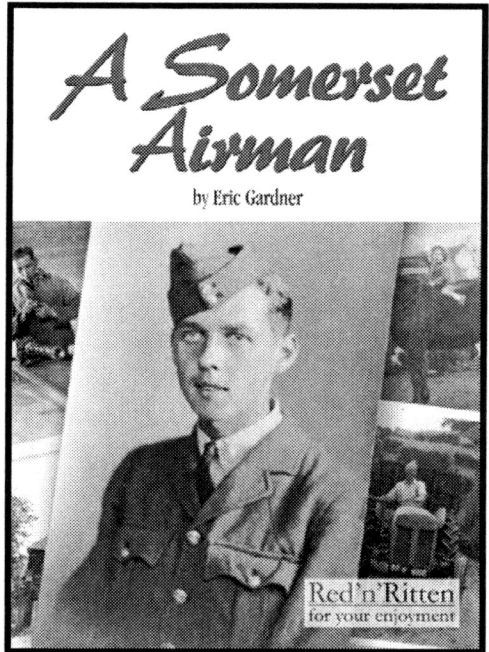

A Somerset Airman
by Eric Gardner

Red'n'Ritten
for your enjoyment

Eric Gardner grew up in Frome on a small family farm. The *Introduction* to this book is his account of the farm itself, daily routines and the animals with which he shared his childhood, and paints an engaging picture of rural life in 1930's Somerset.

At the age of 19 he joined the RAF. His witty observations of day-to-day life as an Airman in wartime Britain and Canada give a fascinating insight into the life experienced by many ordinary men and women, from all backgrounds, who were brought together by World War Two.

Like many of his generation, Eric Gardner did not receive a higher education, and was unable to fulfil his obvious potential. In later life he often commented that the RAF had been his university.

Eric thought his wartime experiences would be of little interest to anyone else, because he did not see any active service. His family did not agree and encouraged him to commit his memories to paper.

He finished the manuscript for *A Somerset Airman* just days before his sudden death at the age of 82 and so, sadly, Eric never saw it in print.

Autobiography:

The story of a Swiss girl who becomes a Section Officer in Photography in the WAAF

ISBN 978 1904278 481

Bamby

by Barbara Dallas

Born to a German actress mother and Swiss artist father, Barbara (Bamby) Dallas's life, (née Schmidbauer and Bamberger) was destined to be anything but straightforward.

Part One (1921-41) tells of her rural life in Upper Silesia; and then her school days, after her mother's second marriage to a Merchant Banker of Jewish origin, in a Pestalozzi school in the Reinland and a finishing school in Switzerland. When the Nazis took over the Bank in 1938, her parents fled to England, and Barbara joined them travelling alone via Berlin and Amsterdam just in time for World War Two …

Even though her parents were Enemy Aliens, she joined the WAAF as a photographer, and met her Army pilot husband. **Part Two** (1941-45) is a transcript of Bamby's diary, written whilst serving in the WAAF. She met an Army Pilot during the war and they married just after VE Day. Ian's family insisted he join the family firm of Insurance Brokers, but it enabled them to bring up a family in comfort. In **Part Three** (1945-2005) we see that Barbara's life was never going to be problem or adventure free…

We also learn more about her very young childhood from her stepmother and stepbrother, and the fate of those who did not escape to or stay in England.

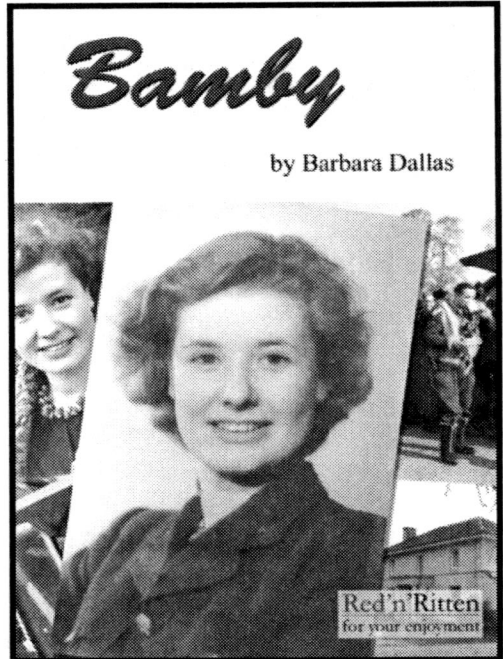

Red'n'Ritten
for your enjoyment